Beginning LoRa Radio Networks with Arduino

Build Long Range, Low Power Wireless IoT Networks

Pradeeka Seneviratne

Apress®

Beginning LoRa Radio Networks with Arduino: Build Long Range, Low Power Wireless IoT Networks

Pradeeka Seneviratne
Mulleriyawa, Sri Lanka

ISBN-13 (pbk): 978-1-4842-4356-5   ISBN-13 (electronic): 978-1-4842-4357-2
https://doi.org/10.1007/978-1-4842-4357-2

Library of Congress Control Number: 2019932795

Managing Director, Apress Media LLC: Welmoed Spahr
Acquisitions Editor: Natalie Pao
Development Editor: James Markham
Coordinating Editor: Jessica Vakili

Cover designed by eStudioCalamar

Cover image designed by Freepik (www.freepik.com)

Distributed to the book trade worldwide by Springer Science+Business Media New York, 233 Spring Street, 6th Floor, New York, NY 10013. Phone 1-800-SPRINGER, fax (201) 348-4505, e-mail orders-ny@springer-sbm.com, or visit www.springeronline.com. Apress Media, LLC is a California LLC and the sole member (owner) is Springer Science + Business Media Finance Inc (SSBM Finance Inc). SSBM Finance Inc is a **Delaware** corporation.

For information on translations, please e-mail rights@apress.com, or visit www.apress.com/rights-permissions.

Apress titles may be purchased in bulk for academic, corporate, or promotional use. eBook versions and licenses are also available for most titles. For more information, reference our Print and eBook Bulk Sales web page at www.apress.com/bulk-sales.

Any source code or other supplementary material referenced by the author in this book is available to readers on GitHub via the book's product page, located at www.apress.com/978-1-4842-4356-5. For more detailed information, please visit www.apress.com/source-code.

Printed on acid-free paper

Table of Contents

About the Author

 **Pradeeka Seneviratne** is a software engineer with more than ten years of experience in computer programming and systems design. He is an expert in the development of Arduino and Raspberry Pi–based embedded systems and is currently a full-time software engineer working with embedded systems and highly scalable technologies. Previously, Pradeeka worked as a software engineer for several IT infrastructure and technology servicing companies. He is the author of several books, including *Beginning BBC micro:bit* (Apress), *Building Arduino PLCs* (Apress), and *Internet of Things with Arduino Blueprints* (Packt).

About the Technical Reviewer

Fabio Claudio Ferracchiati is a senior consultant and a senior analyst/
developer using Microsoft technologies. He works at BluArancio S.p.A
(**www.bluarancio.com**) as senior analyst/developer and Microsoft
Dynamics CRM specialist. He is a Microsoft Certified Solution Developer
for .NET, a Microsoft Certified Application Developer for .NET, a Microsoft
Certified Professional, and a prolific author and technical reviewer. Over the
past ten years, he's written articles for Italian and international magazines
and co-authored more than ten books on a variety of computer topics.

CHAPTER 1

Introduction to LoRa and LoRaWAN

Radios are exciting pieces of hardware that can be used to build wireless communication links. Radios used to listen to voice and audio are known as *receivers*; your home radio, for example, can only tune into and receive radio stations. Radios that can be used to transmit voice and audio are known as *transmitters*; radio stations use transmitters to broadcast programs. Radios that can do both (transmit and receive) are known as *transceivers*; a walkie-talkie is an example of a two-way radio transceiver.

Transceivers use different types of modulations to send and receive data. The network coverage and data capacity are highly dependent on the frequency and type of modulation used. By using LoRa modulation, you can send data to long distances.

By reading this chapter, you will gain a basic understanding of LoRa, LoRaWAN, and LoRaWAN's architecture.

What Is LoRa?

The LoRa spread spectrum is a patented modulation developed by Semtech (https://www.semtech.com/) based on the chirp spread spectrum (CSS) modulation. LoRa (short for "long range") provides long-range and low-power consumption, a low data rate, and secure data

© Pradeeka Seneviratne 2019
P. Seneviratne, *Beginning LoRa Radio Networks with Arduino*,
https://doi.org/10.1007/978-1-4842-4357-2_1

transmission. LoRa can be used with public, private, or hybrid networks to achieve a greater range than cellular networks. LoRa technology can easily integrate with existing networks and enables low-cost, battery-operated Internet of Things (IoT) applications.

Let's try to understand how the LoRa Spread Spectrum Modulation works. A plain radio signal carries no information besides the transmitter being left on. The signal must be modified in some way to convey information. There are several ways in which this can be done. Two of the most popular methods are to modify the amplitude and to modify the frequency.

Amplitude Modulation

In *amplitude modulation* (AM), the signal strength (amplitude) of the carrier wave is varied in proportion to that of the message signal being transmitted. Figure 1-1 shows how the information signal (modulating signal) is transformed into the modulated signal. First, the information signal is mixed with the carrier signal using a mixer (indicated with an X). The carrier signal has a constant frequency and amplitude, generated by an oscillator. During the transformation, the resulting modulated signal varies its amplitude, but the frequency remains constant. This simple modulation technique simplifies the transmitter and receiver design and is cost effective.

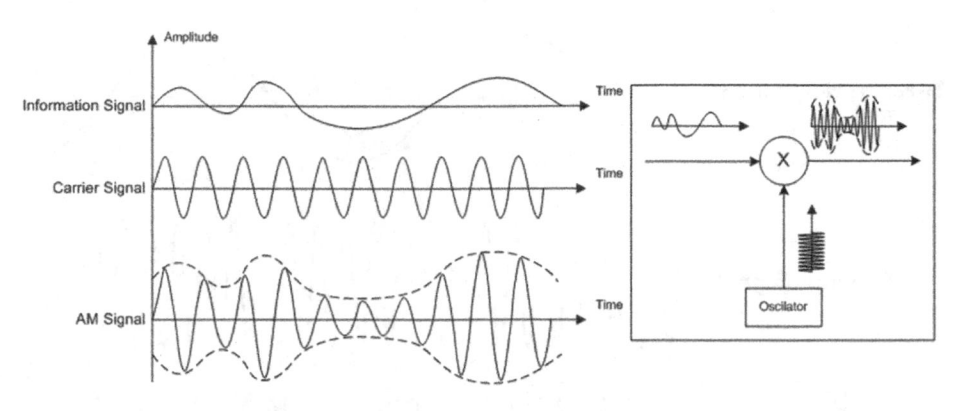

Figure 1-1. *Amplitude modulation, including the information signal, carrier signal, and AM signal (source:* `https://en.wikipedia.org/wiki/Amplitude_modulation#/media/File:Illustration_of_Amplitude_Modulation.png` *by Ivan Akira,* `https://creativecommons.org/licenses/by-sa/3.0`*)*

Amplitude-modulated signals are less resistant to noise and deliver poor sound quality compared with frequency modulation. However, amplitude modulation signals can be sent over long distances.

Frequency Modulation

Frequency modulation (FM) is widely used for FM radio broadcasting. In frequency modulation, the frequency of the carrier wave is changed in accordance with the intensity of the signal. The amplitude and the phase of the carrier wave remain constant. Only the frequency of the carrier wave changes in accordance with the signal.

Figure 1-2 shows the frequency modulation technique. The information signal is mixed with the carrier signal using a mixer. The carrier signal has a constant frequency and amplitude. When the information signal voltage is 0, the carrier frequency is unchanged. When the information signal approaches its positive peaks, the carrier frequency is increased to a maximum. But during the negative peak of a signal, the carrier frequency is reduced to a minimum. Therefore, the resulting modulated signal has a constant amplitude with varied frequencies.

3

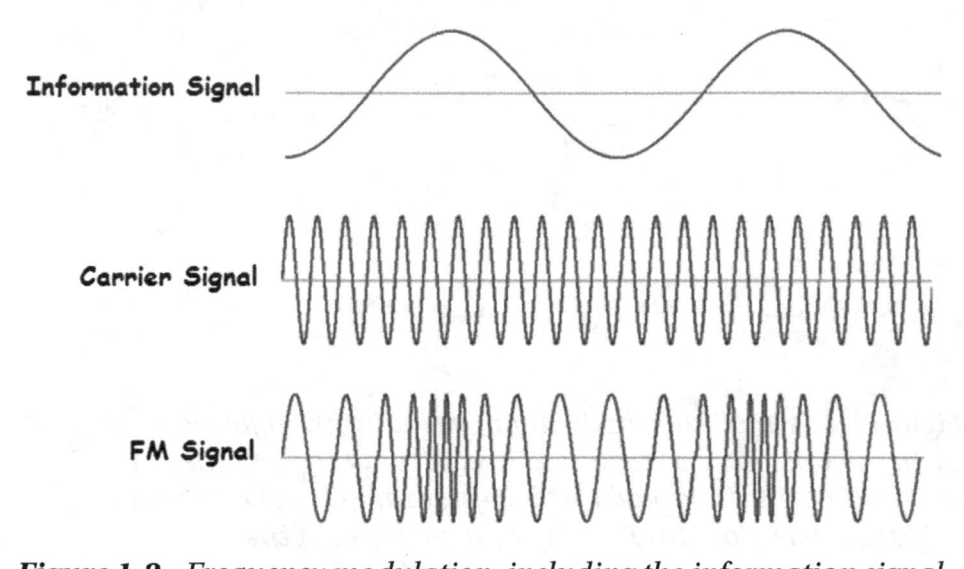

Figure 1-2. *Frequency modulation, including the information signal, carrier signal, and FM signal*

Frequency-modulated signals are more resistant to noise and deliver better sound quality compared with AM. They can't travel long distances and can be blocked by tall buildings or mountains.

Frequency Shift Keying

Frequency shift keying (FSK) represents a digital signal with two frequencies. One frequency could be used to represent digital 1, and the second frequency could be used to represent digital 0. Figure 1-3 shows how a digital signal is transformed into a modulated analog signal using FSK modulation. A carrier signal and two different frequencies are used to represent digital states, HIGH and LOW. The digital data signal is mixed with the carrier signal and encoded into a modulated analog signal.

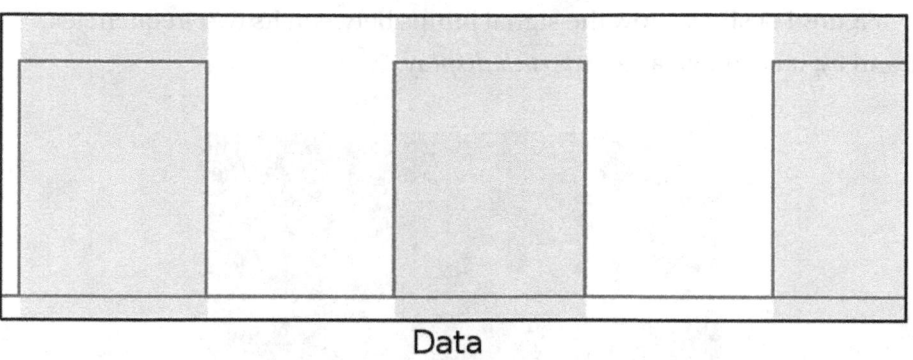

Data

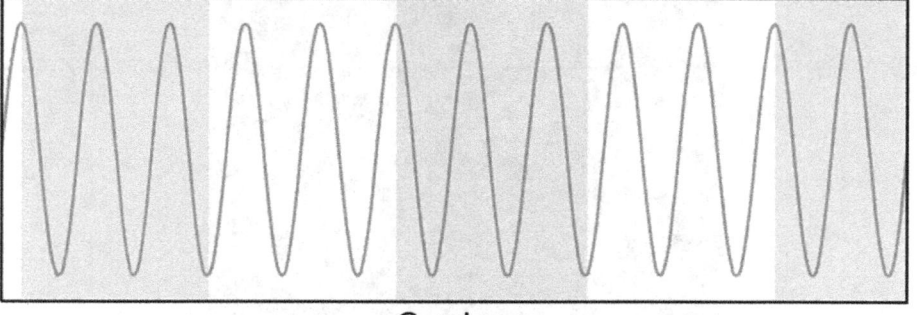

Carrier

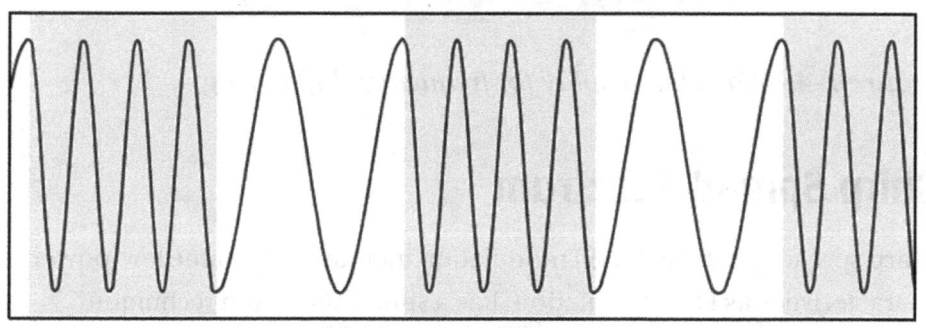

Modulated Signal

Figure 1-3. *FSK modulation transformed digital signal into an analog signal using two frequencies. Each frequency represents a digital state. (Source:* `https://en.wikipedia.org/wiki/ Frequency-shift_keying#/media/File:Fsk.svg;` *license:* `https:// creativecommons.org/licenses/by-sa/3.0/`*)*

Figure 1-4 shows how the signal jumps between its two frequencies (1 and 0); it is known as a *waterfall display*.

Figure 1-4. *Waterfall display for frequency shift keying*

Chirp Spread Spectrum

Chirp spread spectrum (CSS) modulation maintains the same low-power characteristics as FSK modulation. It is a spread spectrum technique that uses wideband linear frequency-modulated chirp pulses to encode information.

CSS was developed for radar applications in the 1940s. It has been used in military and space communications for decades because of its long communication distances, low transmission power requirements, and less interference.

LoRa Spread Spectrum Modulation

You already know that LoRa modulation uses the chirp spread spectrum to encode data. Each bit is spread by a chipping factor. The number of chips per bit is called the *spreading factor* (SF). CSS uses spreading factors from 7 to 12. Small spreading factors provide high data rates and require less over-the-air time. Large spreading factors provide low data rates and require more over-the-air time.

LoRa modulation is more complex and resilient to background noise. Rather than just use the two frequencies of SFK, it sweeps between the two frequencies, as shown in Figure 1-5. The bottom part of the image shows the frequency sweeps from up to down. The top part of the image shows the frequency sweeps from down to up.

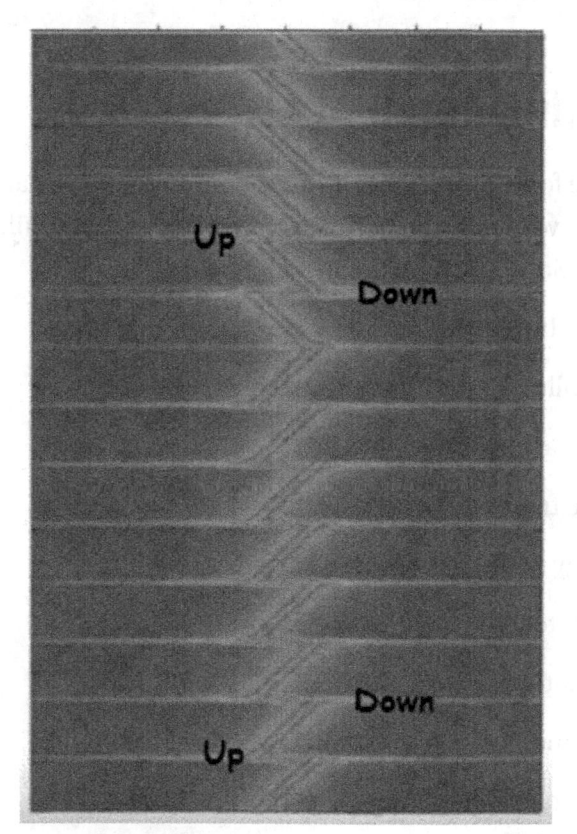

Figure 1-5. *Sweeping between the two frequencies (up to down and down to up)*

The LoRa Spread Spectrum Modulation has the following properties:

- Bandwidth scalable

- Constant envelope/low power

- High robustness

- Multipath/fading resistance

- Doppler resistance

- Long-range capability

- Enhanced network capacity

- Ranging/localization

LoRa Applications

LoRa is suitable for building long-range communication channels with low data rates. LoRa wireless sensor networks can be used to build a wide array of applications. Some of them are as follows:

- Agriculture processing

- Air pollution monitoring

- Asset tacking

- Cattle tracking

- Energy management and sustainability

- Fall detection

- Fire detection

- Fleet management

- Fleet tracking

- Home security
- Indoor air quality management
- Industrial temperature management
- Liquid presence detection
- Locating stolen vehicles and cargo
- Medical refrigerator monitoring
- Parking management
- Precision farming
- Predictive maintenance
- Radiation leak detection
- Shipment quality
- Smart home asset tracking
- Smart irrigation
- Smart lighting
- Smart parking
- Tank flow monitoring
- Waste management
- Water flow monitoring
- Water management and protection
- Wireless gas-level monitoring

Network Coverage

A single gateway can cover entire cities or hundreds of square miles/kilometers. The coverage highly depends on obstructions (buildings, trees, hills), the environment (heavy rain), and technical factors (high-level radio interference, antenna type). Figure 1-6 shows a coverage map of LoRa gateways distributed in New Zealand by Spark Digital.

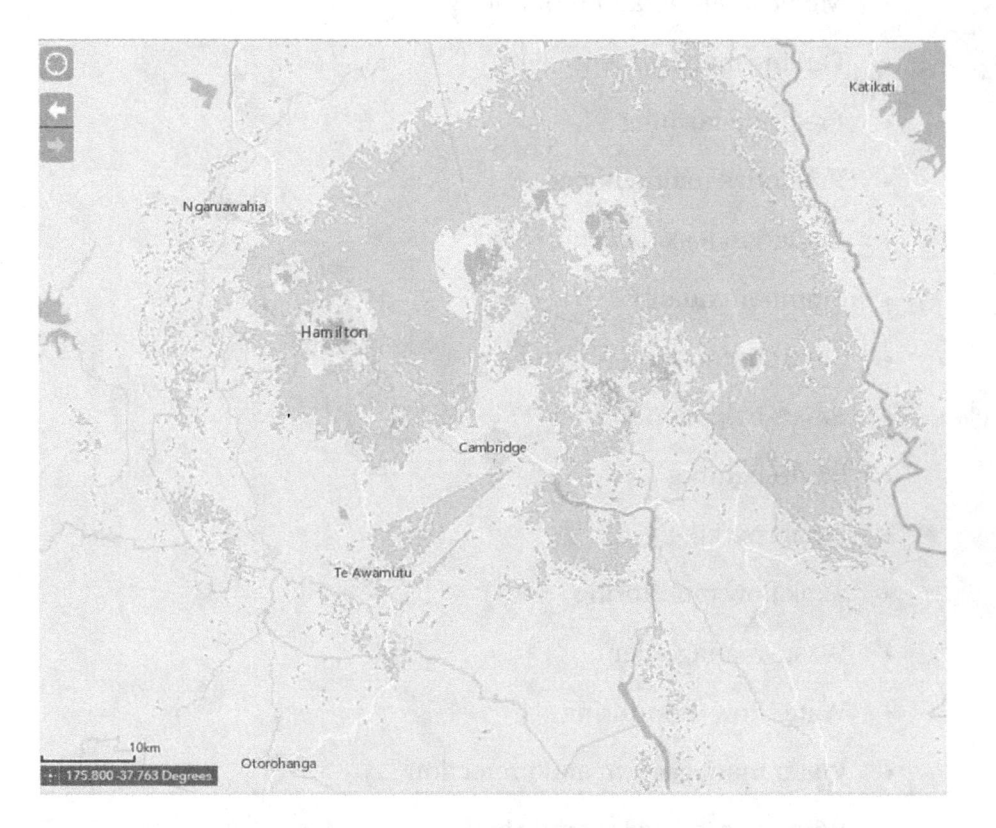

Figure 1-6. *Source: https://www.SparkDigital.co.nz/solutions/mobility/iot/loracoverage/*

The coverage is greater than any other standardized communication technologies such as Bluetooth, ZigBee, Wi-Fi, or cellular. The link budget is the primary factor in determining the range in a given environment for any communication link, typically given in decibels (dB). LoRa modulation can be used to replace some parts of new or existing IoT networks that require small payloads and data rates.

Example

Let's assume we have a vehicle tracking system based on traditional GPS trackers. Each vehicle transmits its current geographical location periodically to a GPS server through a cellular network. Each GPS tracker has a data plan. Let's also assume an organization has 100 vehicles, so they should pay $100 for the Internet plan.

If we replace each GPS tracker with a LoRa sensor node and a few LoRa gateways, we will only require cellular data plans for the gateways. Let's say we installed ten gateways to cover the entire geographical area. With this implementation, we can highly reduce the cost for cellular data and increase the portion of ownership of the network.

Low-Power Wide Area Networks

LoRa networks are considered low-power wide area networks (LPWANs). The nodes can be battery powered, and the lifetime of the battery is about ten years. The nodes transmit data in small amounts over long distances and a few times per hour (for example, every ten minutes).

What Is LoRaWAN?

Long Range Wide Area Network (LoRaWAN) is the communication protocol and system architecture for the network, while the LoRa physical layer enables the long-range communication link. LoRaWAN has the capacity to have an effect on the following:

- Battery lifetime of the node

- Network capacity

- Quality of service

- Security

- Applications served by the network

LoRaWAN consists of end nodes (end devices), gateways (concentrators), a network server, and application servers (Figure 1-7). In a LoRaWAN network, data transmitted by an end node is typically received by multiple gateways. Once the data is received, each gateway will forward the received packet to the network server through cellular, Ethernet, Wi-Fi, or satellite. The software running on the gateway is responsible for forwarding any incoming data packet to the network server. This software is known as a *packet forwarder*.

The network server sends and receives LoRaWAN messages to and from devices and communicates with upstream application servers. The application server is the destination for device application data sent as the payload in LoRaWAN messages.

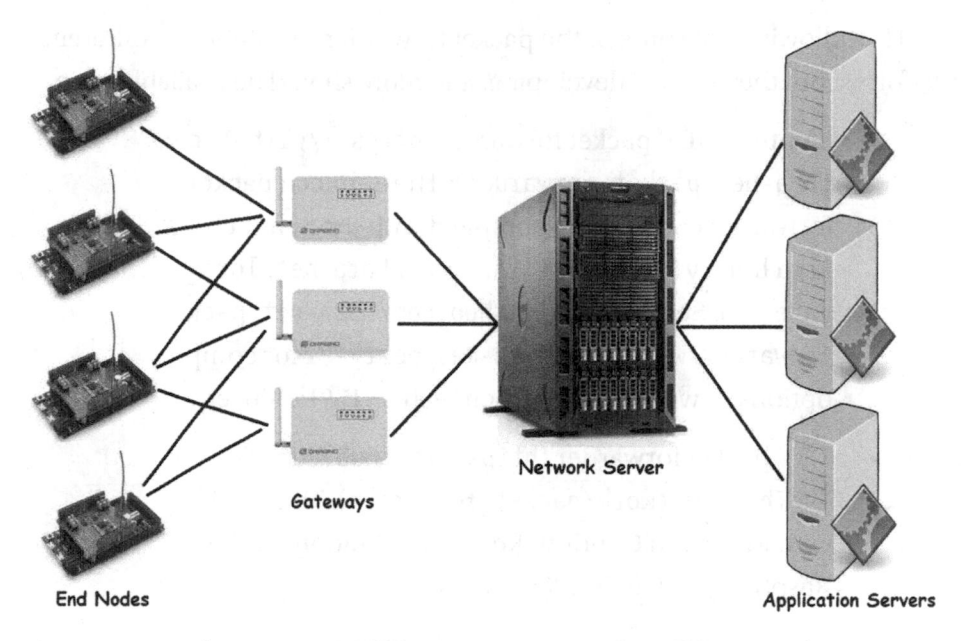

Figure 1-7. *Elements of LoRaWAN*

Packet Forwarders

A *packet forwarder* is software running on the LoRa gateway. It allows the
LoRa concentrator to transmit and receive LoRa packets for both uplinks
and downlinks from end nodes to network servers and from network
servers to end nodes. Packet forwarders can be categorized into single-
channel packet forwarders and multichannel packet forwarders. Only
multichannel packet forwarders are LoRaWAN compatible.

Usually a packet forwarder does the following:

- Forwards LoRa packets received by the concentrator
  (LoRa module) to the network server through the IP/
  UDP link

- Emits LoRa packets that are sent by the network server

13

The following are some of the packet forwarders available for different platforms. But they are still developing, and more should be available soon.

- Semtech UDP packet forwarder (`https://github.com/Lora-net/packet_forwarder`): The Semtech packet forwarder code can be compiled with the Semtech Lora library (`https://github.com/Lora-net/lora_gateway`). See `https://github.com/Lora-net/packet_forwarder/wiki/Use-with-Raspberry-Pi` for compile options. It works with the Semtech SX1301 chipset.

- TTN packet forwarder (`https://github.com/TheThingsNetwork/packet_forwarder`): This works with Multitech Conduit, Kerlink IoT Station, and Raspberry Pi and iC880a setups.

- Dragino single-channel packet forwarder (`www.dragino.com/downloads/index.php?dir=motherboards/lg01/sketch/&file=Single_pkt_fwd_v004.ino.hex`): This software is written for Dragino LoRa gateways. It works with Semtech SX1272, SX1276, and SX1278 chips.

- Raspberry Pi single-channel packet forwarder (`https://github.com/tftelkamp/single_chan_pkt_fwd`): This works with the Semtech SX1272 transceiver (HopeRF RFM92W) and SX1276 (HopeRF RFM95W).

Hardware for End Devices

Semtech offers a wide range of chipsets for building end devices to work with different frequency ranges. Table 1-1 shows some of the popular chipsets that can be used to build end devices with the Arduino and Raspberry Pi.

Table 1-1. *Chipsets for End Devices /End Nodes*

Part Number	Description	Source
SX 1272	Long-range, low-power RF transceiver 860–1000 MHz with LoRa technology	https://www.semtech.com/ products/wireless-rf/ lora-transceivers/SX1272
SX 1276	137–1020 MHz long-range, low-power transceiver	https://www.semtech.com/ products/wireless-rf/ lora-transceivers/SX1276
SX 1278	137–525 MHz long-range, low-power transceiver	https://www.semtech.com/ products/wireless-rf/ lora-transceivers/SX1278

Some transceiver modules are available for building end devices without heavy soldering and additional electronic components. Figure 1-8 shows a LoRa transceiver breakout based on the SX1276/SX1278 chipset. It can be easily used with the Arduino or Raspberry Pi to build end nodes and single-channel gateways.

Figure 1-8. *Adafruit RFM96W LoRa radio transceiver breakout, 433 MHz*

Hardware for Gateways

LoRa gateways can handle data coming from many end devices simultaneously. These gateways can be built from scratch with Semtech chipsets.

Semtech offers the chipsets in Table 1-2 for designing and building multichannel LoRa gateways.

Table 1-2. *Chipsets for Multichannel Gateways*

Part Number	Description	Source
SX 1301	Digital baseband chip for outdoor LoRaWAN macro gateways	https://www.semtech.com/products/wireless-rf/lora-gateways/SX1301
SX 1308	Digital baseband chip for indoor LoRaWAN pico gateways	https://www.semtech.com/products/wireless-rf/lora-gateways/SX1308

However, single-channel LoRa gateways can be built with the same chipsets designed for the end devices (Table 1-3).

Table 1-3. *Chipsets for Single-Channel Gateways*

Part Number	Description	Source
SX 1272	Long-range, low-power RF transceiver 860–1000 MHz with LoRa technology	https://www.semtech.com/products/wireless-rf/lora-transceivers/SX1272
SX 1276	137–1020 MHz long-range, low-power transceiver	https://www.semtech.com/products/wireless-rf/lora-transceivers/SX1276
SX 1278	137–525 MHz long-range, low-power transceiver	https://www.semtech.com/products/wireless-rf/lora-transceivers/SX1278

Also, there are hundreds of ready-to-use LoRa gateways available on the market. Some of them are as follows:

- Dragino LG01-P IoT gateway (`www.dragino.com/products/lora/item/117-lg01-p.html`): This is a single-channel, indoor gateway (Figure 1-9) and is available in different frequencies such as 868, 915, and 433 MHz.

Figure 1-9. *Dragino LG01-P IoT gateway (courtesy of Dragino,* `www.dragino.com`*)*

- Dragino LG02 Dual Channels LoRa IoT gateway (`www.dragino.com/products/lora/item/135-lg02.html`): This gateway can simultaneously receive two channels. It also can transmit data on a single channel (Figure 1-10). It is available in different frequencies such as 868, 915, and 433 MHz.

Figure 1-10. *Dragino LG02 Dual Channels LoRa IoT gateway (courtesy of Dragino,* `www.dragino.com`*)*

- Waspmote gateway SX1272 LoRa module SMA 4.5 dBi, 868 MHz (`https://www.cooking-hacks.com/ waspmote-gateway-sx1272-lora-sma-4-5-dbi-868- mhz`): See Figure 1-11.

Figure 1-11. *Waspmote gateway SX1272 (courtesy of* https://www.
cooking-hacks.com*)*

- Waspmote Plug & Sense (www.libelium.com/
products/plug-sense/): See Figure 1-12.

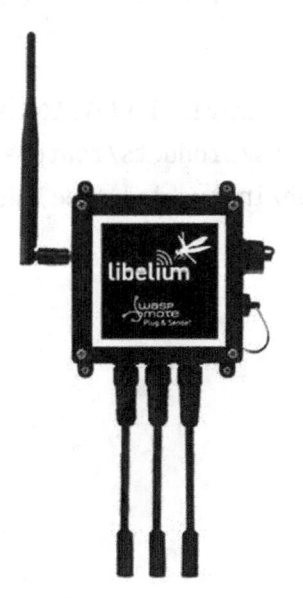

Figure 1-12. *Waspmote Plug & Sense (courtesy of* www.libelium.com*)*

- The Things gateway (https://www.element14.com/
  community/docs/DOC-83605/1/things-gateway-use-
  a-long-range-and-low-power-radio-frequency-
  protocol-called-lorawan-and-for-short-range-
  bluetooth-42): See Figure 1-13.

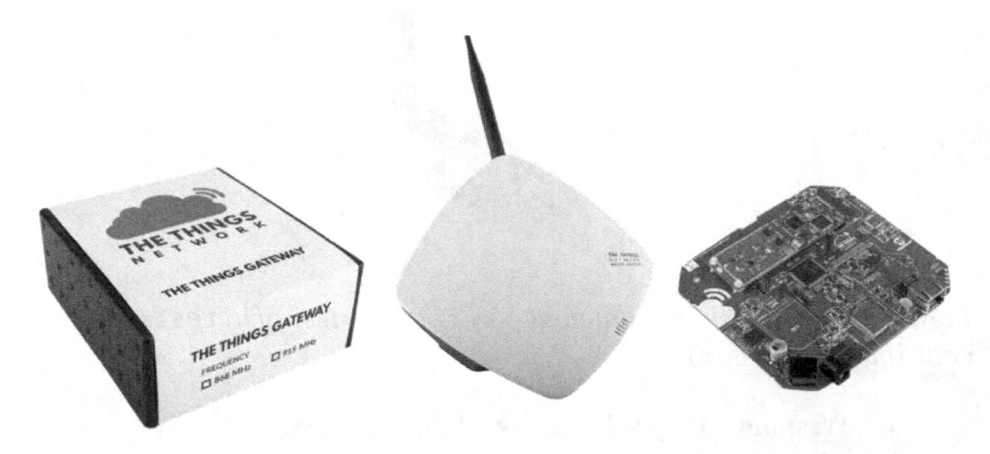

Figure 1-13.   *The Things gateway (courtesy of* https://www.
element14.com/*)*

- Cisco Wireless Gateway for LoRaWAN (https://www.
  cisco.com/c/en/us/products/routers/wireless-
  gateway-lorawan/index.html): See Figure 1-14.

Figure 1-14. *Cisco Wireless Gateway for LoRaWAN (courtesy of* `https://www.cisco.com`*)*

- Figure 1-15 shows the SX1301 and SX1278 eight-channel LoRaWAN gateway module that can be used to build LoRa gateways with the Raspberry Pi. These modules are expensive, so in this book we will focus on building single-channel LoRa gateways.

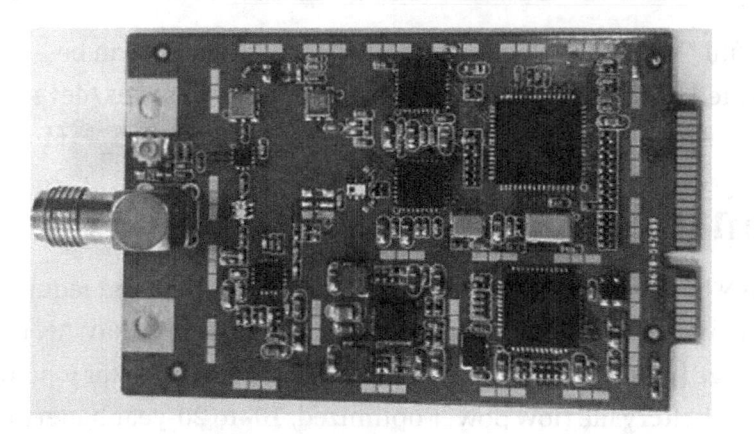

Figure 1-15. *SX1301-based eight-channel LoRa gateway module*

21

LoRaWAN Frequencies

LoRa Alliance defines regional frequency profiles to operate LoRaWAN for different regulatory regions worldwide. Table 1-4 lists the frequencies allowed to be used in some countries.

Table 1-4. *LoRaWAN Frequencies and Channel Plans*

Country	Band/Channels	Channel Plan
United States	902–928 MHz	US902-928, AU915-928
United Kingdom	433.05–434.79 MHz	EU433
	863–873 MHz	EU863-870
	918–921 MHz	Other
Canada	902–928 MHz	US902-928, AU915-928
Australia	915–928 MHz	AU915-928, AS923
India	865–867 MHz	IN765-867
France	433.05–434.79 MHz	EU433
	863–870 MHz	EU863-870
Sri Lanka	433.05–434.79 MHz	EU433

The full "LoRaWAN Regional Parameters" document can be downloaded from https://www.lora-alliance.org/sites/default/files/2018-04/lorawantm_regional_parameters_v1.1rb_-_final.pdf.

Summary

LoRaWAN has significant cost savings in its deployment and required infrastructure compared to existing systems. LoRa and LoRaWAN provide a long range (greater than cellular, deep indoor coverage, star topology), maximum battery life (low power optimized, 10- to 20-year battery life), multiple uses (high capacity, multitenant, public network), and low cost (minimal infrastructure, low-cost end nodes, open software).

CHAPTER 2

Obtaining and Preparing Hardware

In Chapter 1, you learned that the LoRaWAN architecture consists of end nodes (also known as *end devices* or *sensor LoRa nodes*) and gateways. End nodes and gateways can be built with various hardware and software options. This chapter introduces some easy-to-find hardware that you can use to build end nodes and single-channel gateways.

The radio transceivers we will be using for this book don't support building LoRaWAN-compatible multichannel gateways. You should use them for educational and testing purposes only. In fact, using them for industrial purposes may violate the LoRaWAN specification and some of the LoRa regional regulations.

LoRa End Node

A LoRa end node consists of a LoRa radio, sensors, an antenna, and a power supply. Some have actuators too. The LoRa radio can transmit or receive data. It is also known as a *transceiver*. An end node can be built by combining various hardware and software options. Some end nodes are physically fixed and transmit sensor data to a LoRa gateway. Some end nodes transmit data to multiple LoRa gateways. Some end nodes are mobile and transmit data while moving. As an example, a LoRa

© Pradeeka Seneviratne 2019
P. Seneviratne, *Beginning LoRa Radio Networks with Arduino*,
https://doi.org/10.1007/978-1-4842-4357-2_2

end node with a GPS module fixed to a vehicle can send geolocation periodically to the LoRa gateway while moving within the network coverage. A LoRa end node can receive data through the downlink from the LoRa gateway.

Figure 2-1 shows a breadboard implementation of a simple LoRa sensor end node. Normally, a LoRa end node consists of a LoRa radio, microcontroller, sensor, power supply unit (PSU), and an antenna.

Figure 2-1. *Simple LoRa sensor end node built with Arduino*

Let's get started filling up our toolbox with commonly available and widely used hardware. At the end of this chapter, you will find a list of hardware with purchase links from leading hardware manufacturers, suppliers, and vendors.

RFM9x LoRa Radio Transceiver Breakouts

Adafruit manufactures and sells LoRa radio transceiver breakouts based on Hope RFM9x LoRa modules (www.hoperf.com/rf_transceiver/lora/). Each LoRa radio transceiver breakout consists of a 74HC4050D logic level translator (which converts Arduino 5V logic to 3.3 V logic that Hope RFM9x can understand) and an AP2112 CMOS process low-dropout linear regulator (which provides the regulated 3.3 V to the LoRa module) that allows you to easily wire it with an Arduino Uno board without requiring any additional components.

These breakouts allow you to build prototypes faster with prewritten software libraries such as RadioHead, Dragino's modified RadioHead library, HopeRFLib, and so forth. You will install some of the libraries on the Arduino in Chapter 3.

Adafruit LoRa radio transceiver breakouts are available in two versions: 868/915 MHz and 433 MHz. Both versions look identical but use different chipsets.

With a simple wire antenna, you can achieve a transmission range of approximately 2 km, but it can be tweaked up to 20 km with various hacks such as avoiding obstructions; changing the frequency (F), bandwidth (BW), spreading factor (SF), code rate (CR), and power output in the software; or using different antenna options.

Let's explore two versions of the radio transceiver breakouts.

868 MHz/915 MHz Version

The 868 MHz/915 MHz LoRa radio transceiver breakout (Figure 2-2) is based on the Hope RFM95W module, which features the Semtech SX1276 chipset.

Figure 2-2. *Adafruit RFM9x LoRa radio transceiver breakout for 868/915 MHz (https://www.adafruit.com/product/3072)*

This radio transceiver breakout is suitable for operating over the 868 MHz and 915 MHz license-free Industry Scientific and Medical (ISM) frequency bands in the following regions:

- European ISM at 868 MHz

- American ISM at 915 MHz

The operation frequency can be configured as 868 MHz or 915 MHz with software (e.g., the RadioHead library).

Figure 2-3 shows the Hope RFM96W module that can be found on the 868 /915 MHz version of this radio transceiver breakout.

Figure 2-3. Hope RFM96W module and chipset

433 MHz Version

The 433 MHz version of the radio transceiver breakout (Figure 2-4) is based on the Hope RFM98W module, which features the Semtech SX1278 chipset.

Figure 2-4. *Front of the Adafruit RFM9x LoRa radio transceiver breakout, 433 MHz*

Figure 2-5 shows the RFM98W module that can be found on the 433 MHz version of the radio transceiver breakout.

Figure 2-5. *Hope RFM98W module and chipset*

The 433 MHz version is suitable for operating over amateur or license-free ISM bands in the following regions:

- ITU "Europe" license-free ISM

- ITU "American" amateur with limitations

Finding the Frequency

The frequency of the radio transceiver breakout can be found on the plastic bag (Figure 2-6), or sometimes you may receive it in a different form. As a good practice, write down the correct frequency on the back side of the PCB. A "Freq" field is provided for this (Figure 2-7).

These breakout boards are much smaller than the figures shown in this book, so you will need a tool like a helping third-hand magnifier (https://www.adafruit.com/product/291) to tightly hold them while magnifying to clearly see the things on the board.

Figure 2-6. *The frequency of the radio transceiver breakout is printed on a sticker affixed to the plastic bag. This one says it is a 433 MHz LoRa radio transceiver breakout. The product page at* https:// www.adafruit.com/product/3073 *named this product as "Adafruit RFM96W LoRa Radio Transceiver Breakout - 433 MHz - RadioFruit." The bag also includes a 0.1-inch male header stripe and a sticker with the MAC address printed on it.*

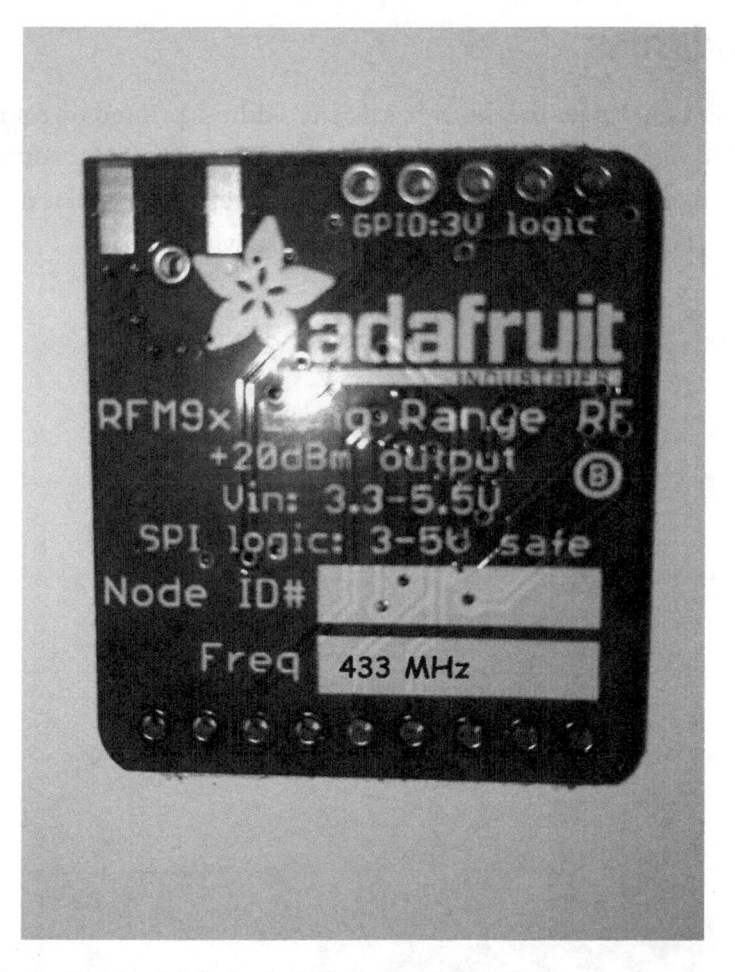

Figure 2-7. *Back of Adafruit RFM9x LoRa radio transceiver breakout, 433 MHz (`https://www.adafruit.com/product/3073`). Note that two spaces are provided, Node ID and Freq.*

To build a peer-to-peer link (or master-slave link), you will need two LoRa radio transceiver breakouts. Before purchasing anything, please check the regulations for operating LoRa radios over license-free ISM frequency bands.

MAC Address

Every radio transceiver breakout has a MAC address printed on a sticker (Figure 2-8) that can be found inside the plastic bag. The MAC address can be used to identify the radio transceiver universally, and it is unique. A LoRaWAN uses these addresses in the MAC payload.

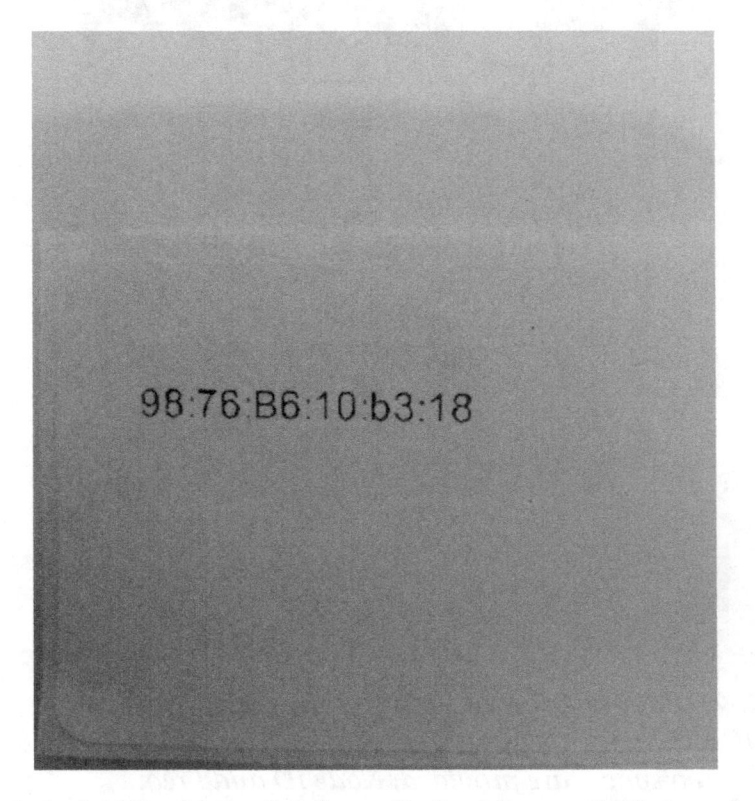

Figure 2-8. MAC address for the radio breakout, which is universally unique

Pins

The LoRa radio transceiver breakout exposes different types of pins such as power, SPI, and GPIO. This is common for both versions.

Power

The pins can be used to power the breakout and shut down the radio
(Figure 2-9).

Power Pins

Figure 2-9. *Power pins: VIN, GND, and EN*

- *VIN*: Through the power in pin, you can supply between 3.3 and 6 VDC. The peak current draw of the radio is about 150 mA, so make sure to supply that much of the current to work it properly. The Arduino Uno can supply 150 mA through the 5 V pin.

- *GND*: The ground is for the logic and power.

- *EN*: This pin is internally connected to the enable pin of the regulator. It is pulled high to VIN by default. You can completely cut power to the radio by connecting it to the GND pin.

Serial Peripheral Interface

These breakouts support the Serial Peripheral Interface (SPI). SPI is the protocol used by microcontrollers for communicating with one or more peripheral devices quickly over short distances. All the communication will be handled through SPI between the radio transceiver and the Arduino or Raspberry Pi. The SPI pins on the radio transceiver support the 3.3 V and 5 V logic levels (Figure 2-10). As pointed out earlier, the level shifter included with the radio transceiver breakout makes the 3.3 V to 5 V logic level conversion. It automatically selects the logic level conversion depending on the VIN pin (power in pin).

SPI Pins

Figure 2-10. *SPI pins: G0, SCK, MISO, MOSI, CS, and RST*

The following pins on the radio transceiver can be used for SPI communication with the microcontroller (Arduino Uno or Raspberry Pi):

- *MISO*: This is the Master In Slave Out pin; it's for data sent from the radio transceiver to your microcontroller.

- *MOSI*: This is the Master Out Slave In pin; it's for data sent from your microcontroller to the radio transceiver.

- *CS*: This is the Chip Select pin; drop it low to start an SPI transaction. It is an input to the chip.

35

- *SCK*: This is the SPI Clock pin; it's an input to the chip.

- *RST*: This is the Reset pin for the radio. It's pulled high by default. Pull it down to ground to put it into reset.

- *G0*: This is used for interrupt request notification from the radio to the microcontroller.

Assembling Headers

Each LoRa radio transceiver breakout comes with a male header strip (0.1 inch). You should first solder them onto the breakout to use it with a breadboard. The following steps will show how to assemble male headers:

- Cut part of nine pins from the male header (Figure 2-11).

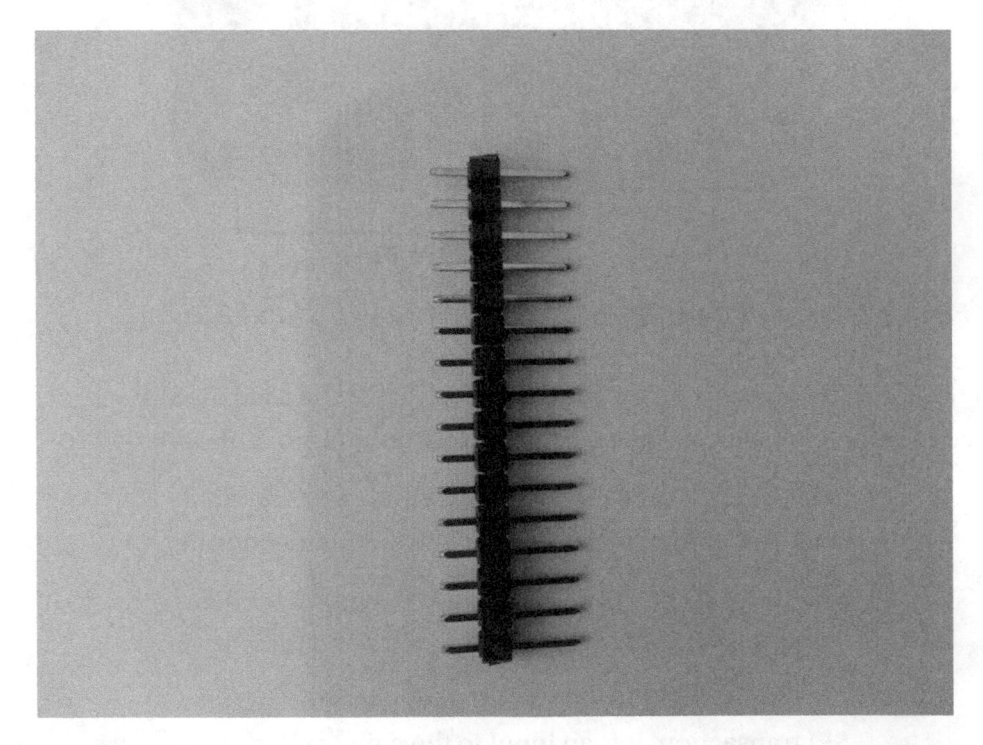

Figure 2-11. *0.1-inch male header strip*

- Insert the long end of the pins into the breadboard (Figure 2-12).

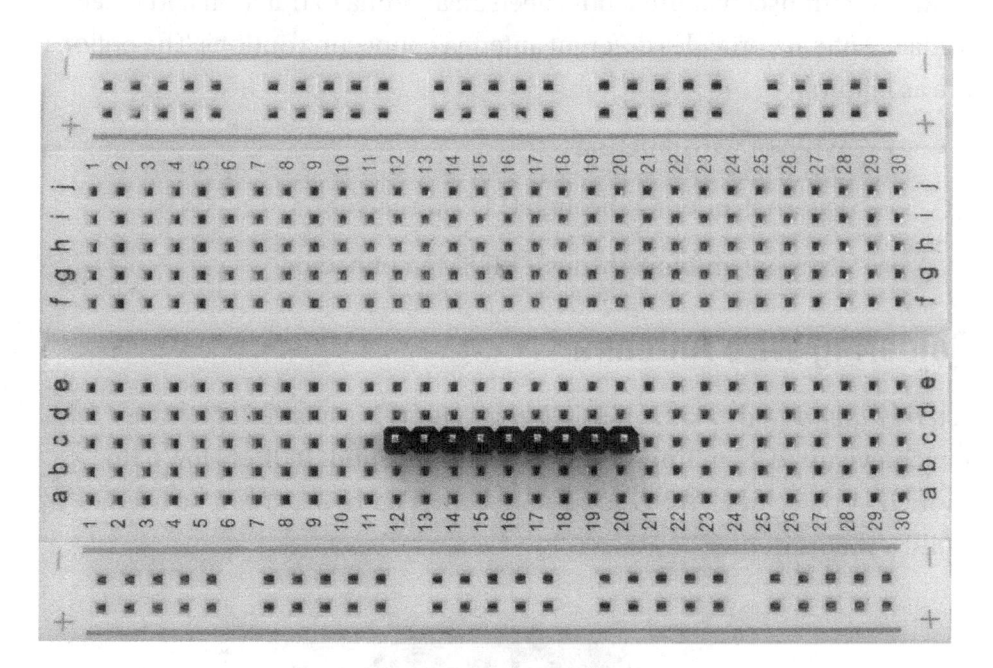

Figure 2-12. *Inserting male headers into the breadboard*

- Place the breakout board over the header pins (Figure 2-13).

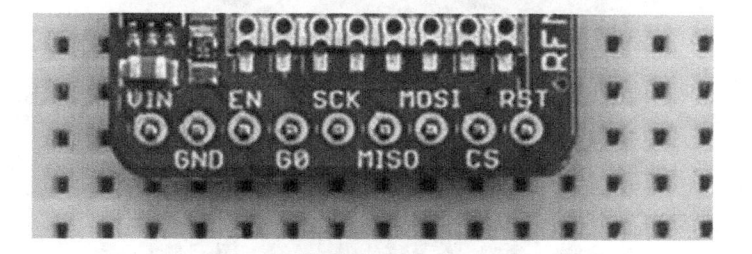

Figure 2-13. *Placing breakout over the header pins*

- Solder all the breakout pads.

Antenna

LoRa radio transceiver breakouts need an antenna to transmit and receive signals. Antenna provides different antenna connecting options. The options are as follows:

- Whip or wire antenna

- External antenna through U.FL connector

- External antenna through RP-SMA connector

Soldering Wire Antenna

A *wire antenna* (also known as *whip antenna*) is a cost-effective way to achieve up to 2 km line-of-sight communication. It offers low gain, though. A piece of 22 AWG solid-core wire (Figure 2-14) can be used to build a wire antenna.

Figure 2-14.   *A solid-core wire spool. They come in different colors.*

The length of the antenna wire depends on the frequency of the radio transceiver breakout. This is known as *quarter-wave whip antenna* because the length is one-quarter a full wavelength at the transmission frequency. A simple formula can be used to calculate the wavelength, as shown here:

wavelength (λ) = wave velocity (v) / frequency (f)

Here, the wavelength is in meters (m), the wave velocity of the radio signal in a vacuum or air is 299,792,458 m/s, and the frequency is in Hertz.

The following example shows how to calculate the antenna length for the 433 MHz frequency:

Wavelength = 299792458 ms^{-1} / 433000000 Hz

= 0.69 m

= 69 cm

1/4 of the wavelength = 69 cm /4

= 17.3 cm

Approximately, the previous formula will produce an antenna length of 17.3 cm.

In practical use, you can use the following values for different frequencies:

- *433 MHz*: 6.5 inches, or 16.5 cm

- *868 MHz*: 3.25 inches, or 8.2 cm

- *915 MHz*: 3 inches, or 7.8 cm

In this exercise, you will solder a piece of solid-core wire onto the radio transceiver breakout to build a wire antenna. Follow these steps:

- Take a spool of solid-core wire and cut a piece of wire using a wire cutter that matches with the frequency of your radio transceiver breakout.

39

- Strip a millimeter or two off the end of the wire using a wire stripper. First, tin both the wire and the ANT pad. Then, solder the wire onto the ANT pad of the breakout. Use a mini vise to hold the PCB while soldering.

- Once you have soldered the wire antenna, the breakout should look like Figure 2-15.

Figure 2-15. *wire antenna*

- Keep the antenna as vertical as possible for the signal to reach the maximum distance.

Arduino

Arduino is an open source prototyping platform. It consists of a processor, RAM, and an I/O line to connect to external peripherals. In this book, you will be using the Arduino Uno board to build LoRa end nodes. It is based on the ATmega328P microcontroller.

Let's take a look at some useful features that can be found on the Arduino Uno board.

- 14 digital input/output pins (6 pins can be used as PWM outputs). These pins have 5 V logic and provide 20 mA each.

- Six analog inputs.

- One SPI interface.

- One I2C interface.

- Built-in hardware serial and software-defined software serial.

- Recommended input voltage: 7 V to 12 V.

- 32 KB of flash memory (ATmega328P) of which 0.5 KB is used by the bootloader

The price of the Arduino Uno REV3 as of this writing is USD $22 on the Arduino USA store (`https://store.arduino.cc/usa/arduino-uno-rev3`). It is a little bit expensive compared to the Adafruit Metro (Figure 2-16). The Adafruit Metro is only about USD $17 and is recommended to build the projects in this book. The Adafruit Metro even provides some extra features.

- Optibooth bootloader

- Switch to cut off the power from DC power jack

- Micro-USB port for programming and powering

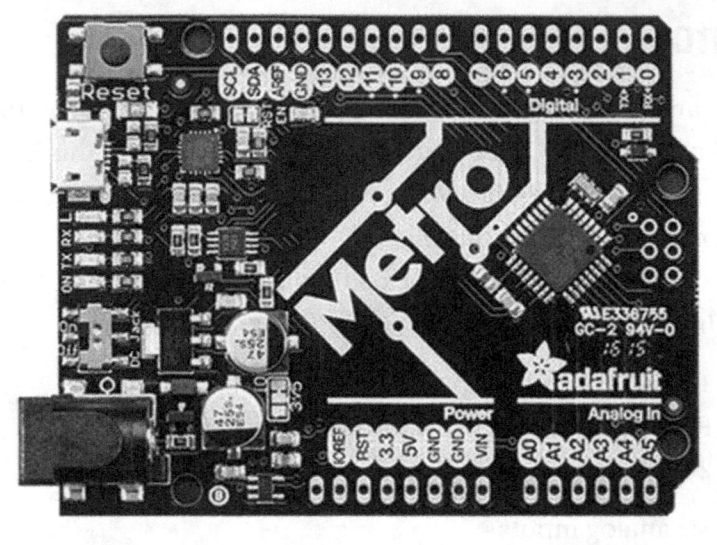

Figure 2-16. *Adafruit Metro (image courtesy of Adafruit,* https:// www.adafruit.com/)

The Adafruit Metro doesn't have an ICSP header for a USB interface. A micro-USB cable (Figure 2-17) is needed to upload sketches to the Metro, and the cable can also be used to power up the board through a computer. The Metro will automatically switch between USB and DC. The switch labeled "DC Jack" can be used to cut off the power supply from the 9 V power adapter.

Figure 2-17. *Micro-USB cable (image courtesy of Adafruit, https://www.adafruit.com/)*

Mounting Plate

A plastic mounting plate (Figure 2-18) can be used to attach the Arduino Uno/Metro and the breadboard. Breadboards can be affixed by removing the protective sticker on the bottom. The Arduino can be attached using four machine screws and hex nuts. This will make your hardware setup neater and more organized. You can use solid-core wires to hook up components with the Arduino Uno/Metro.

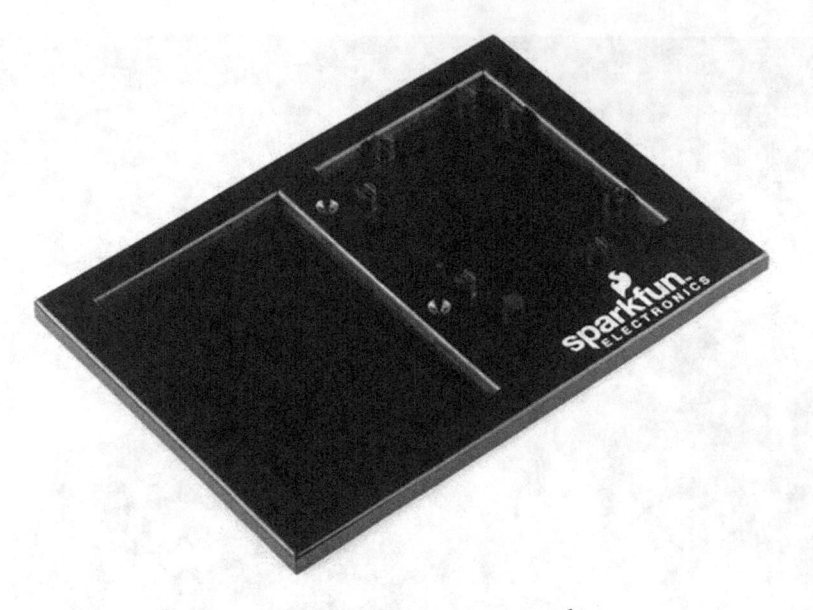

Figure 2-18. *Arduino and breadboard holder (image courtesy of SparkFun,* https://www.sparkfun.com/*)*

Arduino SPI

The SPI of the Arduino Uno is accessible with digital pins 10, 11, 12, and 13. The Adafruit Metro also follows this pin layout (Figure 2-19). These pins use the 5 V logic level. Table 2-1 shows the Arduino SPI pin numbers and their functions.

Table 2-1. *Arduino SPI pins and their functions*

Pin Number	Function
10	SS (slave)
11	MOSI
12	MISO
13	SCK

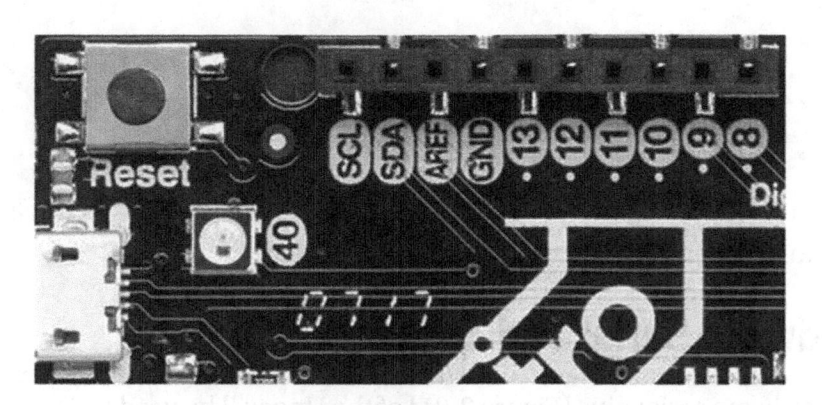

Figure 2-19. *Arduino Uno/Adafruit Metro SPI pins 10, 11, 12, and 13*

The Arduino Uno has a 2×3 pin header marked "ICSP." ICSP stands for "in-circuit serial programming." It breaks out the SPI pins of the microcontroller, power, ground, and reset. Also, there is another 2×3 pin header you can find on the Uno, and it breaks out the SPI pins of the USB interface chip. Figure 2-20 shows that the pinout of the ICSP header belongs to the ATmega328P microcontroller.

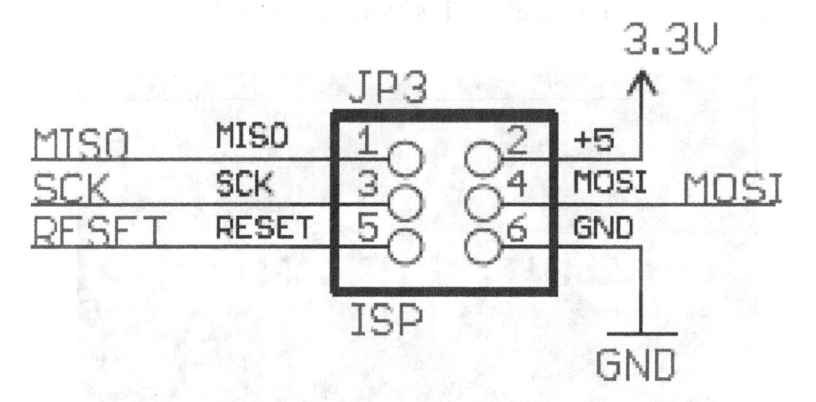

Figure 2-20. *Pinout of the Arduino ICSP header. It breaks out the SPI pins of the Arduino MCU.*

- *MOSI*: ICSP-4

- *MISO*: ICSP-1

- *SCK*: ICSP-3

You will be using the Arduino SPI interface to perform bidirectional communication with LoRa radio transceivers.

Hardware Serial and Software Serial

The hardware serial pins (Figure 2-21) of the Uno will be used to communicate with the GPS module and to get NMEA strings for further processing. The following are the hardware serial pins. The Uno has one hardware serial interface.

- *0*: RX

- *1*: TX

You can bypass the limitations of the hardware serial interfaces by using software serial interfaces. With the Arduino SoftwareSerial library, you can define any pair of digital pins as a serial interface.

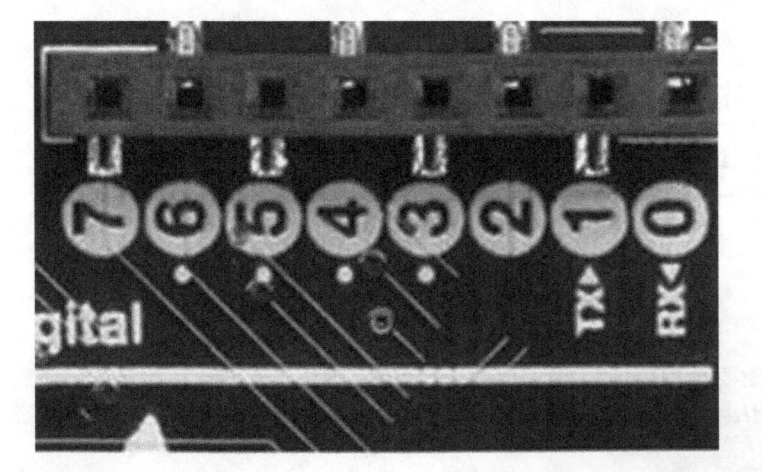

Figure 2-21. *Arduino Uno/Adafruit Metro hardware serial pins marked with "TX" and "RX"*

Power Supply Unit

A power supply is needed to power up the node. You can use any power source that can provide 5 V and enough current to run the microcontroller and the radio transceiver. The radio transceiver normally takes power from the microcontroller, so you don't need a separate power supply for that. An uninterruptable power supply (UPS) unit is a best solution to continuously supply power to the node during the mains power outage.

Here is the list of powering options for the Arduino Uno and Adafruit Metro:

- 9 VDC 1000 mA regulated switching power adapter (https://www.adafruit.com/product/63) [Arduino Uno/Adafruit Metro]

- 9 V alkaline battery (https://www.adafruit.com/product/1321) plus 9 V battery clip with 5.5 mm/2.1 mm plug (https://www.adafruit.com/product/80) [Arduino Uno/Adafruit Metro]

- 9 V alkaline battery (https://www.adafruit.com/product/1321) plus 9 V battery holder with switch and 5.5 mm/2.1 mm plug (https://www.adafruit.com/product/67) [Arduino Uno/Adafruit Metro]

- 5 V 2.4 A switching power supply with 20 AWG micro-USB cable (https://www.adafruit.com/product/1995) [Adafruit Metro only]

Sensors

Sensors measure changes in their environment or detect events and send them to a computer for further processing. To understand how the sensor data can be transmitted with LoRa wireless, we will be using two cheap hardware devices. Specifically, we will be using the following sensors with LoRa end devices:

- *DHT11 sensor*: Measures temperature and humidity in the environment

- *GPS module*: Tracks the current geolocation and sends NEMA strings

Let's take a look at some important features of them.

DHT11 Basic Temperature-Humidity Sensor

The DHT11 (Figure 2-22) will be used to gather temperature and humidity data and upload it to a cloud service such as the Things Network, ThingsSpeak, or Adafruit IO. You can plug the DHT11 into any breadboard. The DHT11 sensor comes with a 4.7 k or 10 k pullup resistor as an extra.

Figure 2-22. *DHT11 sensor*

Figure 2-23 shows how to connect the DHT11 sensor to the Arduino Uno or Adafruit Metro. The figure also shows the pinout of the sensor, marked from left to right if you hold the sensor face up.

- 1 is VCC (connect to Arduino 5 V power).

- 2 is data out. This is the data line.

- 3 is not connected.

- 4 is ground.

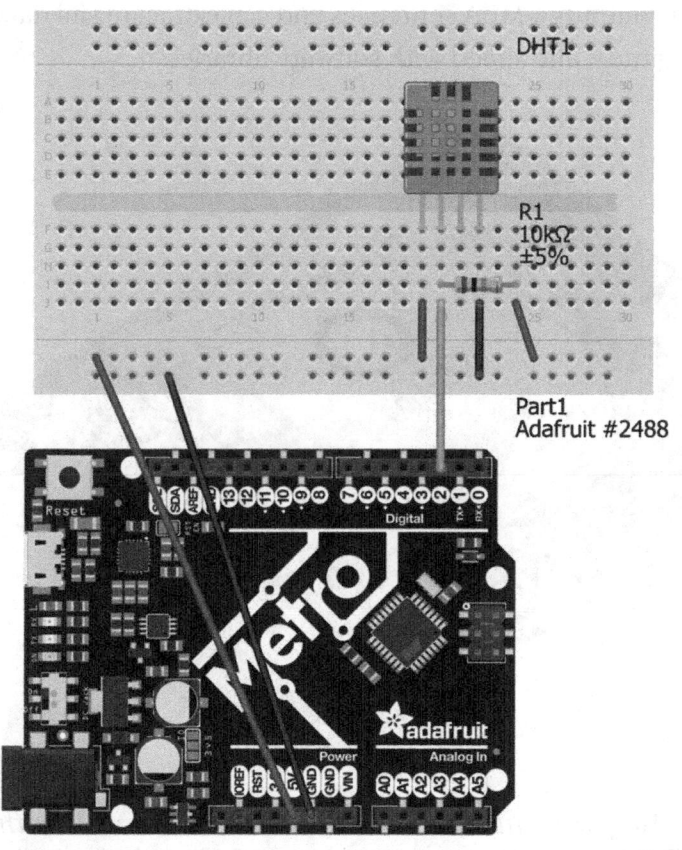

Figure 2-23. *Using a pull-up resistor between the data pin and VCC, which is 5 V*

GPS Breakout

The Adafruit Ultimate GPS breakout (Figure 2-24) is based on the MTK3339 chipset. It can track up to 22 satellites on 66 channels. The breakout can be powered with an Arduino 3.3 V pin. It uses hardware serial or software serial to communicate with the host microcontroller. The module has two antenna options: a built-in standard ceramic patch antenna and an external antenna. The breakout has a U.LF connector, so you can connect a GPS antenna using a U.LF to SMA adapter.

The module outputs NMEA sentences and can extract useful data such as latitude, longitude, and speed with software libraries.

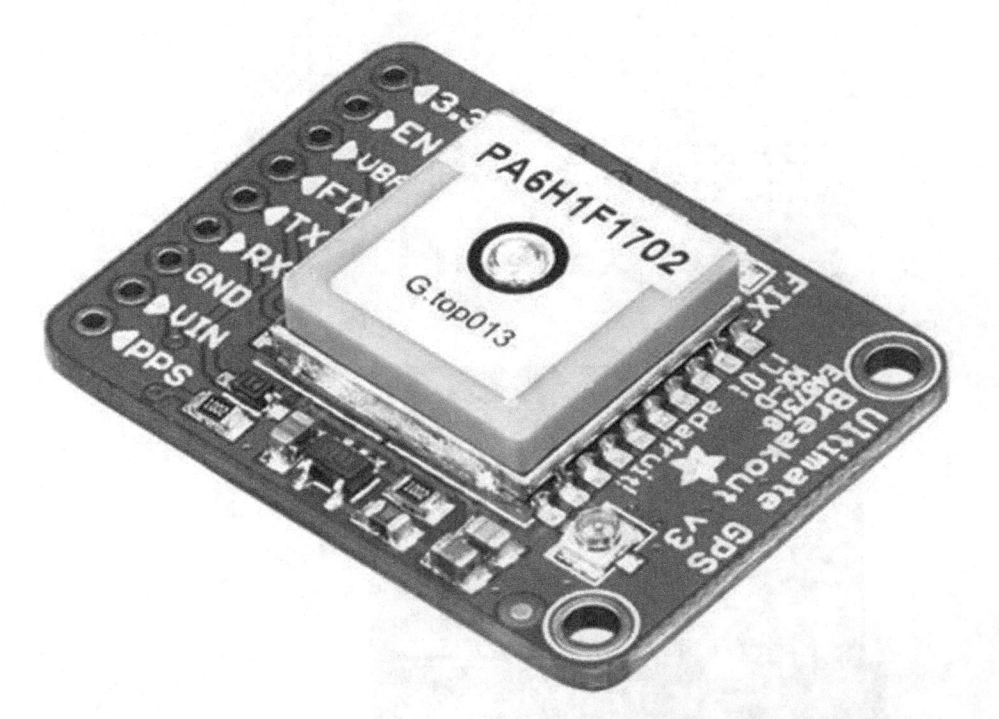

Figure 2-24. *Adafruit Ultimate GPS breakout, 66 channels with 10 Hz updates, version 3 (image courtesy of Adafruit, https://www. adafruit.com/)*

LoRa Gateway

LoRa gateways should have more processing power than the end nodes. A single-channel LoRa gateway can be built with the Raspberry Pi, the Arduino Yun Shield, or a similar hardware platform. These single-channel gateways are not LoRaWAN compliant. However, they can be used to start exploring LoRa radio networks. They can receive LoRa packets on a single frequency and hence offer poor coverage. Assume you have a LoRa end node sending data to a single-channel LoRa gateway using eight different frequencies at different times. But the single-channel LoRa gateway can receive data with only one frequency, and all other frequencies with data are ignored.

A multichannel concentrator consists of a digital baseband chip (SX1301) and one or more RF front ends to digital I and Q modulator/demodulator Multi-PHY mode transceivers (SX1257). The baseband chip is capable of receiving data on multiple frequencies at the same time.

Figure 2-25 shows a breadboard implementation of the Raspberry Pi–based single-channel LoRa gateway.

Figure 2-25. *Raspberry Pi–based single-channel LoRa gateway*

A single-channel LoRa gateway consists of a radio transceiver, microprocessor, power supply, and antenna. For multichannel LoRa gateways, the radio transceiver is known as *a concentrator*.

Chapter 5 shows how to build single-channel LoRa gateways with the Raspberry Pi. Building multichannel gateways is beyond the scope of this book.

Raspberry Pi

The Raspberry Pi 3 (Figure 2-26) is cheaper than other similar hardware (the Arduino Yun Shield) and ideal for building LoRa gateways. Older Raspberry Pi versions also should work with compatible gateway software packages and packet forwarders. They can be easily installed on Raspbian.

Figure 2-26. *Raspberry Pi 3, model B, ARMv8 with 1 GB RAM*

Raspberry Pi boards can be powered with a 5.1 V 2.5 A switching power supply (Figure 2-27) that has a micro-USB plug. A Pi board should connect to the micro-USB port on the Raspberry Pi board. Don't use 5 V/2 A–regulated power supplies with the Raspberry Pi 3; they consume more power (current) than previous versions of the Pi, though.

Figure 2-27. *Connecting a 5 V-regulated power supply to the micro-USB port of the Raspberry Pi*

The Pi 3 comes with a built-in Wi-Fi chip, so you don't want an external Wi-Fi dongle unless you really need more gain.

Raspberry Pi Pin Header

The Raspberry Pi 3 has a 2×20 pin header and can be started to count from the top-left pin, which is pin 1. Figure 2-28 shows the pin numbering and the functions of each pin.

```
[pi@raspberrypi3:~ $ gpio readall
+-----+-----+---------+------+---+---Pi 3---+---+------+---------+-----+-----+
| BCM | wPi |   Name  | Mode | V | Physical | V | Mode |   Name  | wPi | BCM |
+-----+-----+---------+------+---+----+-----+---+------+---------+-----+-----+
|     |     |    3.3v |      |   |  1 ||  2 |   |      | 5v      |     |     |
|   2 |   8 |   SDA.1 | ALT0 | 1 |  3 ||  4 |   |      | 5v      |     |     |
|   3 |   9 |   SCL.1 | ALT0 | 1 |  5 ||  6 |   |      | 0v      |     |     |
|   4 |   7 |  GPIO. 7 |  IN | 1 |  7 ||  8 | 1 | ALT5 | TxD     | 15  | 14  |
|     |     |      0v |      |   |  9 || 10 | 1 | ALT5 | RxD     | 16  | 15  |
|  17 |   0 |  GPIO. 0 |  IN | 0 | 11 || 12 | 0 |  IN  | GPIO. 1 | 1   | 18  |
|  27 |   2 |  GPIO. 2 |  IN | 0 | 13 || 14 |   |      | 0v      |     |     |
|  22 |   3 |  GPIO. 3 |  IN | 0 | 15 || 16 | 0 |  IN  | GPIO. 4 | 4   | 23  |
|     |     |    3.3v |      |   | 17 || 18 | 0 |  IN  | GPIO. 5 | 5   | 24  |
|  10 |  12 |    MOSI | ALT0 | 0 | 19 || 20 |   |      | 0v      |     |     |
|   9 |  13 |    MISO | ALT0 | 0 | 21 || 22 | 0 |  IN  | GPIO. 6 | 6   | 25  |
|  11 |  14 |    SCLK | ALT0 | 0 | 23 || 24 | 1 | OUT  | CE0     | 10  | 8   |
|     |     |      0v |      |   | 25 || 26 | 1 | OUT  | CE1     | 11  | 7   |
|   0 |  30 |   SDA.0 |  IN  | 1 | 27 || 28 | 1 |  IN  | SCL.0   | 31  | 1   |
|   5 |  21 | GPIO.21 |  IN  | 1 | 29 || 30 |   |      | 0v      |     |     |
|   6 |  22 | GPIO.22 |  IN  | 1 | 31 || 32 | 0 |  IN  | GPIO.26 | 26  | 12  |
|  13 |  23 | GPIO.23 |  IN  | 0 | 33 || 34 |   |      | 0v      |     |     |
|  19 |  24 | GPIO.24 |  IN  | 0 | 35 || 36 | 0 |  IN  | GPIO.27 | 27  | 16  |
|  26 |  25 | GPIO.25 |  IN  | 0 | 37 || 38 | 0 |  IN  | GPIO.28 | 28  | 20  |
|     |     |      0v |      |   | 39 || 40 | 0 |  IN  | GPIO.29 | 29  | 21  |
+-----+-----+---------+------+---+----+-----+---+------+---------+-----+-----+
| BCM | wPi |   Name  | Mode | V | Physical | V | Mode |   Name  | wPi | BCM |
+-----+-----+---------+------+---+---Pi 3---+---+------+---------+-----+-----+
```

Figure 2-28. *Pin organization of the Raspberry Pi 2x20 header. Each pin is marked with the pin number, name, and function.*

Raspberry Pi SPI

Like the Arduino, the SPI pins of the Raspberry Pi can be used to communicate with the concentrator (the LoRa radio transceiver module). Figure 2-29 shows the SPI pins that can be found in the middle part of the 2×20 pin header.

Pin 19	MOSI
Pin 21	MISO
Pin23	SCLK
Pin 24	CE0
Pin 26	CE1

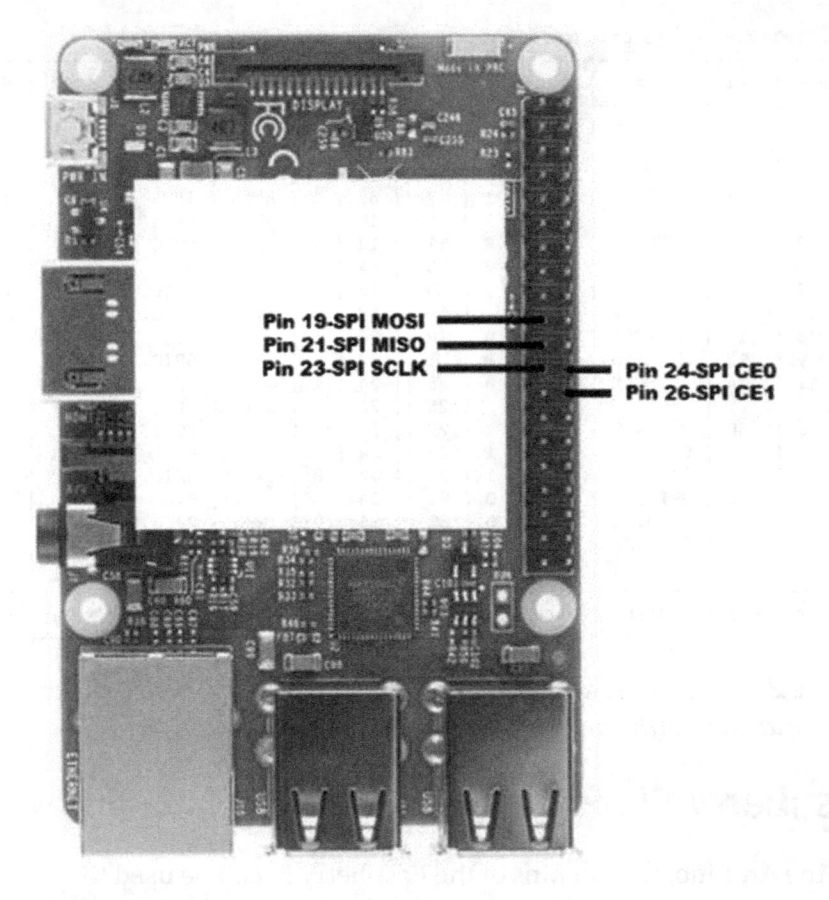

Pin 19-SPI MOSI
Pin 21-SPI MISO
Pin 23-SPI SCLK
Pin 24-SPI CE0
Pin 26-SPI CE1

Figure 2-29. *SPI pins*

You can use female-to-male hookup wires to make a connection with
the Raspberry Pi pins. The female end should connect with the pin header.
It could start getting messy if you connect more wires to the header.
To avoid this, you can use the Adafruit Pi T-Cobbler Plus breakout or
SparkFun Pi Wedge.

Pi T-Cobbler Plus

The Pi T-Cobbler Plus breaks out all the power, SPI, I2C, and GPIO pins
to any standard breadboard and labels them clearly. It also comes with a

40-pin ribbon cable. You can plug the 40-pin GPIO cable between the Pi computer and the Pi T-Cobbler breakout. The T-Cobbler can plug into any solderless breadboard.

Let's take a look at where you can find the SPI pins on the Pi T-Cobbler. Figure 2-30 highlights the SPI pins.

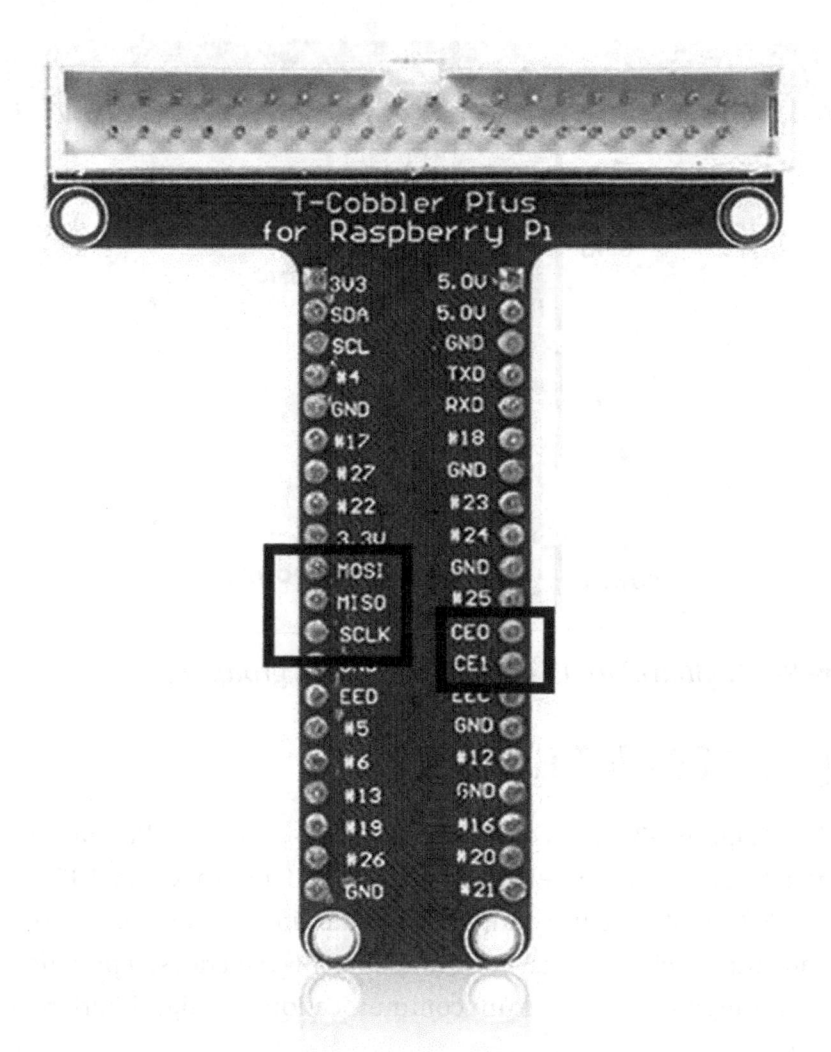

Figure 2-30. *Pi T-Cobbler*

Plug the Pi T-Cobbler to the breadboard and connect the ribbon cable between the T-Cobbler and the Raspberry Pi.

SparkFun Electronics offers another type of Raspberry Pi pin header breakout called the Pi Wedge (Figure 2-31). It organizes the GPIO, SPI, I2C, UART, and power pins so you can easily find them.

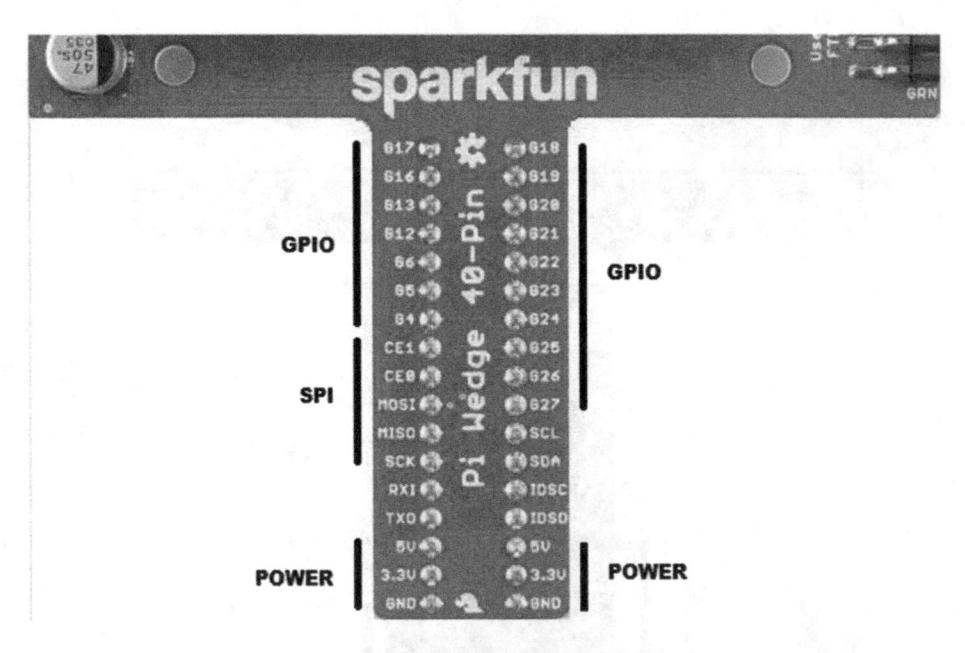

Figure 2-31. *SparkFun Pi Wedge, functional grouping of pins*

Dragino LG01 IoT Gateway

The LG01 (Figure 2-32) is an open source single-channel LoRa gateway. It lets you bridge a LoRa wireless network to an IP network via Wi-Fi, Ethernet, 3G cellular, or 4G cellular. The LoRa wireless allows users to send data and reach extremely long ranges at low data rates. It provides ultra-long-range spread spectrum communication and high-interference immunity.

The LG01-S has a Wi-Fi interface, Ethernet port, and USB host port. These interfaces provide flexible methods for users to connect their sensor networks to the Internet.

The LG01-S runs the open source OpenWrt system, and users are free to modify the source file or compile the system to support their customized applications.

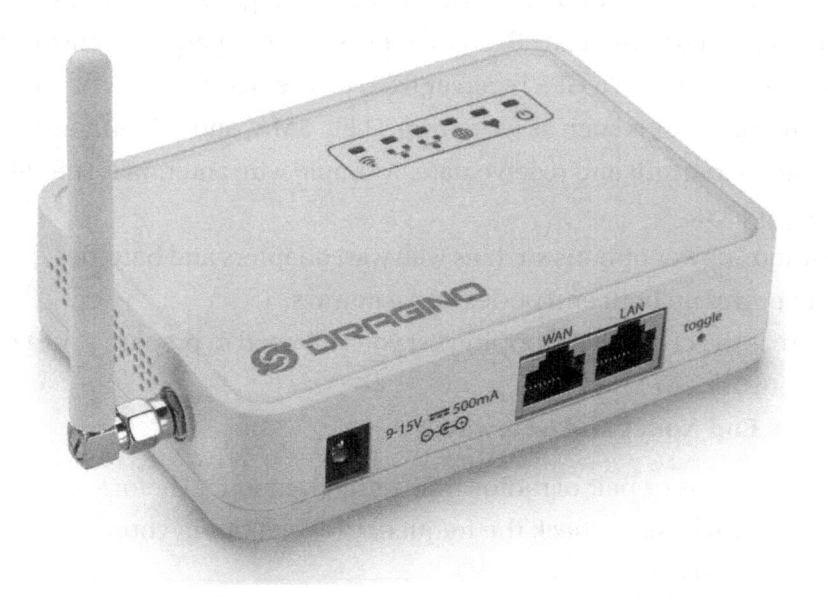

Figure 2-32. *Dragino LG01 IoT gateway (image courtesy of Dragino, www.dragino.com)*

The LG01 has a built-in web server. You can manage it using the web UI or SSH through Ethernet or Wi-Fi.

Summary

Now you know that LoRa end nodes/devices and gateways can be built with Adafruit RFM9x LoRa radio transceiver breakouts. The term *transceiver* is used if you use them with end nodes, and the term *concentrator* (not the correct term for single-channel gateways) is used if you used them with gateways. A microcontroller like the Arduino can be used as the processing unit for the end nodes. For gateways, you will need a microcontroller with more processing power (Raspberry Pi, Dragino Yun Shield for Arduino), known as a *microcomputer*.

Sensors can also be connected to the end nodes so they can periodically send sensor data to the gateway through LoRa wireless. End nodes can be physically fixed (a node with a temperature sensor) or portable (a node with a GPS receiver fixed to a vehicle).

Antenna options such as wire whip, U.FL, SMA, and RP-SMA are available to transmit and receive data. A simple wire antenna is suitable for indoor projects.

Various power options such as wall wart adapters and batteries can be used to power up both end nodes and gateways.

Here is the complete shopping list you will need to prepare your LoRa radio network:

LoRa End Nodes and Gateway

- Choose a pair of radios from either frequency (before purchasing, check the frequency regulations in your area).

    - Two Adafruit RFM95W LoRa radio transceiver breakouts, 868 or 915 MHz, RadioFruit (`https://www.adafruit.com/product/3072`)

    - Two Adafruit RFM96W LoRa radio transceiver breakouts, 433 MHz, RadioFruit (`https://www.adafruit.com/product/3073`)

LoRa End Nodes

- Two Adafruit Metro 328 with headers, ATmega328 (`https://www.adafruit.com/product/2488`)

- One DHT11 basic temperature-humidity sensor plus extras (https://www.adafruit.com/product/386)

- One Adafruit Ultimate GPS breakout, 66 channels with 10 Hz updates, version 3 (https://www.adafruit.com/product/746)

- Two USB cables, A/Micro B, 3 ft (https://www.adafruit.com/product/592)

Power Supply Options

- Two 9 VDC 1000 mA–regulated switching power adapter, UL listed (https://www.adafruit.com/product/63)

- One of the following, with 9 V alkaline battery

  - Two 9 V battery holders with switch and 5.5 mm/2.1 mm plug (https://www.adafruit.com/product/67)

  - Two 9 V battery clips with 5.5 mm/2.1 mm plug (https://www.adafruit.com/product/80)

- Two alkaline 9 V batteries (https://www.adafruit.com/product/1321)

- Two half-size breadboards (https://www.sparkfun.com/products/12002)

- Two Arduino and breadboard holders (https://www.sparkfun.com/products/11235)

- One hook-up wire spool set, 22 AWG solid core, 10 by 25 ft (https://www.adafruit.com/product/3174)

LoRa Gateway

- One Raspberry Pi 3, model B, ARMv8 with 1 B RAM (https://www.sparkfun.com/products/13825)

- One wall adapter power supply, 5.1 V DC 2.5 A (USB Micro-B) (https://www.sparkfun.com/products/13831)

Ready-to-Use LoRa Gateway

- LG01 LoRa OpenWrt IoT gateway (https://www.tindie.com/products/edwin/lg01-lora-openwrt-iot-gateway/?pt=ac_prod_search) (before purchasing, check frequency regulations in your area)

Soldering

- Soldering iron, 30W/60W

- Helping third-hand magnifier W/magnifying glass tool, MZ101 (https://www.adafruit.com/product/291)

- Solder wire, RoHS lead free, 0.5mm/.02-inch diameter, 50 g (https://www.adafruit.com/product/2473)

Cutting and Stripping

- Multi-size wire stripper and cutter, 5023 (https://www.adafruit.com/product/147)

The next chapter introduces the essential software components that you will need to build LoRa radio networks.

CHAPTER 3

Setting Up the Software Development Environment

This chapter covers how to set up the software development environment to build single-channel LoRa wireless radio networks. First, you will learn how to install and configure the Arduino IDE on the Windows operating system to work with Arduino boards, RFM9x radio transceivers, GPS modules, temperature sensors, and so forth, for building LoRa end nodes (sensor nodes). In the latter part of this chapter, you will learn how to install PuTTY on Windows as a prerequisite to building a single-channel LoRa gateway with the Raspberry Pi.

Arduino Integrated Development Environment

The Arduino integrated development environment (IDE) allows you to write and upload code to the Arduino board. It also provides facilities for compiling and debugging code. The Arduino IDE is available for Windows (XP and up), Windows Mobile (8.1 or 10), Mac OS X (10.7 Lion and up), and Linux (32-bit, 64-bit, and ARM). It can be downloaded from

© Pradeeka Seneviratne 2019
P. Seneviratne, *Beginning LoRa Radio Networks with Arduino*,
https://doi.org/10.1007/978-1-4842-4357-2_3

http://arduino.cc/en/Main/Software. There is an online Arduino editor for coding known as Arduino Create, available at https://create. arduino.cc/editor (Figure 3-1).

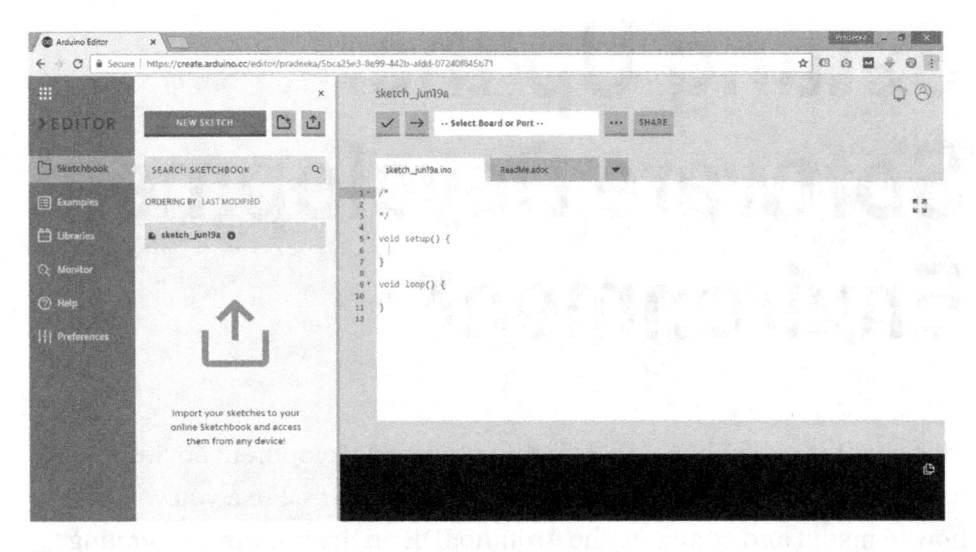

Figure 3-1. *Arduino Create online editor*

Arduino for Windows

The Arduino software is available as a ZIP file for nonadmin installation and comes with an installer for Windows XP and up. An app is also available for Windows 8.1 and 10. You can use either the admin or nonadmin installation method to set up the IDE on your computer.

Admin Install

Follow these steps:

1. Download the installer by clicking "Windows Installer, for Windows XP and up."

2. Once the installer has been downloaded, double-click the EXE file to start the installation process.

3. Follow the instructions shown in the wizard to install the Arduino software correctly on your computer.

Nonadmin Install

Follow these steps:

1. Download the ZIP file by clicking "Windows ZIP file for non-admin install."

2. Once downloaded, extract the ZIP file to any convenient directory in your computer.

3. You will get a folder named arduino<version>. Inside that folder, you can find an application file named arduino along with other files and folders. Simply, double-click it to start the Arduino software. It will take some time for the Arduino software to load.

Figure 3-2 shows the main areas of the Arduino IDE labeled with numbers.

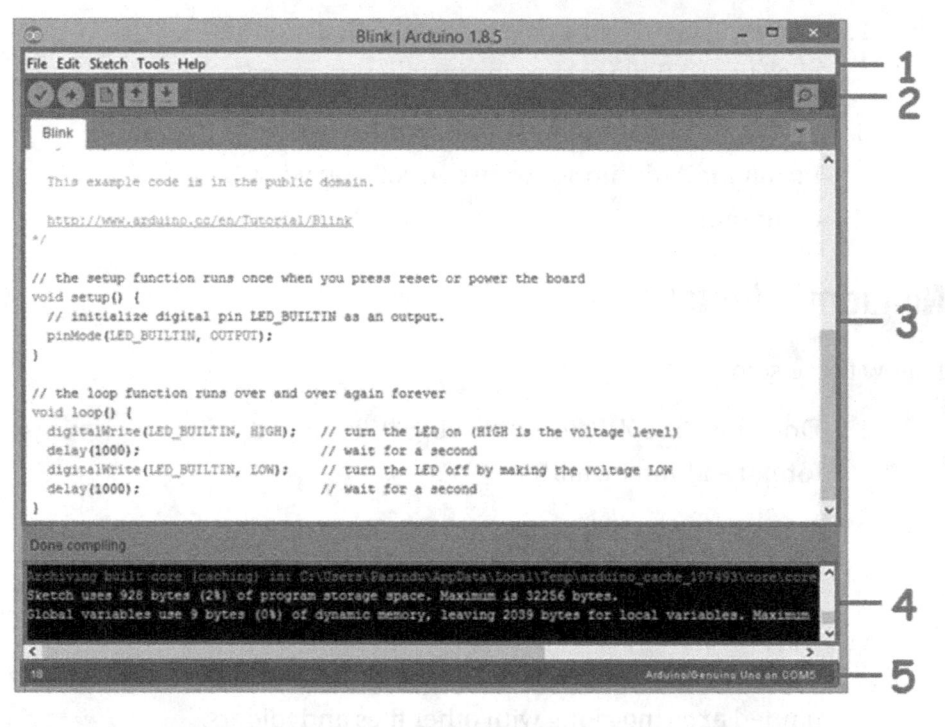

Figure 3-2. *Main areas of the Arduino IDE*

Here's what each element shown in Figure 3-2 is:

1. *Menu bar*: Provides useful commands

2. *Toolbar*: Provides the most important commands

3. *Sketch editor*: The area you can use to type your code

4. *Text console*: Shows status and error messages

5. *Status bar*: Displays the currently configured microcontroller board with the COM port

Table 3-1 summarizes the function of each button in the toolbar. You can view the name of a toolbar button by placing the mouse pointer over it. A tooltip will show the name of the button.

Table 3-1. *Function of Each Toolbar Button in the Arduino IDE*

Icon	Name	Function
	New	Creates a new sketch
	Open	Opens a sketch
	Save	Saves the sketch
	Verify	Compiles your code and shows whether it has any errors
	Upload	Compiles and uploads the code to the microcontroller board
	Serial Monitor	Opens the serial monitor window

Installing Drivers for the Arduino

Drivers allow operating systems to properly recognize the Arduino board. The following sections will describe how to install drivers for the Arduino Uno and Arduino Metro on the Windows operating system.

Installing Drivers for Uno

If you have installed the Arduino IDE on your Windows computer using the ZIP file, you will need to install the drivers manually. The following steps show how to install the drivers on Windows 8:

1. Connect the Arduino Uno with your Windows computer using a USB type A to B cable (Figure 3-3). Use the type B end to connect with the Arduino (Figure 3-4) and the type A end to connect with the computer.

Figure 3-3. *USB type A to B cable (courtesy of SparkFun Electronics)*

Figure 3-4. *Connecting a USB cable to the Arduino Uno. Use the type B end of the cable to connect with Arduino's USB port B.*

2. Open the Device Manager with Windows 8 by typing
    Device Manager in the Search box (Figure 3-5).

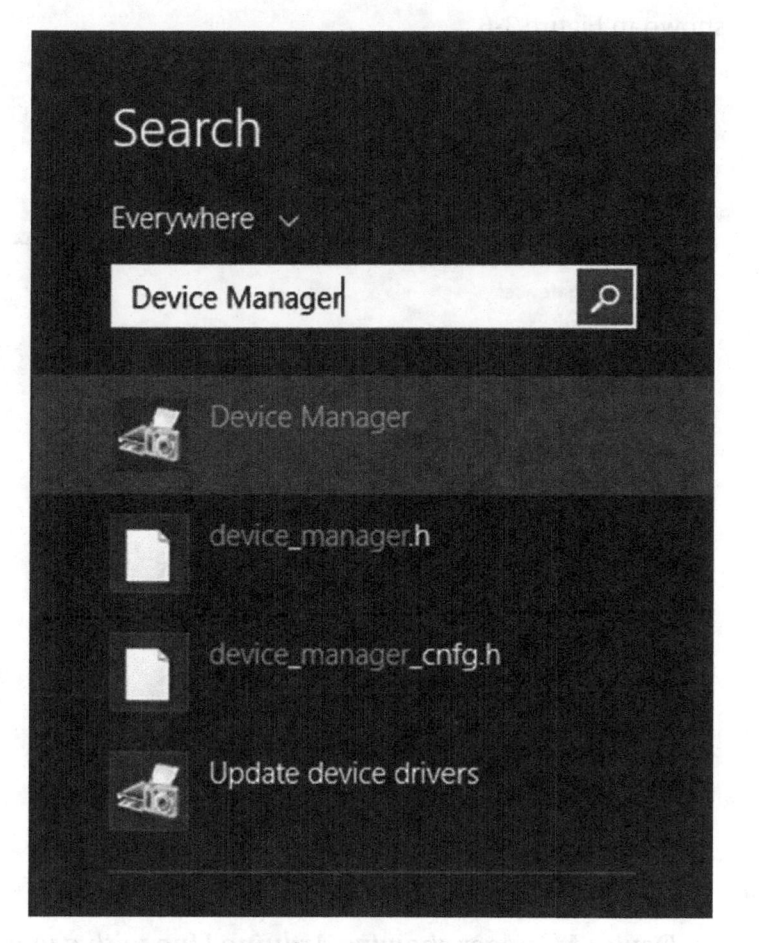

Figure 3-5. *Opening an application with Windows Search*

3. In the Device Manager, under "Other devices," you should see a node named Arduino Uno (with a yellow triangle with a black exclamation mark), as shown in Figure 3-6.

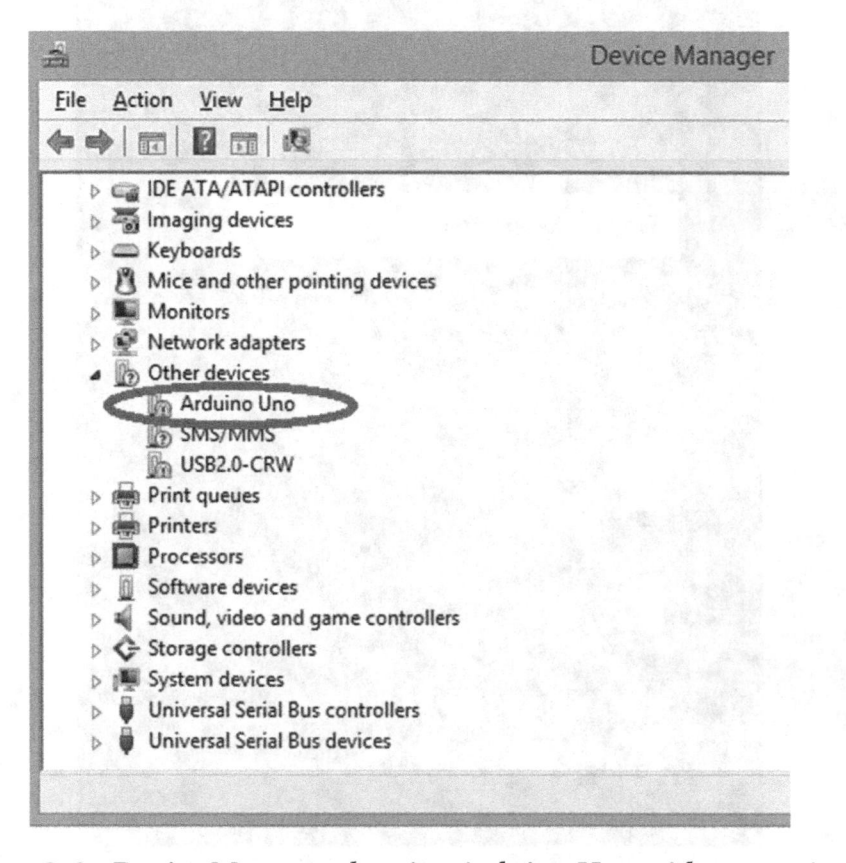

Figure 3-6. *Device Manager showing Arduino Uno with a warning*

4. Right-click the node Arduino Uno, and from the
    shortcut menu, choose Update Driver Software
    (Figure 3-7).

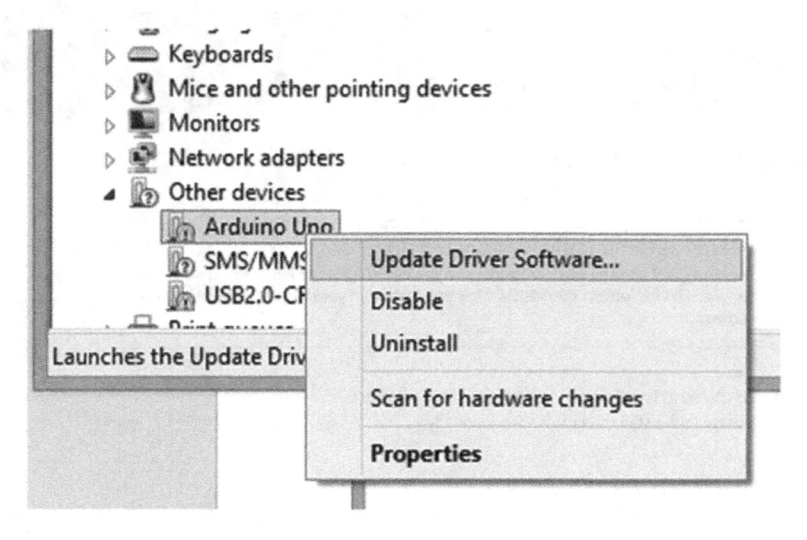

Figure 3-7. Updating the driver software

5. Click the "Browse my computer for driver software" option to locate and install the driver software manually (Figure 3-8).

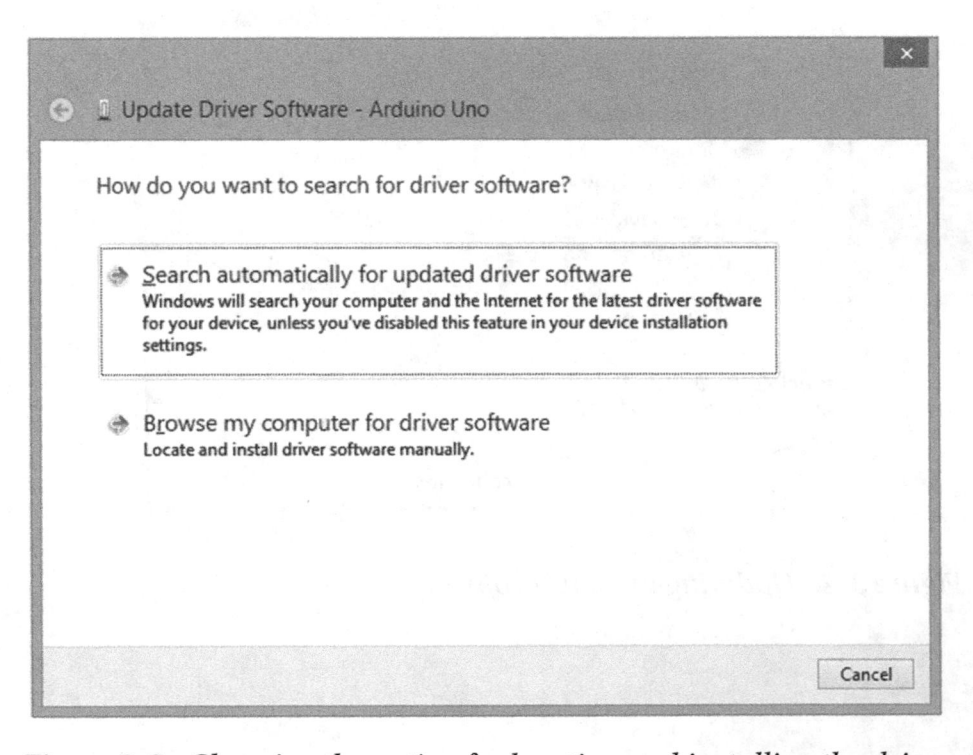

Figure 3-8. *Choosing the option for locating and installing the driver software manually*

6.   Click the Browse button (Figure 3-9).

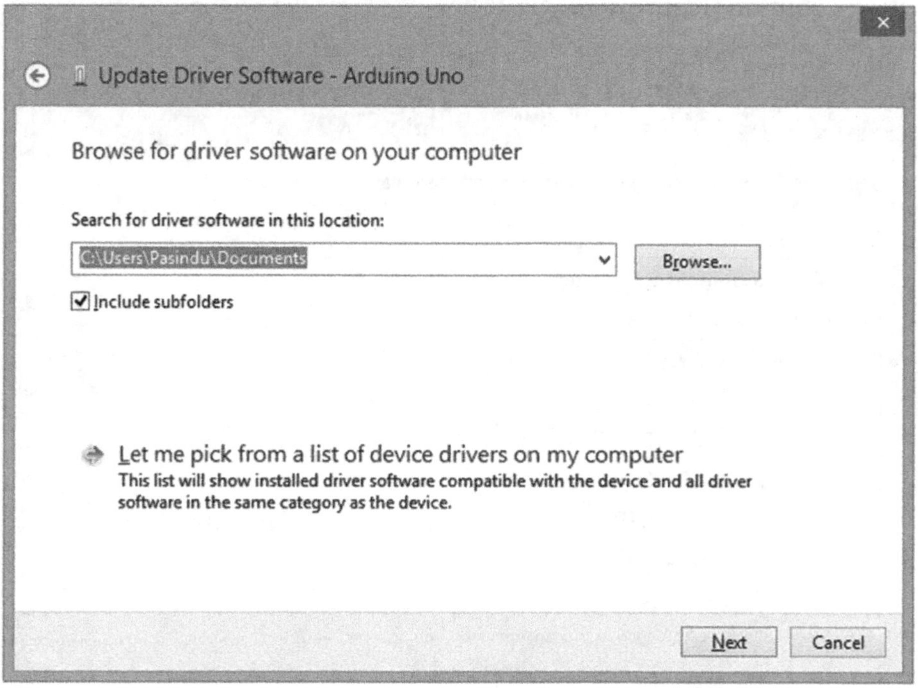

Figure 3-9.   *Searching for the driver software*

7. Browse and select the folder named drivers from the Arduino software download. Then click the OK button (Figure 3-10).

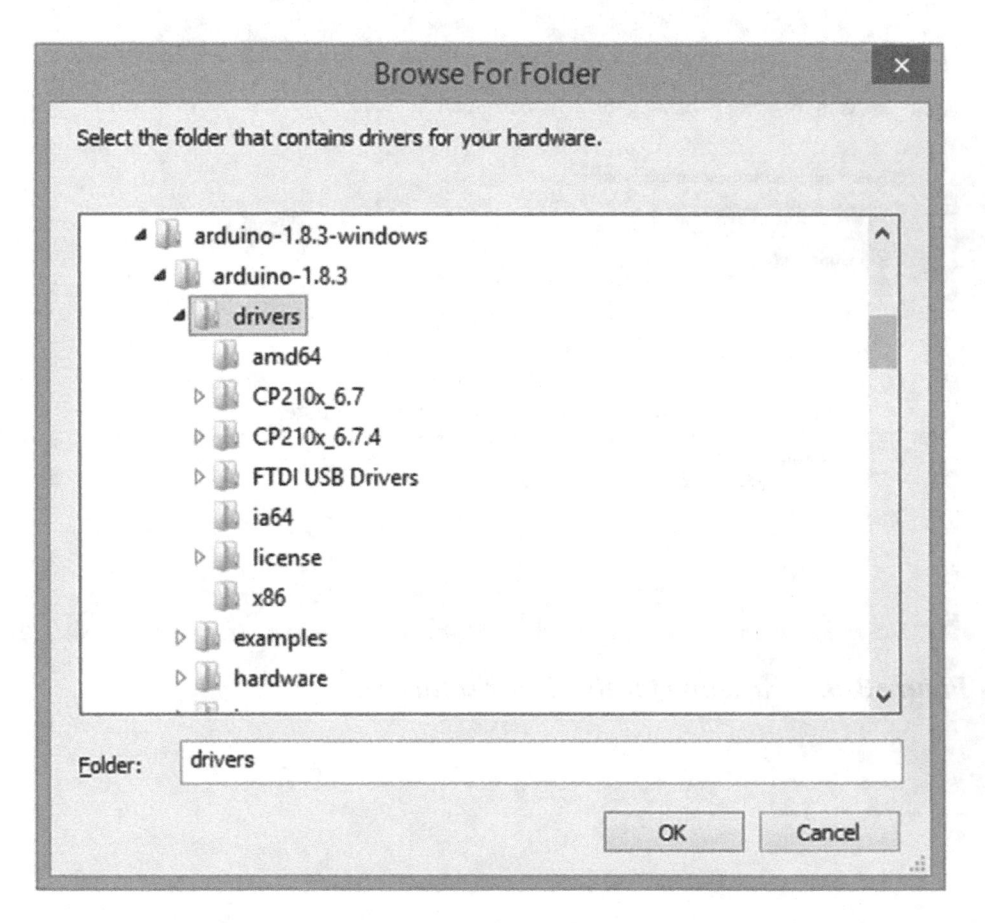

Figure 3-10. *The drivers for Arduino Uno can be found in the drivers folder*

8. Click the Next button. Windows will start to install the drivers for the Arduino Uno.

9. Click the Close button to exit the wizard (Figure 3-11).

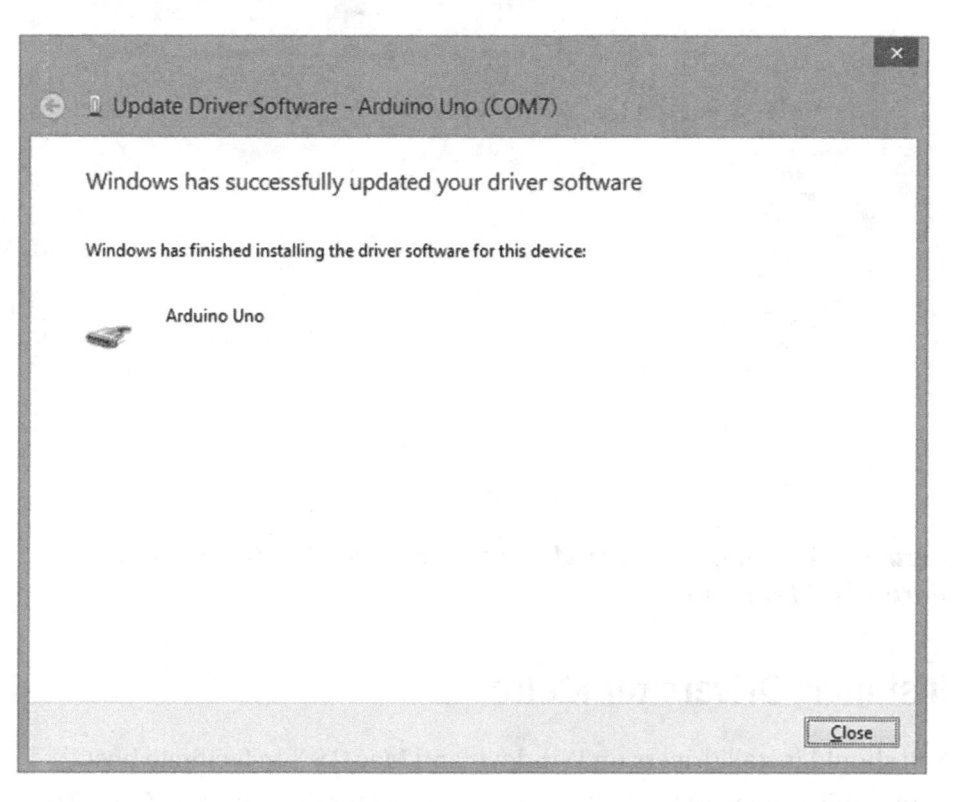

Figure 3-11. *This step will confirm that Windows has successfully updated your driver software*

10.   Now you can see your Arduino Uno under Ports
(COM & LPT), as shown in Figure 3-12.

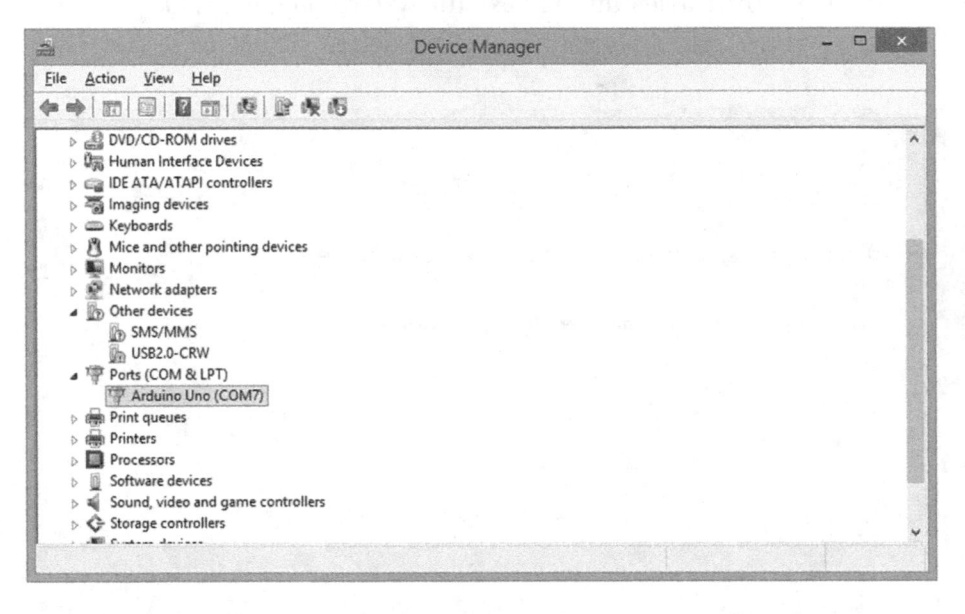

Figure 3-12.   *In the Device Manager, Arduino Uno is listed under*
Ports (COM & LPT)

Installing Drivers for Metro

You should install drivers on Windows and Mac OS X to facilitate host
communication with the USB/serial chip used for the Adafruit Metro. The
USB/serial chip is marked as "CP2014" and can be found near the micro-
USB port of the Metro board (Figure 3-13).

Figure 3-13. *CP2014 USB/serial chip*

1. The drivers can be downloaded from Silicon
   Labs (https://www.silabs.com/products/
   development-tools/software/usb-to-uart-
   bridge-vcp-drivers), as shown in Figure 3-14.
   Click the link labeled as the default (e.g., Download
   VPC (5.3 MB) (Default)).

Platform	Software
Windows 7/8/8.1/10	Download VCP (5.3 MB) (Default)
Windows 7/8/8.1/10	Download VCP with Serial Enumeration (5.3 MB) Learn More »

Figure 3-14. *CP2014 USB/serial chip drivers for Windows 7 and up. Download the software marked as the default.*

2. After downloading the drivers, extract the ZIP file and find the relevant installer for your Windows version. (For 32-bit Windows, run CP210xVCPInstaller_x86, and for 64-bit Windows, run CP210xVCPInstaller_x64.) Follow the instruction in the setup wizard to install them.

3. Once installed, connect the Adafruit Metro with your computer using the micro-USB cable. Now you can find your Adafruit Metro under Ports (COM & LPT), as shown in Figure 3-15.

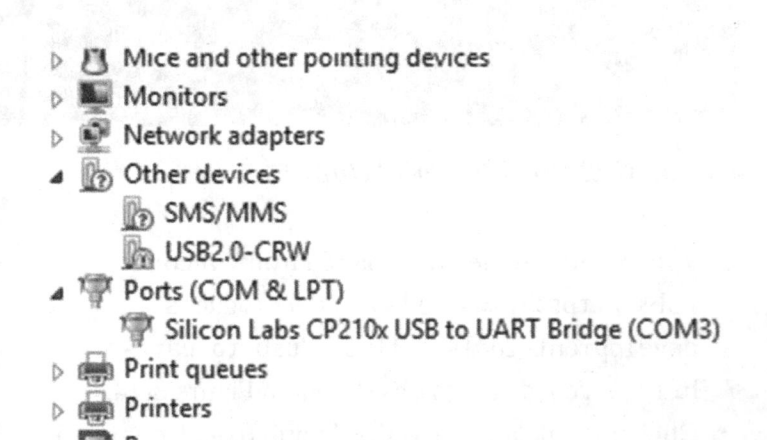

Figure 3-15. *The Adafruit Metro is listed as Silicon Labs CP210x USB to UART Bridge under Ports (COM & LPT)*

4. The drivers for Mac OSX can also be downloaded from the same page under the section, **Download for Macintosh OSX (vX)** by clicking on the link, **Download VCP**. After downloading the driver, follow the instaructions mentioned in the page at https://learn.adafruit.com/experimenters-guide-for-metro/mac-setup to setting it up on your Mac OSX.

Your First Arduino Sketch

The Arduino Uno and other Arduino-compatible boards have a built-in LED connected to digital pin 13. This LED can be controlled with a sample sketch bundled with the Arduino IDE.

Usually, the Adafruit Metro comes with the preflashed Blink sketch. When you apply power to the board, the red LED (internally connected to digital pin 13, marked with an *L*) will start to blink. If not, upload the sample sketch provided with the Arduino IDE to make sure that the board is working properly. The following steps will show you how to upload a sketch into the Metro board:

1. Open the sample sketch from the menu bar by choosing File ➤ Examples ➤ 01. Basics ➤ Blink. Listing 3-1 shows the Arduino sketch that can be used to blink an LED connected to digital pin 13.

Listing 3-1. Blinks the Built-in LED Connected to Digital Pin 13

```
// the setup function runs once when you press reset or power
the board
void setup() {
  // initialize digital pin LED_BUILTIN as an output.
  pinMode(LED_BUILTIN, OUTPUT);
}

// the loop function runs over and over again forever
void loop() {
  digitalWrite(LED_BUILTIN, HIGH);   // turn the LED on (HIGH
                                        is the voltage level)
  delay(1000);                       // wait for a second
  digitalWrite(LED_BUILTIN, LOW);    // turn the LED off by
                                        making the voltage LOW
  delay(1000);                       // wait for a second
}
```

2. Choose the board you're going to use by selecting
    Tools ➤ Board ➤ Arduino/Genuino Uno under
    Arduino AVR Boards (Figure 3-16).

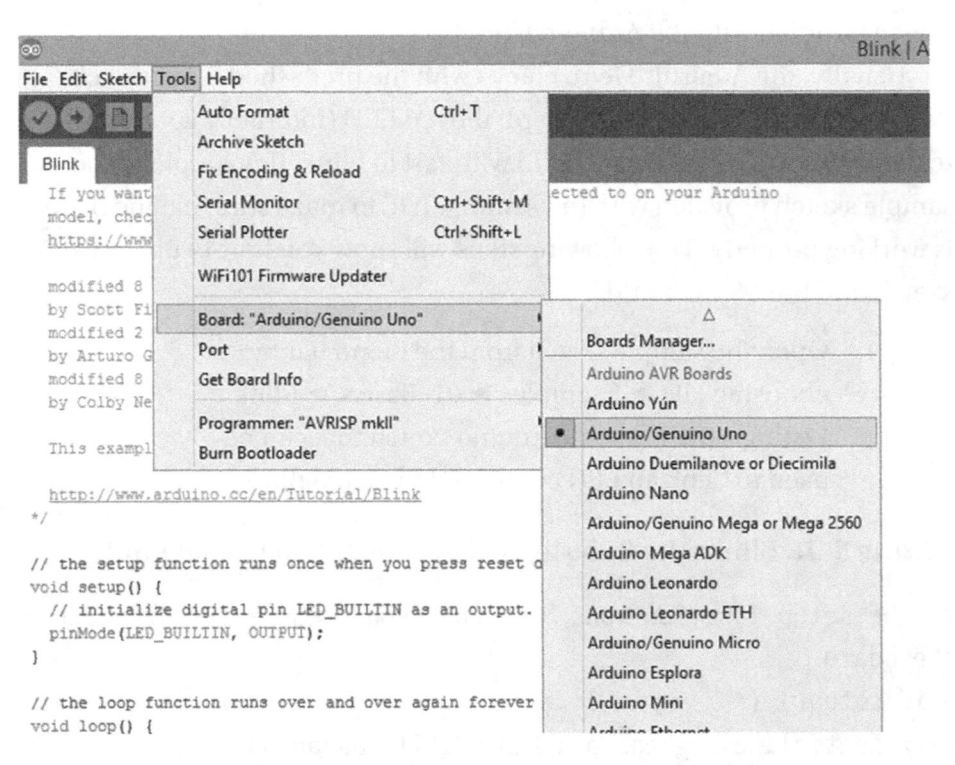

Figure 3-16. *Choosing the type of microcontroller board*

3. Choose the port associated with the Arduino Uno/
    Metro board by selecting Tools ➤ Serial Port ➤
    PORT (Figure 3-17).

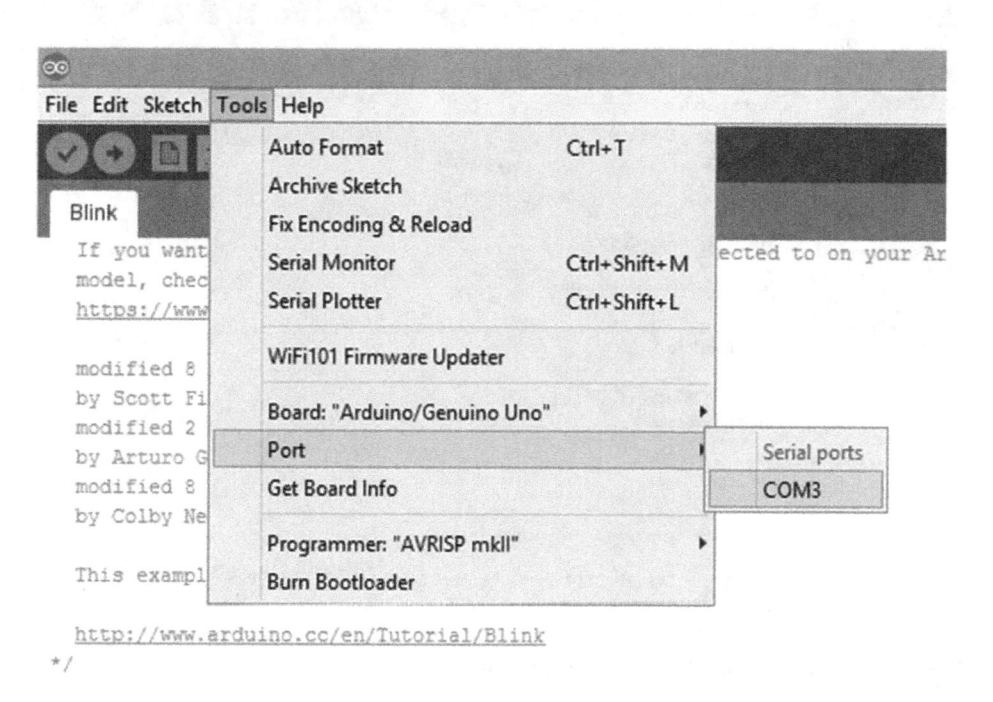

Figure 3-17. *Choosing the port*

4. Choose the programmer as AVRISP mkll by selecting
    Tools ➤ Programmer ➤ AVRISP mkll (Figure 3-18).

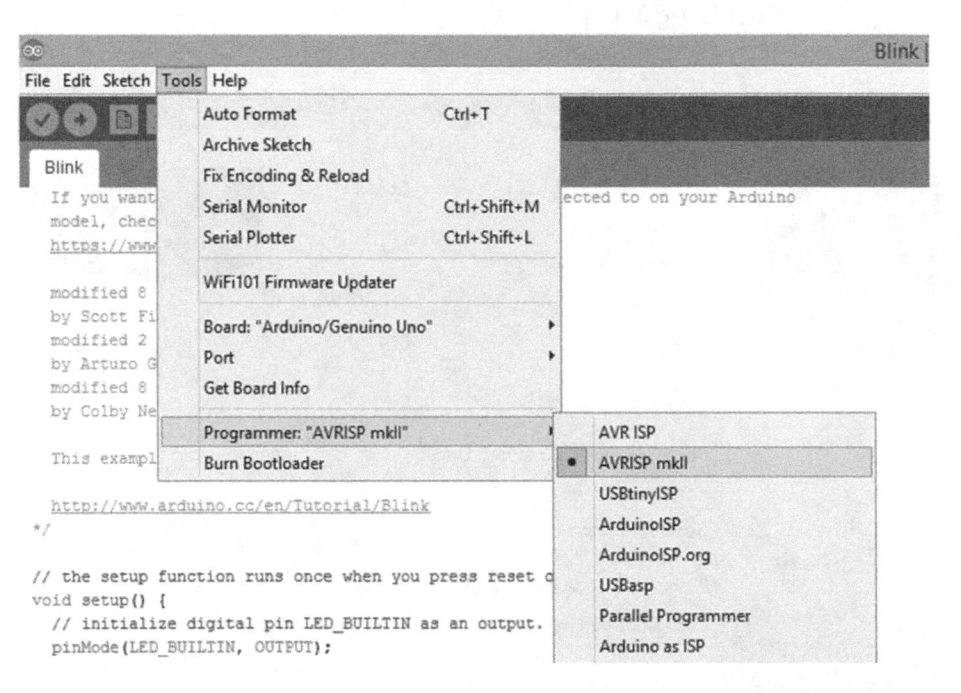

Figure 3-18. *Choosing a programmer*

5. Verify and compile the sketch by choosing Sketch ➤
    Verify/Compile or pressing Ctrl+R. When the compiler
    is compiling your sketch, it will report problems that it
    finds in your sketch. Find and correct them all. This is
    known as *debugging*. Then compile the sketch again and
    see whether there are more errors still in the code.

6. Upload the sketch by choosing Sketch ➤ Upload or
    pressing Ctrl+U. You can also use the Upload button
    (the button has a right arrow icon) on the toolbar.

7. After the upload finishes, you should see the LED on
    the Arduino Uno/Metro start to blink.

Installing the Arduino Libraries

Arduino libraries should be copied to the `libraries` folder in the Arduino sketch book. There are two ways to install Arduino libraries.

- Manually copy the library master folder to the `libraries` folder.

- Use the Boards Manager to search, install, and update libraries (some libraries don't support the Boards Manager).

Follow these steps to install an Arduino library:

1. Find your Arduino sketchbook location by selecting File ➤ Preferences in the Arduino IDE (Figure 3-19).

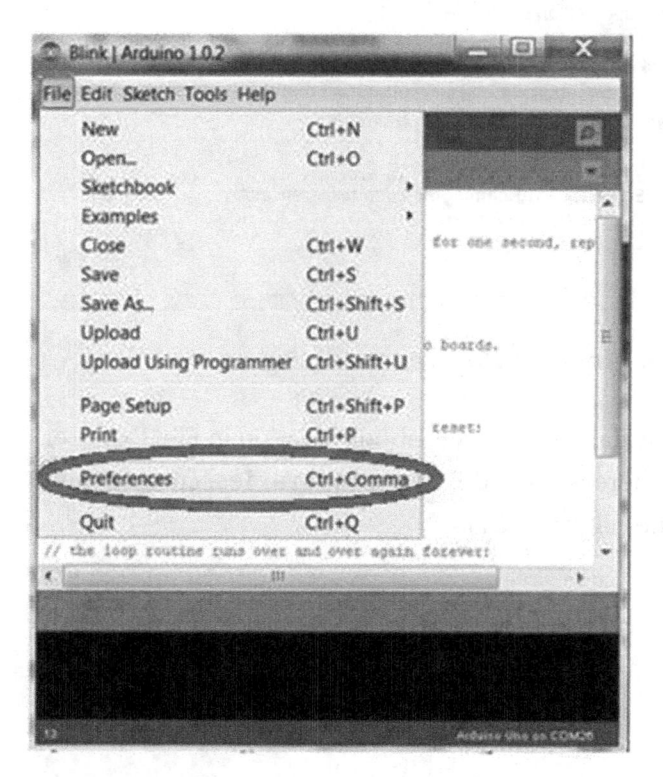

Figure 3-19. *Finding the Sketchbook location*

2. Usually, the sketchbook location is a folder named
    Arduino in the Documents folder (Figure 3-20).

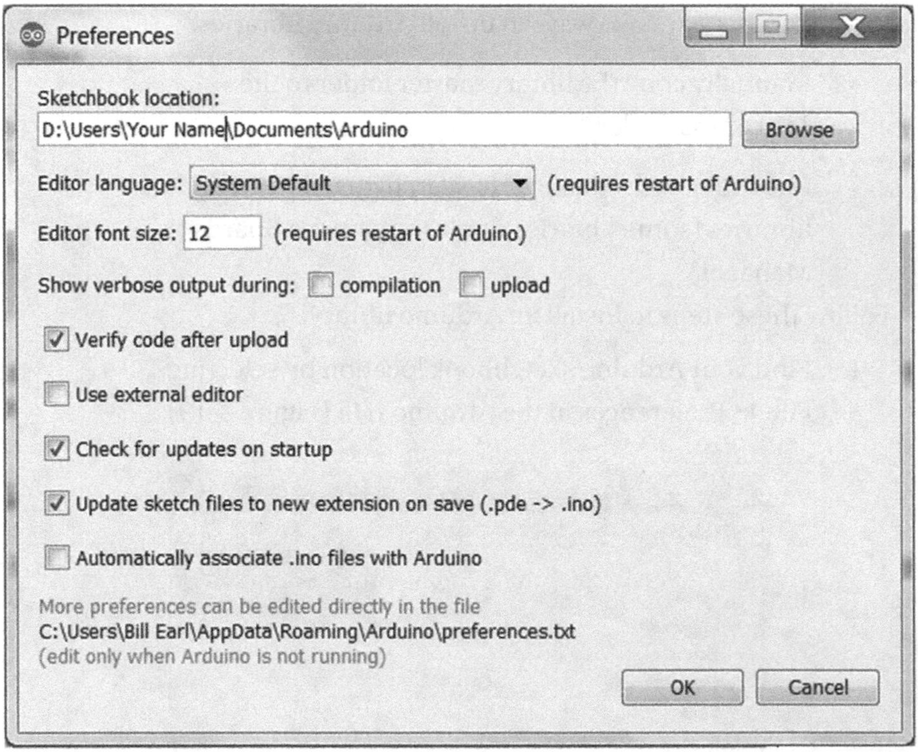

Figure 3-20. *Arduino Preferences dialog*

3. Navigate to the sketchbook location in File Explorer.
    If there is no folder named libraries, create a new
    one (Figure 3-21).

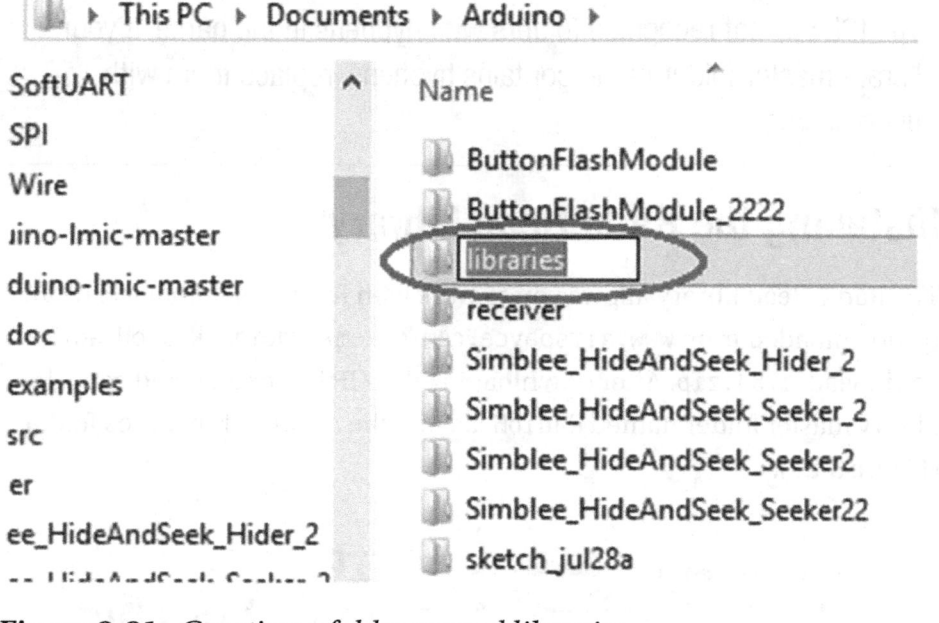

Figure 3-21. *Creating a folder named libraries*

4. Now close all instances of the Arduino IDE.

5. When you download a library from GitHub, Arduino
    Playground, or any other location on the Internet,
    usually you will get a ZIP file.

6. Open the ZIP file and navigate until you find the
    library master folder. This is the folder that has the
    name of your library.

7. Copy the library master folder and paste it in the
    libraries folder.

8. Restart the Arduino IDE and verify that the library
    appears in the Sketch ➤ Include Library menu.

The IDE will not recognize folders with hyphens in the name. If your
library master folder name contains hyphens, replace them with
underscores.

Installing the RadioHead Library

The RadioHead library allows you to work with RFM95/96 modules. It can
be downloaded from www.airspayce.com/mikem/arduino/RadioHead/
RadioHead-1.84.zip. After downloading the ZIP file, open it and copy the
library master folder named RadioHead into the Arduino libraries folder
(Figure 3-22).

Figure 3-22. *RadioHead library*

The RadioHead library provides drivers for a wide range of chipsets and
modules. For this book, you will need the RH_RF95 class. It allows the driver
to send and receive unaddressed, unreliable datagrams via a Lora-capable
radio transceiver. The RH_RF95 class supports both 833/915 and 433MHz
Adafruit radio transceiver breakouts.

However, Dragino provides an improved version of the RadioHead
library known as Dragino's Modified RadioHead library. It provides
additional functions to configure the following things:

- Spreading factor

- Signal bandwidth

- Coding rate

The library can be downloaded from https://github.com/dragino/
RadioHead. After downloading the ZIP file, open it and copy the library
master folder named RadioHead-master into the Arduino libraries
folder (Figure 3-23).

Figure 3-23. *Dragino RadioHead library*

Once that's copied, rename the folder to RadioHead_master.

Installing the Adafruit DHT11 Library

Adafruit provides an easy-to-use library for the DHT11 and DHT 22
temperature and humidity sensors. You can download it from https://
github.com/adafruit/DHT-sensor-library. After downloading the
ZIP file, open it and copy the library master folder named DHT-sensor-
library-master into the Arduino libraries folder (Figure 3-24).

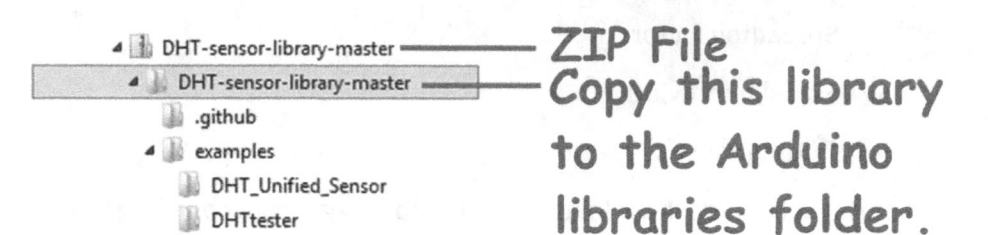

Figure 3-24. *Adafruit DHT11 library*

Once copied, rename the folder to DHT_sensor_library_master.

Installing the TinyGPS Library

TinyGPS allows you to read and parse NMEA sentences to extract actual data from them. It uses background interrupt to read, store, and parse the data. You can download it from https://github.com/mikalhart/ TinyGPS/releases/tag/v13. On the download page, click "Source code (zip)," as shown in Figure 3-25.

Figure 3-25. *Source code for TinyGPS library*

After downloading the ZIP file, open it and copy the library master folder named `TinyGPS-13` into the Arduino `libraries` folder (Figure 3-26).

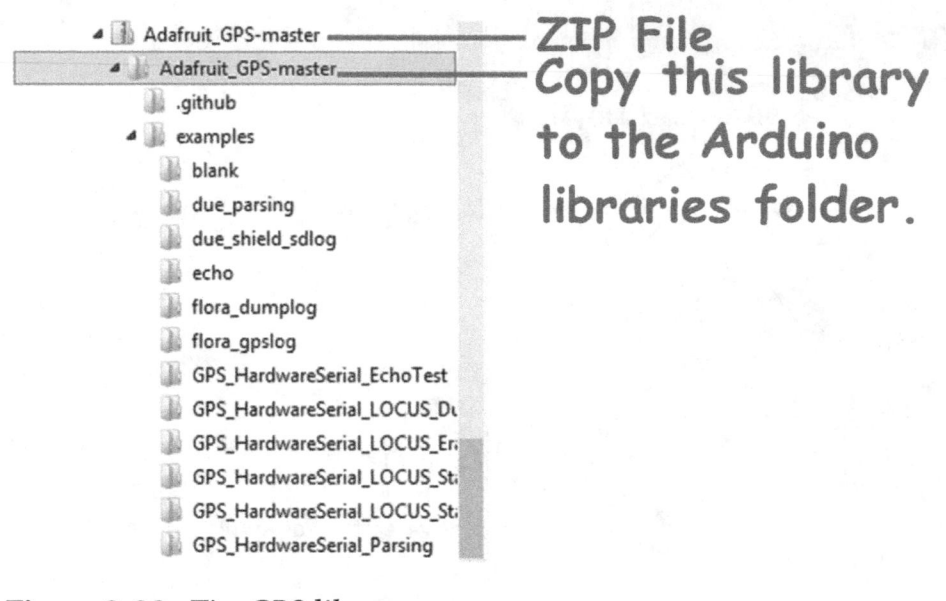

Figure 3-26. *TinyGPS library*

Once copied, rename the folder to TinyGPS_13.

Installing the Arduino LMIC Library

The Arduino-LMIC library allows you to use the SX1272 and SX1276 transceivers and compatible modules (such as some HopeRF RFM9x modules) with the Arduino environment. It is a slightly modified version of the IBM LMIC (LoraMAC-in-C) library.

You can download it from https://github.com/matthijskooijman/arduino-lmic. On the GitHub page, first click the "Clone or download" button and then click the Download ZIP link (Figure 3-27).

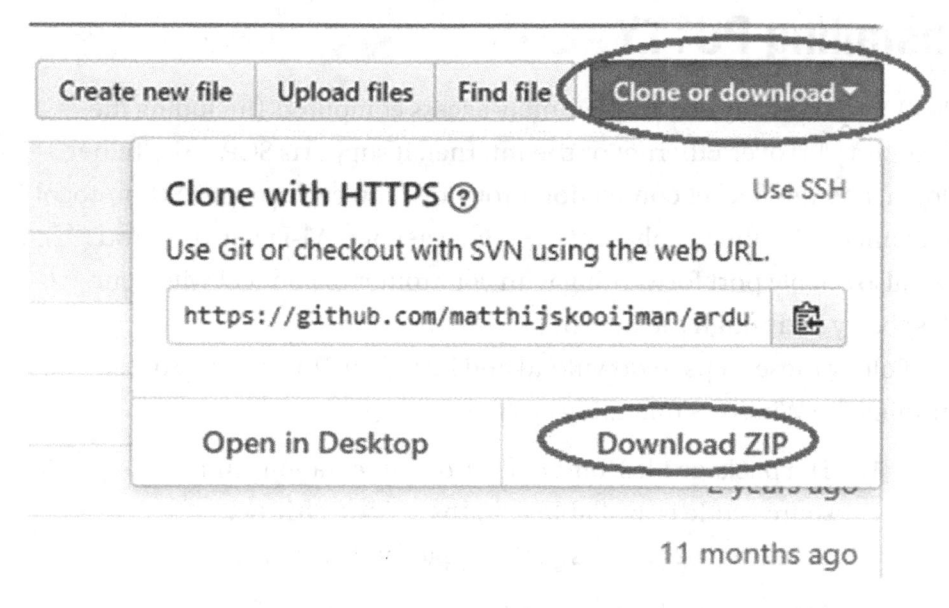

Figure 3-27. *Downloading the Arduino LMIC library from GitHub*

After downloading the ZIP file, open it and copy the library master folder named `arduino-lmic-master` into the Arduino `libraries` folder (Figure 3-28).

Figure 3-28. *Arduino LMIC library*

Once copied, rename the folder to `arduino_lmic_master`.

Now you have installed all the required Arduino libraries for the Arduino IDE.

Installing PUTTY

PuTTY enables any users to remotely access computers (including the Raspberry Pi) over Ethernet or the Internet. It supports SCP, SSH, Telnet, rlogin, and raw socket connection protocols. You can use the SSH protocol to connect with the Raspberry Pi via Ethernet or a Wi-Fi network. You can also enable port forwarding with your router to connect with your Raspberry Pi through the Internet.

Follow these steps to download and install PuTTY on a computer running the Windows operating system:

1. The package files, binary files, documentation, and source code is available at `https://www.chiark.greenend.org.uk/~sgtatham/putty/latest.html`.

2. At the top of the page, under the Package files (Figure 3-1), click `putty-0.70-installer.msi` (for 32-bit Windows) or `putty-64bit-0.70-installer.msi` (for 64-bit Windows), as shown in Figure 3-29.

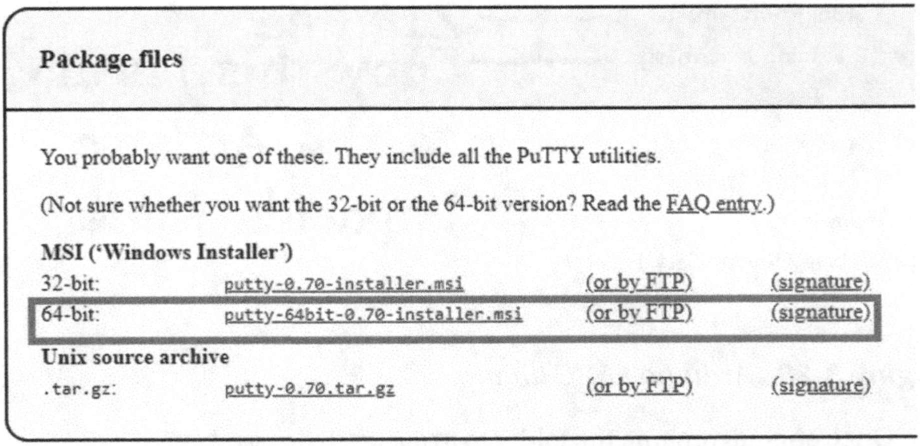

Figure 3-29. *Installers for 32-bit and 64-bit Windows*

3. Once downloaded, run the installer by double-
    clicking it. The setup wizard will open. Click the Next
    button to continue (Figure 3-30).

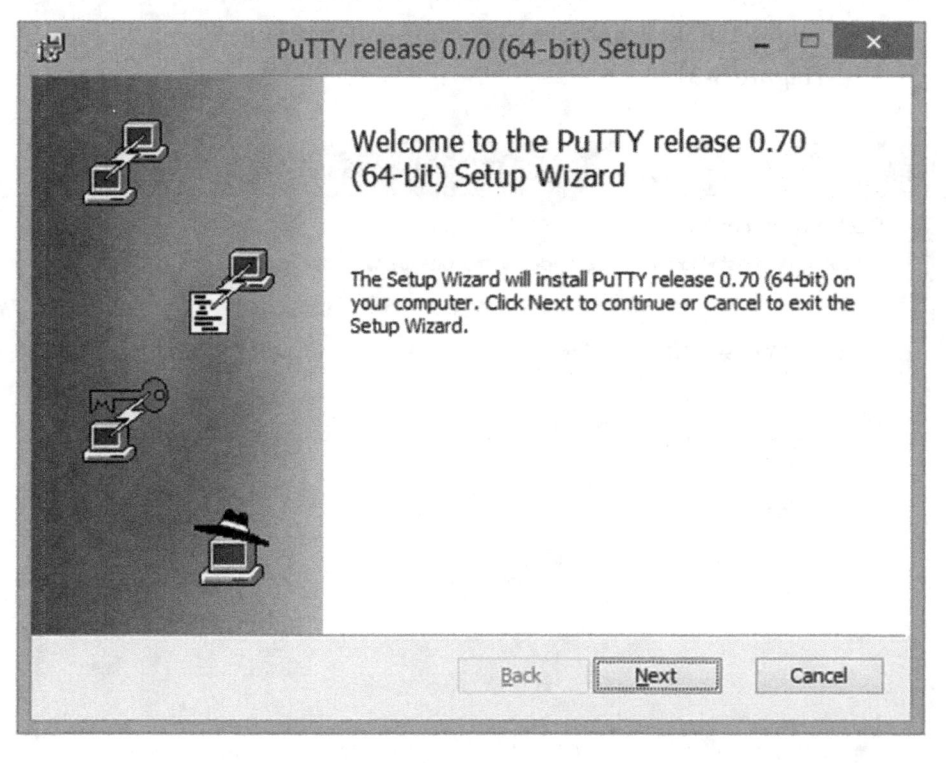

Figure 3-30. PuTTY installation wizard welcome page for 64-bit
Windows OS

4. For the default destination folder, PuTTY will install into C:\Program Files\PuTTY\. If you want to install PuTTY in a different directory, first click the Change button. Then browse to a new destination folder. Finally, click the Next button to continue (Figure 3-31).

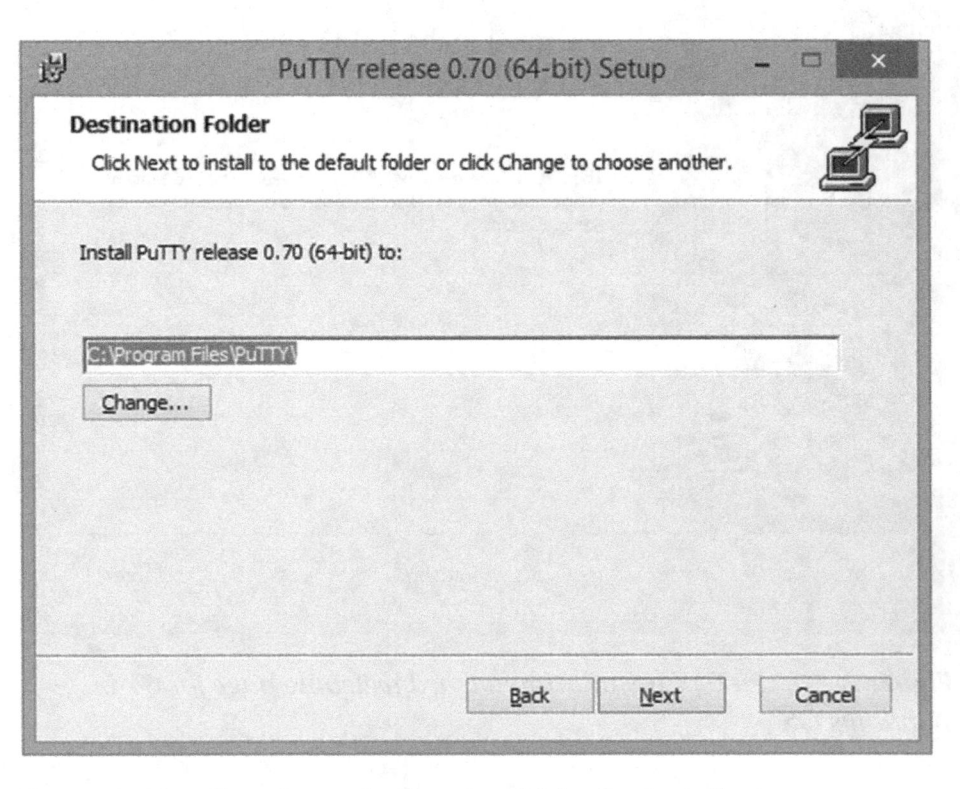

Figure 3-31. *Choosing a destination folder for installation*

5. To add a desktop shortcut for PuTTY, click "Add shortcut to PuTTY on the desktop" (click the button marked with an X), and from the drop-down menu, choose the "Will be installed on the local hard drive" option. Then click the Install button to continue (Figure 3-32).

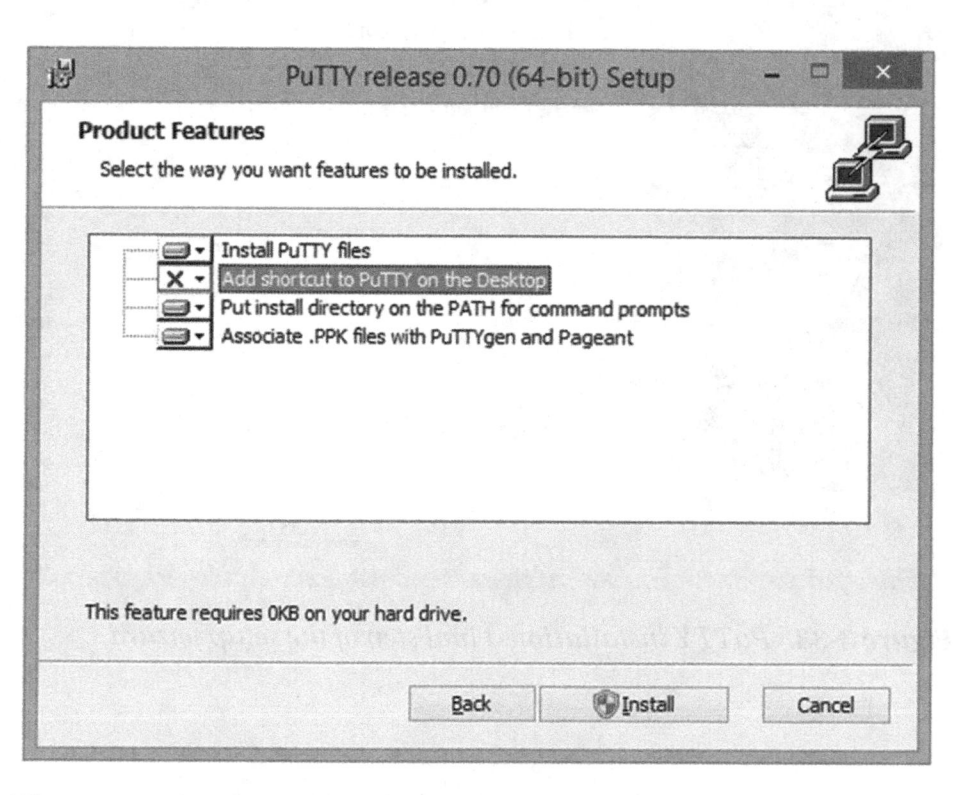

Figure 3-32. *Customizing the product features*

6. In the User Access Control dialog box, click the Yes button to continue.

7. PuTTY will start to install on your computer. Wait until it completes.

8. Click the Finish button to exit from the setup wizard (Figure 3-33).

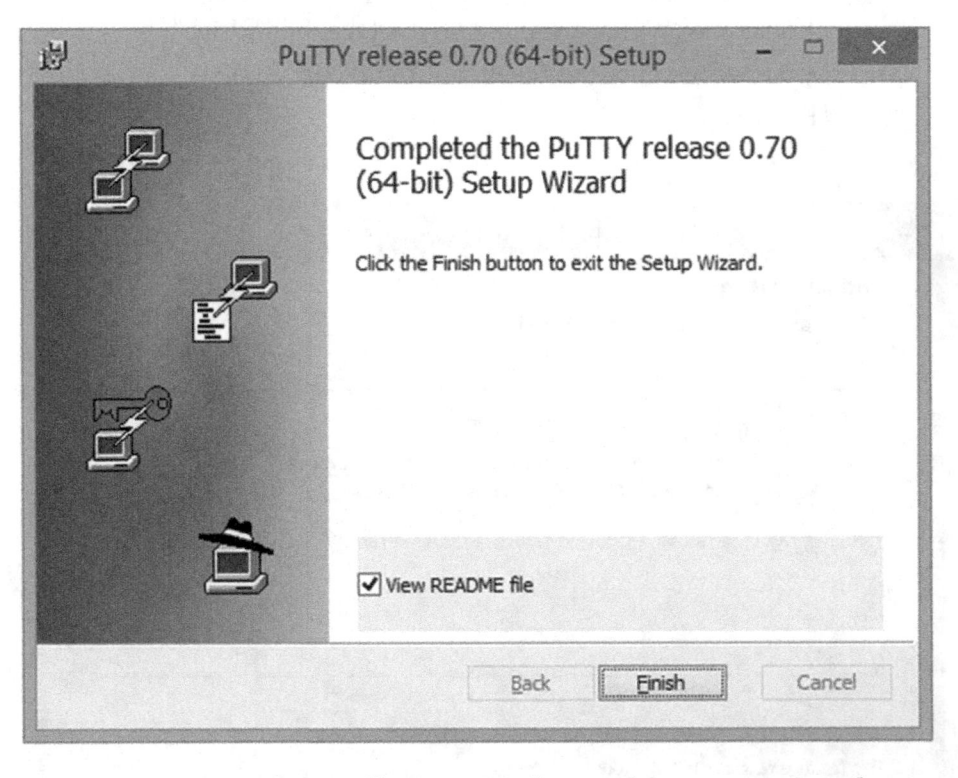

Figure 3-33. *PuTTY installation. Final step of the setup wizard.*

To verify the installation, double-click the PuTTY shortcut icon on the Windows desktop. If it was successfully installed, the PuTTY Configuration window will open (Figure 3-34).

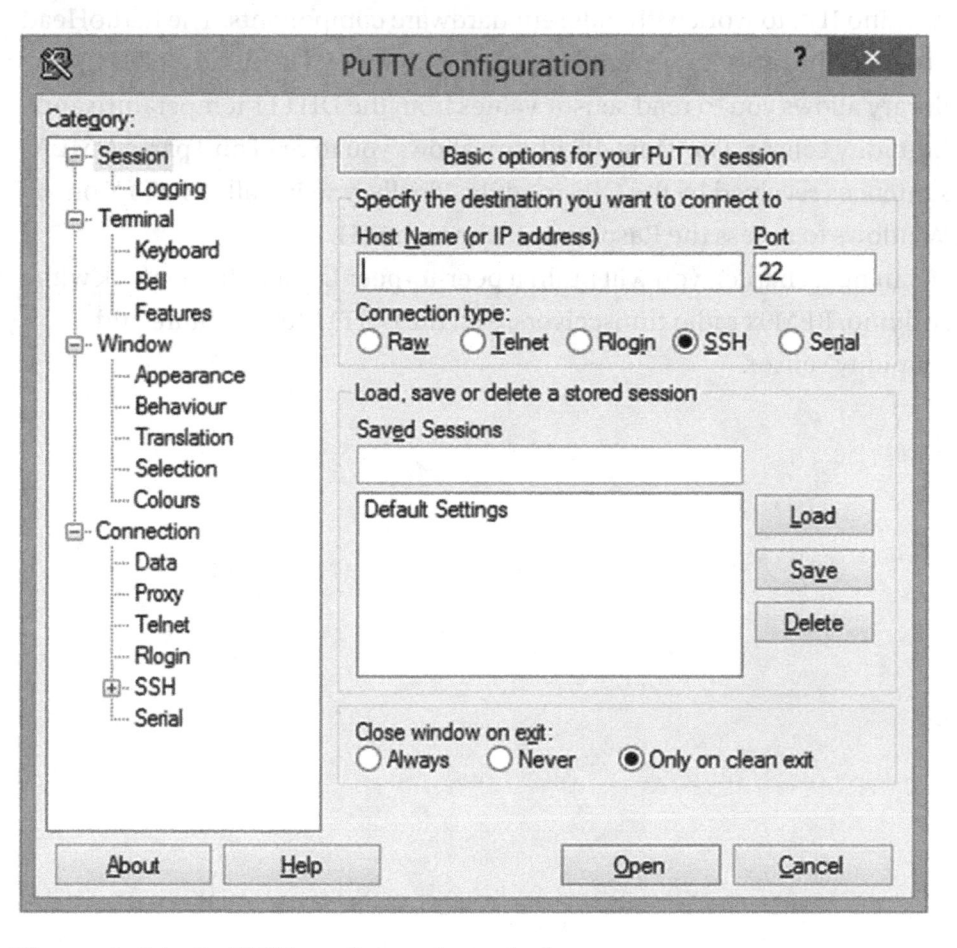

Figure 3-34. *PuTTY configuration window*

Summary

You installed the Arduino IDE on your computer and configured it by installing drivers. Then you installed some software libraries on the Arduino IDE to work with different hardware components. The RadioHead library is the most important software component. The Adafruit DHT11 library allows you to read sensor values from the DHT11 temperature and humidity sensor. The TinyGPS library allows you to read and parse NMEA sentences received by the GPS module. Finally, you installed PuTTY on Windows to access the Raspberry Pi through SSH.

In next chapter, you will build a peer-to-peer LoRa radio network with Arduino, RFM9x radio transceivers, and the DHT11 temperature and humidity sensor.

CHAPTER 4

Building a Peer-to-Peer Channel

In this chapter, you will learn how to build a peer-to-peer communication channel using two LoRa radio transceiver modules. Building a peer-to-peer communication channel is not LoRaWAN compatible, but it provides a way to better understand how messages can be exchanged between two LoRa radio transceivers.

Things You Need

You will need to use the following hardware from your toolbox:

- Two Adafruit Metro or Arduino Uno boards

- Two RFM9x radio transceiver modules

- One DHT11 temperature sensor

- Two mini breadboards

- Two breadboard holders

- A few hook-up wires

© Pradeeka Seneviratne 2019
P. Seneviratne, *Beginning LoRa Radio Networks with Arduino*,
https://doi.org/10.1007/978-1-4842-4357-2_4

In addition, you will need the RadioHead library to work with the LoRa radio transceivers, and you will need the DHT11 library to work with the DHT11 temperature sensor. In the previous chapter, you learned about how to install these libraries on Arduino IDE.

Hardware Setup

Let's get started building hardware for the two LoRa nodes. You will build one node as a sensor node and the other node as a receiving node. The sensor node can be configured to periodically transmit (broadcast) the temperature data in Celsius. The receiving node can listen to the incoming data. Once the data is received, the receiving node can process the data and display it on the Arduino serial monitor. The receiving node can also send an acknowledgment message to the sensor node. Once that message is received, it will display on the sensor node's serial monitor.

Figure 4-1 shows a peer-to-peer communication channel. The LoRa sensor node is also known as the *client*, and the receiving node is also known as the *server*.

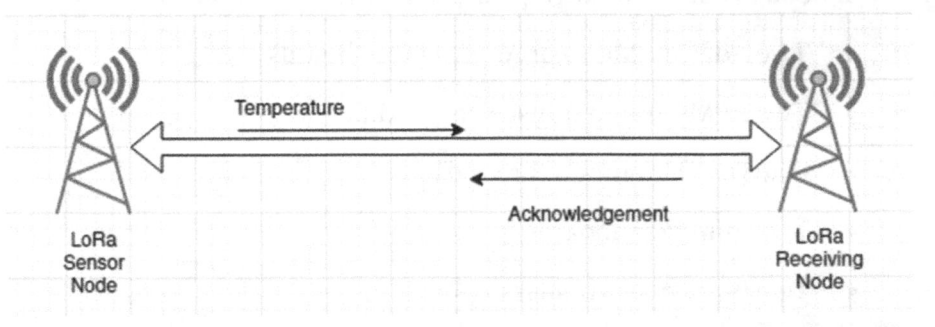

Figure 4-1. *Peer-to-peer communication channel*

Building the Sensor Node

Now you'll build a LoRa sensor node with a temperature sensor. It periodically collects temperature data from the environment and sends (broadcasts) to the receiving node. Follow these steps to build the hardware setup:

1. First, get the following:

   - Breadboard holder

   - Mini breadboard

   - Adafruit Metro or Arduino Uno board

2. Stick the breadboard to the breadboard holder.

3. Usually the breadboard prototyping holder comes with two screws for mounting the Arduino Uno. Place the Arduino Uno on the prototyping plate and apply screws.

4. Insert the LoRa Radio transceiver, the DHT11 temperature sensor, and the current limiting resistor.

5. Using hook-up wires, connect all the data and power lines between the breadboard and the Adafruit Metro/Arduino Uno. Use the Fritzing diagram shown in Figure 4-2 to make the wire connections between components.

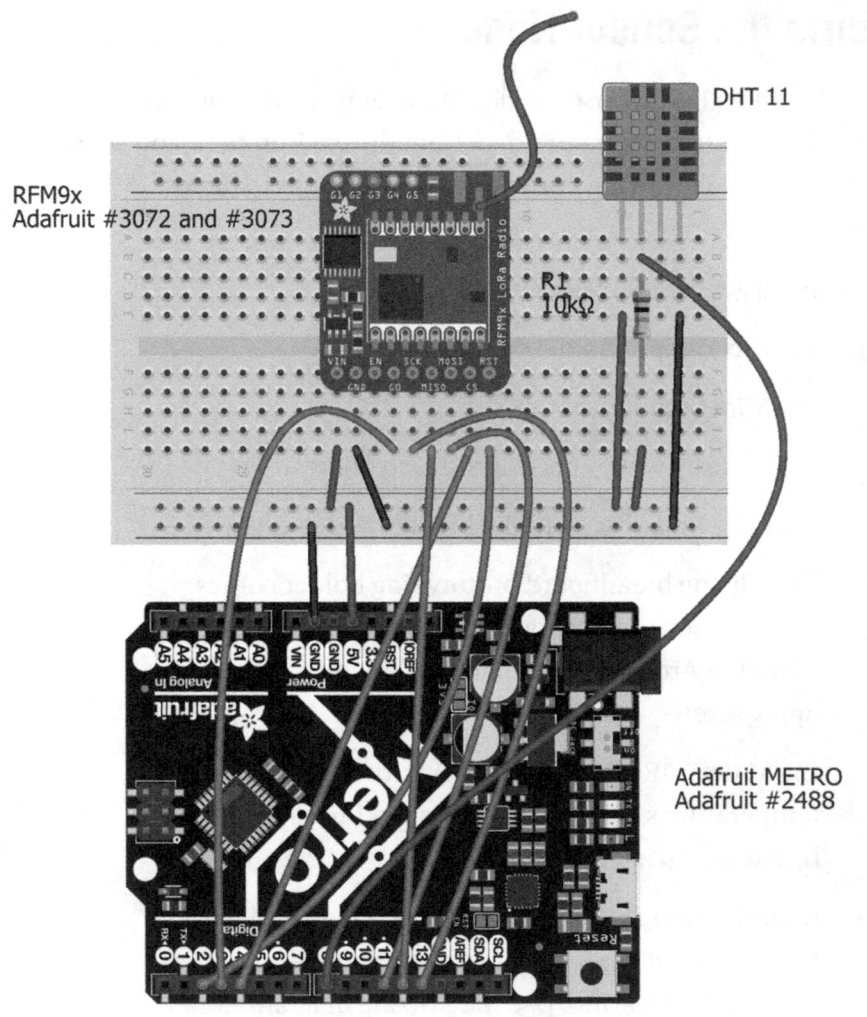

Figure 4-2. *Wiring diagram for the LoRa sensor node*

Table 4-1 shows the connections between the Arduino/Metro, radio transceiver, and DHT11 sensor.

Table 4-1. *Wiring Connections for Sensor Node*

Arduino/Metro	Radio Transceiver	DHT11
VIN	VIN	VIN
GND	GND	GND
2	RST	
3	G0	
4	CS	
8		DATA
11	MOSI	
12	MISO	
13	SCK	

Make sure to keep the antenna wire perpendicular to the LoRa radio transceiver module.

Building the Receiving Node

The receiving node receives the temperature data from the sensor node periodically. The following steps explain how to build the receiving node:

1. Take the other prototyping plate, mini breadboard, and the Adafruit Metro/Arduino Uno.

2. Stick the breadboard to the prototyping plate and then connect the Arduino to the prototyping plate using two screws.

3. Place the RFM9x radio transceiver module on the breadboard, as shown in Figure 4-3, and use hook-up wires to make all the data and power connections.

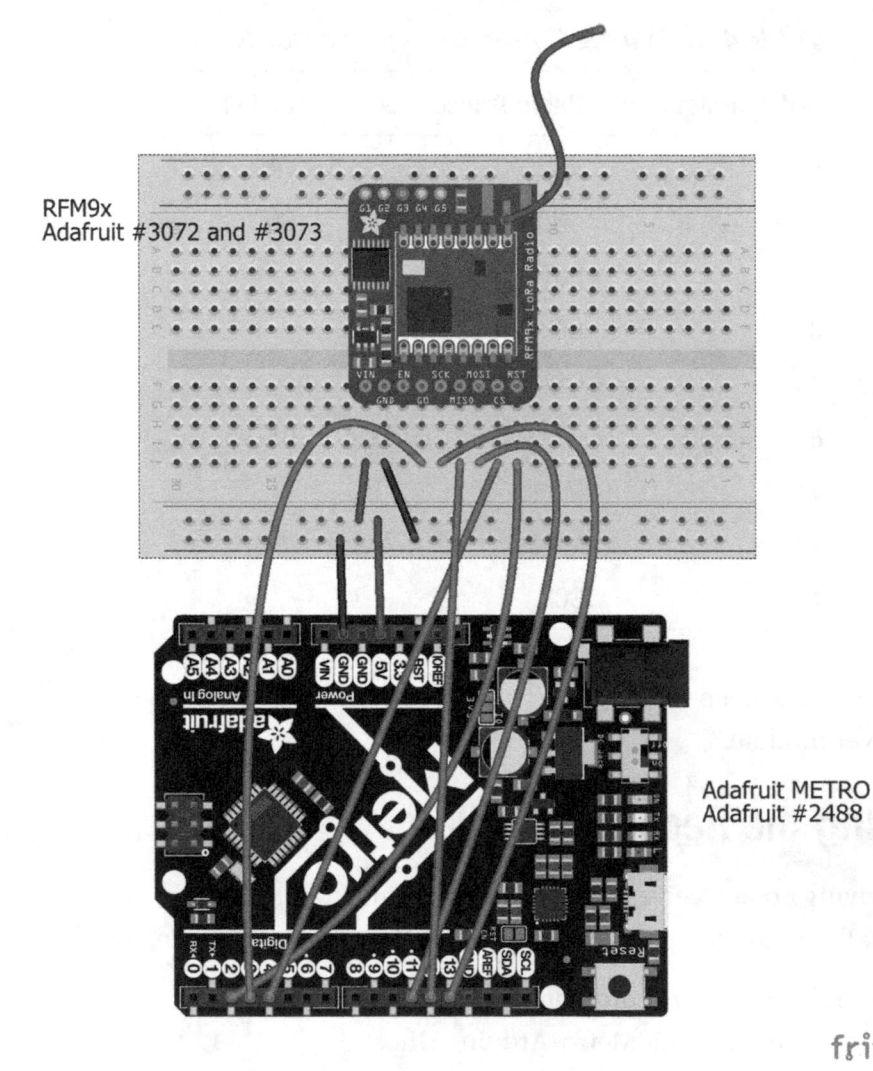

Figure 4-3. *Wiring diagram for the LoRa receiving node*

Table 4-2 shows the connections between Arduino/Metro, radio transceiver, and DHT11 sensor.

Table 4-2. *Wiring Connections for Receiver*

Arduino/Metro	Radio Transceiver
VIN	VIN
GND	GND
2	RST
3	G0
4	CS
8	
11	MOSI
12	MISO
13	SCK

4. Make sure to keep the antenna wire perpendicular to the LoRa radio transceiver module.

Writing Sketches

Once you have assembled the hardware, you will need to load the Arduino sketches for the project. You can download them from following locations:

- *Sensor node*: Chapter 4/sensor.ino

- *Receiving node*: Chapter 4/receiver.ino

You will be using the RadioHead library to write sketches for both the sensor node and the receiving node. In addition, the sensor node will be using the DHT11 library.

Sensor Node

Listing 4-1 lists the Arduino sketch for the sensor node. The sensor node
really works as a client.

Listing 4-1. sensor.ino

```
#include <SPI.h> // Serial Pheripheral Interface library
#include <RH_RF95.h> //RadioHead RFM9x library
#include "DHT.h" //DHT temperature and humidity sensor library

//Radio pinout setup
#define RFM95_CS 4 //CS pin is connected to Arduino digital pin 4
#define RFM95_RST 2 //RST pin is connected to Arduino digital pin 2
#define RFM95_INT 3 //G0 pin is connected to Arduino digital pin 3
//DHT11 sensor pinout setup
#define DHTPIN 8     // Data out pin is connected to Arduino
digital pin 8

#define RF95_FREQ 433.0

#define DHTTYPE DHT11    // DHT 11 sensor

RH_RF95 rf95(RFM95_CS, RFM95_INT);

DHT dht(DHTPIN, DHTTYPE);

void setup()
{
  pinMode(RFM95_RST, OUTPUT);
  digitalWrite(RFM95_RST, HIGH);

  while (!Serial);
  Serial.begin(9600);
  delay(100);
```

```
  digitalWrite(RFM95_RST, LOW);
  delay(10);
  digitalWrite(RFM95_RST, HIGH);
  delay(10);

  while (!rf95.init()) {
    Serial.println("initializing...");
    while (1);
  }
  Serial.println("initialisation succeeded");

  if (!rf95.setFrequency(RF95_FREQ)) {
    Serial.println("setFrequency failed");
    while (1);
  }
  Serial.print("Set Freq to: "); Serial.println(RF95_FREQ);

  rf95.setTxPower(23, false);

  dht.begin();
}

void loop()
{

  float t = dht.readTemperature();

  if (isnan(t)) {
    Serial.println("Failed to read from DHT sensor!");
    return;
  }

  Serial.println("Sending to receiver");

  char radiopacket[20]= "";

  dtostrf(t,5,2,radiopacket);
```

```
  Serial.print("Sending "); Serial.println(radiopacket);

  Serial.println("Sending..."); delay(10);

  rf95.send((uint8_t *) radiopacket, 20);

  Serial.println("Waiting for packet to complete..."); delay(10);
  rf95.waitPacketSent();
// Waiting for the reply
  uint8_t buf[RH_RF95_MAX_MESSAGE_LEN];
  uint8_t len = sizeof(buf);

  Serial.println("Waiting for reply..."); delay(10);
  if (rf95.waitAvailableTimeout(1000))
  {
    // Should be a reply message for us now
    if (rf95.recv(buf, &len))
    {
      Serial.print("Got reply: ");
      Serial.println((char*)buf);
      Serial.print("RSSI: ");
      Serial.println(rf95.lastRssi(), DEC);
    }
    else
    {
      Serial.println("Receive failed");
    }
  }
  else
  {
    Serial.println("No reply, is the receiver running?");
  }
  delay(1000);
}
```

Let's take a look at some of the important sections and functions used in the sketch.

1. First you include all the required libraries at the top of the sketch.

```
#include <SPI.h> // Serial Peripheral Interface library
#include <RH_RF95.h> //RadioHead RFM9x library
#include "DHT.h" //DHT temperature and humidity sensor library
```

2. Then you define the radio and DHT11 sensor pinout setups. INT is the interrupt pin labeled as "G0."

```
//Radio pinout setup
#define RFM95_CS 4 //CS pin is connected to Arduino
digital pin 4
#define RFM95_RST 2 //RST pin is connected to Arduino
digital pin 2
#define RFM95_INT 3 //G0 pin is connected to Arduino
digital pin 3
//DHT11 sensor pinout setup
#define DHTPIN 8     // Data out pin is connected to
Arduino digital pin 8
```

3. Define the frequency in megahertz. The frequency can be 433 or 915 MHz. Change the frequency to match your LoRa radio transceiver module.

```
#define RF95_FREQ 433.0
```

4. Define the DHT sensor type. For the DHT11 sensor, it should be as follows:

```
#define DHTTYPE DHT11    // DHT 11 sensor
```

5. Instantiate the radio object with the CS and INT pin numbers. RH_RF95() is the constructor. You can have multiple instances, but each instance must

have its own slave select and interrupt pin. After constructing, you must call init() to initialize the interface and the radio module. In your hardware setup, the slave select pin is the CS pin connected to the Arduino's digital pin 4. The interrupt pin is the G0 pin connected to the Arduino's digital pin 3.

```
RH_RF95 rf95(RFM95_CS, RFM95_INT);
```

6. Instantiate the DHT object with the data out pin and the DHT sensor type.

```
DHT dht(DHTPIN, DHTTYPE);
```

7. In the setup() function, type the following code:

```
void setup()
{
  pinMode(RFM95_RST, OUTPUT);
  digitalWrite(RFM95_RST, HIGH);

  while (!Serial);
  Serial.begin(9600);
  delay(100);

  digitalWrite(RFM95_RST, LOW);
  delay(10);
  digitalWrite(RFM95_RST, HIGH);
  delay(10);

  while (!rf95.init()) {
    Serial.println("initializing...");
    while (1);
  }
  Serial.println("initialisation succeeded");
```

```
    if (!rf95.setFrequency(RF95_FREQ)) {
        Serial.println("setFrequency failed");
        while (1);
    }
    Serial.print("Set Freq to: "); Serial.println(RF95_FREQ);

    rf95.setTxPower(23, false);

    dht.begin();
}
```

The init() function is used to initialize the radio module. It will return true if the initialization succeeded.

```
while (!rf95.init()) {
    Serial.println("initializing...");
    while (1);
}
Serial.println("initialisation succeeded");
```

The setFrequency() function is used to set the transmitter and receiver center frequency. The center frequency can be a range from 137.0 MHz to 1020.0 MHz. It will return true if the selected center frequency is within the range. Use the following frequencies for the Adafruit RFM9x LoRa radio transceiver breakouts:

- *Adafruit RFM95W*: 868 or 915 MHz

- *Adafruit RFM96W*: 433 MHz

Setting a frequency outside the range of your radio will probably not work.

```
if (!rf95.setFrequency(RF95_FREQ)) {
    Serial.println("setFrequency failed");
    while (1);
}
Serial.print("Set Freq to: "); Serial.println(RF95_FREQ);
```

The setTxPower() function is used to set the transmitter power output level. You can set the transmission power between +5 to +23 in dBm. Set the second parameter to false to enable PA_BOOST for high-power output.

```
rf95.setTxPower(23, false);
```

Inside the loop() function, type in the following code.

```
void loop()
{

  float t = dht.readTemperature();

  if (isnan(t)) {
    Serial.println("Failed to read from DHT sensor!");
    return;
  }

  Serial.println("Sending to receiver");

  char radiopacket[20]= "";

  dtostrf(t,5,2,radiopacket);
  Serial.print("Sending "); Serial.println(radiopacket);

  Serial.println("Sending..."); delay(10);

  rf95.send((uint8_t *) radiopacket, 20);

  Serial.println("Waiting for packet to complete..."); delay(10);
  rf95.waitPacketSent();
// Waiting for the reply
  uint8_t buf[RH_RF95_MAX_MESSAGE_LEN];
  uint8_t len = sizeof(buf);

  Serial.println("Waiting for reply..."); delay(10);
  if (rf95.waitAvailableTimeout(1000))
  {
```

```
    // Should be a reply message for us now
    if (rf95.recv(buf, &len))
    {
      Serial.print("Got reply: ");
      Serial.println((char*)buf);
      Serial.print("RSSI: ");
      Serial.println(rf95.lastRssi(), DEC);
    }
    else
    {
      Serial.println("Receive failed");
    }
  }
  else
  {
    Serial.println("No reply, is the receiver running?");
  }
  delay(1000);
}
```

The dtostrf() function will convert a float to a char array so it can then be printed easily.

The function prototype of the dtostrf() function is as follows:

```
dtostrf(floatvar, StringLengthIncDecimalPoint,
numVarsAfterDecimal, charbuf);
```

Here is what this means:

floatvar	This is a float variable.
StringLengthIncDecimalPoint	This is the length of the string that will be created.
numVarsAfterDecimal	This is the number of digits after the decimal point to print.
charbuf	This is the array to store the results.

The send() function used to send a data packet; it loads a message into the transmitter and starts the transmitter. This function requires the array of data to be sent and the size of data in bytes.

The waitPacketSent() function blocks other things until the transmitter is no longer transmitting. Once transmitted, the recv() function turns the receiver on and, if there is a valid message available, copies it to the buffer and returns true. Otherwise, it returns false.

The println() function is used to print the character buffer.

Receiving Node

Listing 4-2 lists the Arduino sketch for the receiving node. The receiving node works as a server.

Listing 4-2. receiver.ino

```
//This code is based on the original code published by Adafruit
availabe at https://learn.adafruit.com/adafruit-rfm69hcw-and-
rfm96-rfm95-rfm98-lora-packet-padio-breakouts/rfm9x-test

#include <SPI.h>
#include <RH_RF95.h>

#define RFM95_CS 10
```

```
#define RFM95_RST 9
#define RFM95_INT 2

#define RF95_FREQ 433.0

RH_RF95 rf95(RFM95_CS, RFM95_INT);

#define LED 13

void setup()
{
  pinMode(LED, OUTPUT);
  pinMode(RFM95_RST, OUTPUT);
  digitalWrite(RFM95_RST, HIGH);

  while (!Serial);
  Serial.begin(9600);
  delay(100);

  digitalWrite(RFM95_RST, LOW);
  delay(10);
  digitalWrite(RFM95_RST, HIGH);
  delay(10);

  while (!rf95.init()) {
    Serial.println("Initializing failed");
    while (1);
  }
  Serial.println("Initialisation succeeded");

  if (!rf95.setFrequency(RF95_FREQ)) {
    Serial.println("Can't set the specified frequency");
    while (1);
  }
  Serial.print("Set Freq to: "); Serial.println(RF95_FREQ);
```

```
  rf95.setTxPower(23, false);
}

void loop()
{
  if (rf95.available())
  {
    //Read the availabe message
    uint8_t buf[RH_RF95_MAX_MESSAGE_LEN];
    uint8_t len = sizeof(buf);

    if (rf95.recv(buf, &len))
    {
      //Receive the message
      digitalWrite(LED, HIGH);
      RH_RF95::printBuffer("Received: ", buf, len);
      Serial.print("Got: ");
      Serial.println((char*)buf);

      // Send a reply
      uint8_t data[] = "Ack";
      rf95.send(data, sizeof(data));
      rf95.waitPacketSent();
      Serial.println("Sent a reply");
      digitalWrite(LED, LOW);
    }
    else
    {
      //If receive failed
      Serial.println("Receive failed");
    }
  }
}
```

Result

Connect the sensor node and receiving node to your computer using USB cables. Open two instances of the Arduino IDE.

To start a new instance of the Arduino IDE, double-click the Arduino desktop icon (for admin installed) or double-click `arduino.exe` (for nonadmin installed). The File ➤ New command doesn't create a new instance of the IDE.

Using the first instance of the IDE, upload Listing 4-1 to the sensor node. With the second instance of the IDE, upload Listing 4-2 to the receiving node. Make sure to select the correct COM port before uploading the sketch.

Here's an example:

- *Sensor node*: COM3

- *Receiving node*: COM7

After uploading the sketches, open serial monitors in both IDEs. Figure 4-4 shows the output on the serial monitor for the sensor node. For example, the sensor node sends the current temperature 30.00 Celsius. Then it receives the acknowledgment packet "And hello back to you."

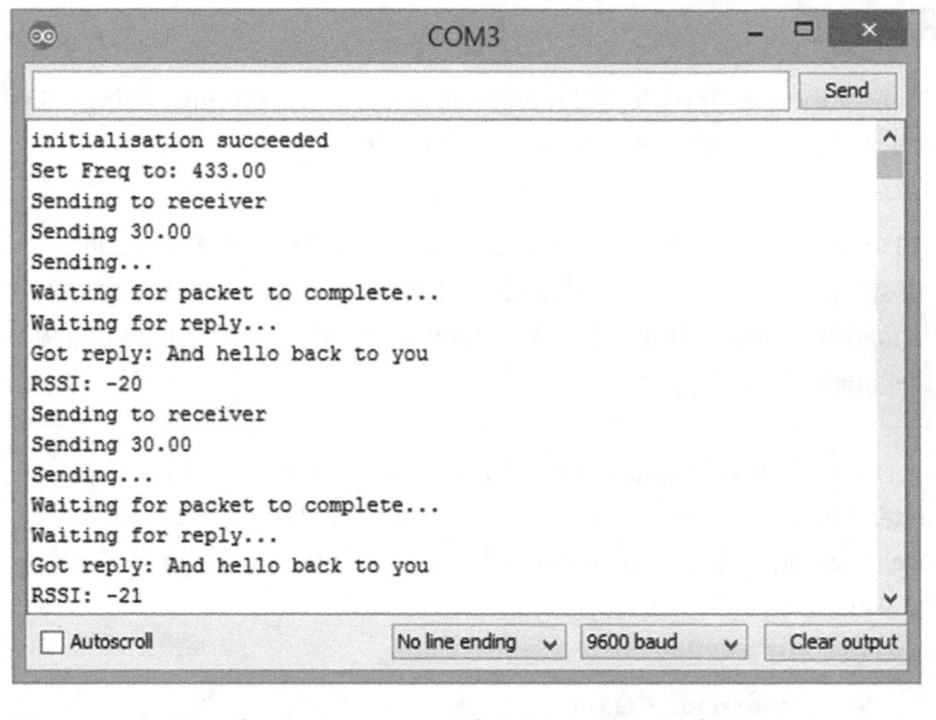

Figure 4-4. *Serial monitor output for the sensor node*

At the receiving end, the receiver receives the data packet containing the temperature, which is 30.00. Then it sends an acknowledgment to the sensor. Figure 4-5 shows the serial monitor output for the receiving node.

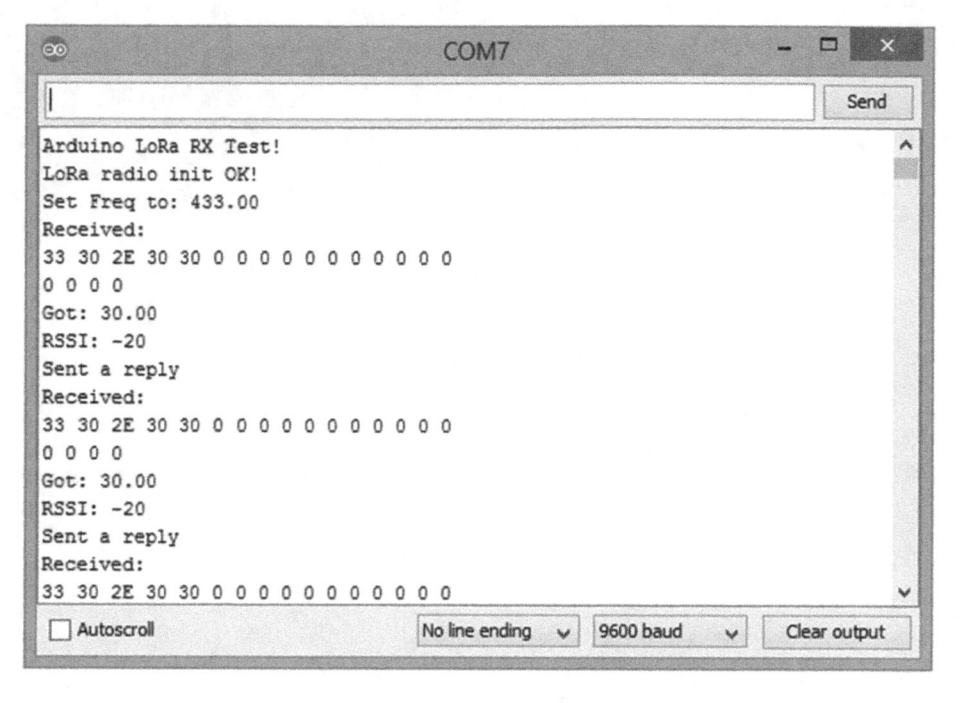

Figure 4-5. *Serial monitor output for the receiving node*

Make sure to use the same frequency for both the sensor and the receiving node.

Summary

Now you know how to use the RadioHead library to send and receive LoRa packets on a specified frequency for both the transmitter and the receiver. In the next chapter, you will build a single-channel LoRa gateway with the Raspberry Pi.

CHAPTER 5

Building a LoRa Gateway

In this chapter, you will learn how to build a low-cost single-channel LoRa gateway based on the Raspberry Pi. The gateway uses a single-channel packet forwarder to forward incoming data packets to the Things Network (https://www.thethingsnetwork.org/). Then, you will create an application on the Things Network to decode the payloads to extract sensor data from the data packet.

Things You Need

You will need following things to build this project:

- One Raspberry Pi 3 (https://www.sparkfun.com/products/13825)

- One microSD card with adapter, 16 GB, Class 10 (https://www.sparkfun.com/products/13833)

- One Arduino Uno or Adafruit Metro (https://www.sparkfun.com/products/11224 or https://www.adafruit.com/product/2488)

- One wall adapter power supply, 5.1 V DC 2.5 A (USB Micro-B) (https://www.sparkfun.com/products/13831)

© Pradeeka Seneviratne 2019
P. Seneviratne, *Beginning LoRa Radio Networks with Arduino*,
https://doi.org/10.1007/978-1-4842-4357-2_5

121

- One 9 VDC 1000 mA--regulated switching power adapter, UL listed (`https://www.adafruit.com/product/63`)

- Two LoRa RFM9x radio transceiver breakouts (`https://www.adafruit.com/product/3072` or `https://www.adafruit.com/product/3073`)

- One DHT11 temperature and humidity sensor (`https://www.adafruit.com/product/386`)

- One 10 K ohm resistor (usually comes with the DHT11 sensor; if not, visit `https://www.adafruit.com/product/2784`)

- Two breadboards (`https://www.sparkfun.com/products/12002`)

- Two breadboard holders (`https://www.sparkfun.com/products/11235`)

- A few hook-up wires (`https://www.sparkfun.com/products/11367`)

- A few male-to-female jumper wires (`https://www.sparkfun.com/products/12794`)

Installing Raspbian on the Raspberry Pi

Your Raspberry Pi doesn't come with a pre-installed operating system. There are plenty of operating systems available for the Raspberry Pi. Among them, Raspbian Stretch LITE is the most suitable lightweight operating system that can be used to build a LoRa single-channel LoRa gateway. It doesn't provide a GUI, but you can access it with the command line. Raspbian Stretch LITE is a minimal image based on Debian Stretch.

1. Go to the official Raspberry Pi download page
    at https://www.raspberrypi.org/downloads/
    raspbian/ and download Raspbian Stretch
    LITE. You can download it from the torrent by
    clicking the Download Torrent button, or you can
    download it as a ZIP file by clicking the Download
    ZIP button (Figure 5-1).

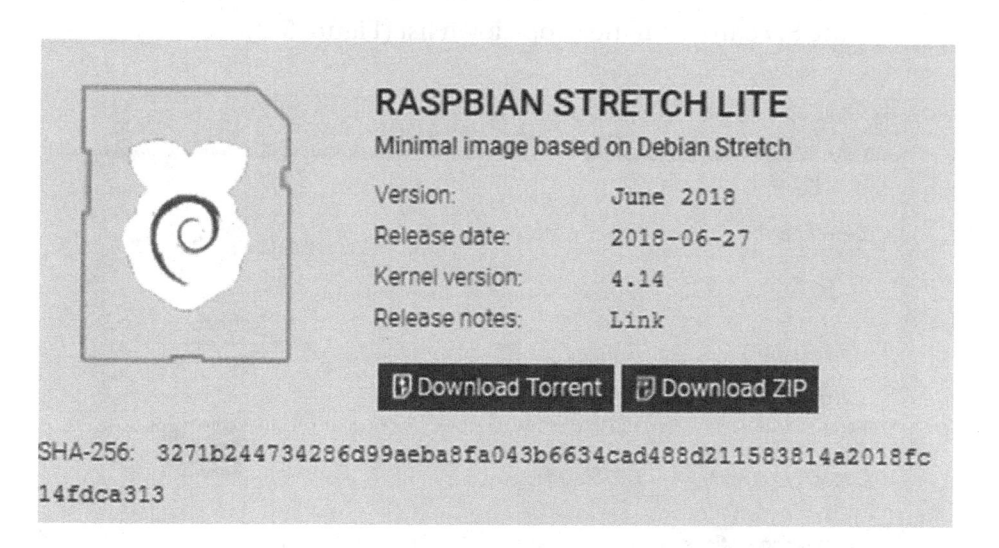

Figure 5-1. *Download options for Raspbian Stretch LITE*

2. After you download the ZIP file, unzip it using 7Zip
    (Windows) or the Unarchiver (Macintosh).

Formatting the SD Card

SD Card Formatter is the best software tool for formatting any type of SD
card. You can download and install the latest version of SD Card Formatter
on your computer by visiting https://www.sdcard.org/downloads/
formatter_4/index.html.

1. Insert the microSD card into the slot of the SD card adapter. Then insert the SD card adapter into the SD card port on your computer (laptop). If you have an SD card reader, insert the microSD card into it and connect the SD card reader to the computer with a suitable USB cable.

2. Start SD Card Formatter and under "Select card," select the SD card from the drop-down list (Figure 5-2).

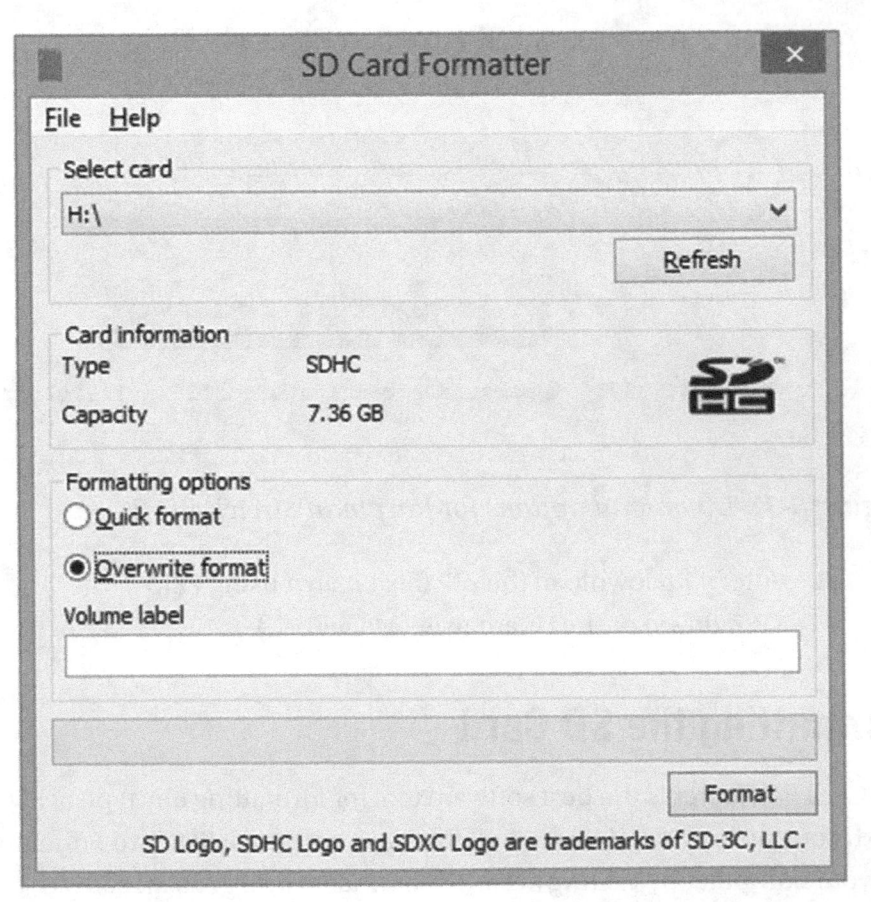

Figure 5-2. Selecting a card and formatting options

3. Under "Formatting options," select "Overwrite format."

4. Click the Format button to start formatting. Click the Yes button to confirm.

5. After completing the formatting process, click the OK button.

Writing Raspbian Stretch LITE to the SD Card

You can use Etcher (`https://etcher.io/`) as the image-writing tool to write Raspbian Stretch LITE to the microSD card. It is a graphical tool that works on Mac OS, Linux, and Windows. Etcher also supports writing images directly from the ZIP file, without any unzipping required.

1. On the Etcher download page, choose the correct operating system that you want to use with Etcher from the drop-down list. Depending on your selection, a portable or installer file will download to your computer (Figure 5-3).

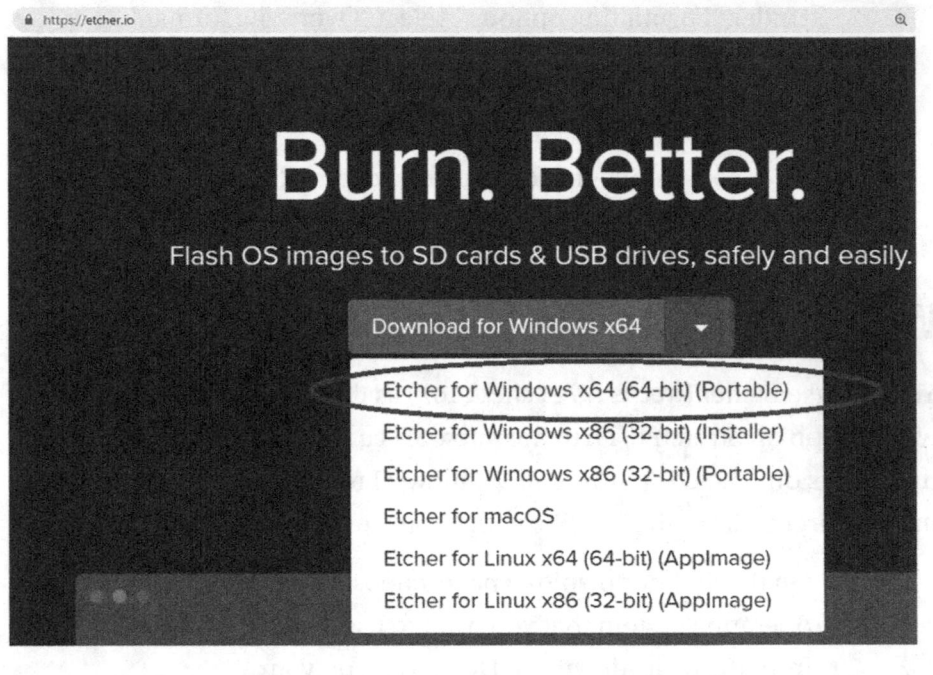

Figure 5-3. *Choosing the Etcher portable or installer for your operating system*

2. If you have a portable file (such as `Etcher-Portable-1.4.5-x64`), simply run it to open Etcher. If you have an installer (such as `Etcher-Setup-1.4.5-x64`), first install it on your computer and then run the program to open the Etcher.

3. In the Etcher window, click the "Select image" button to browse to the downloaded Raspbian Stretch LITE image (IMP or ZIP) from your computer (Figure 5-4).

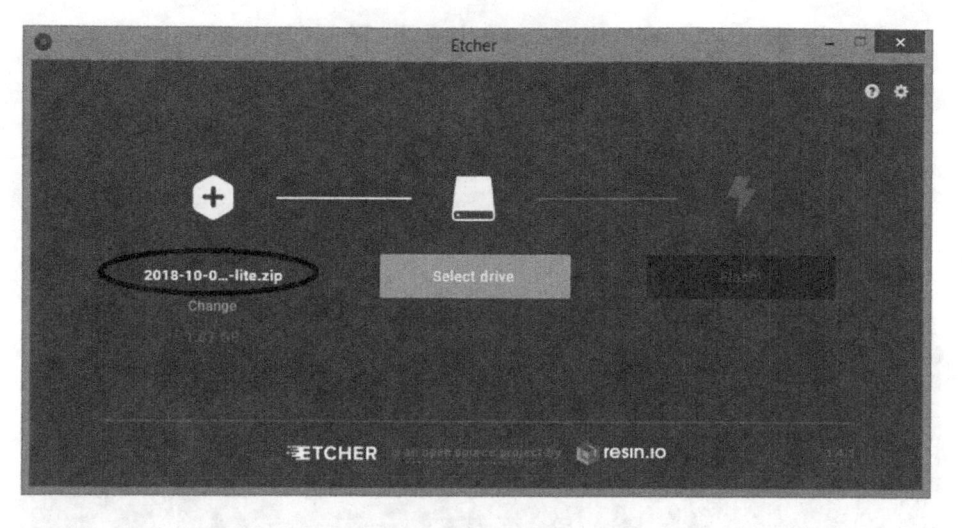

Figure 5-4. *Selecting the downloaded image file*

4. Click the "Select drive" button and select the
   microSD card (Figure 5-5).

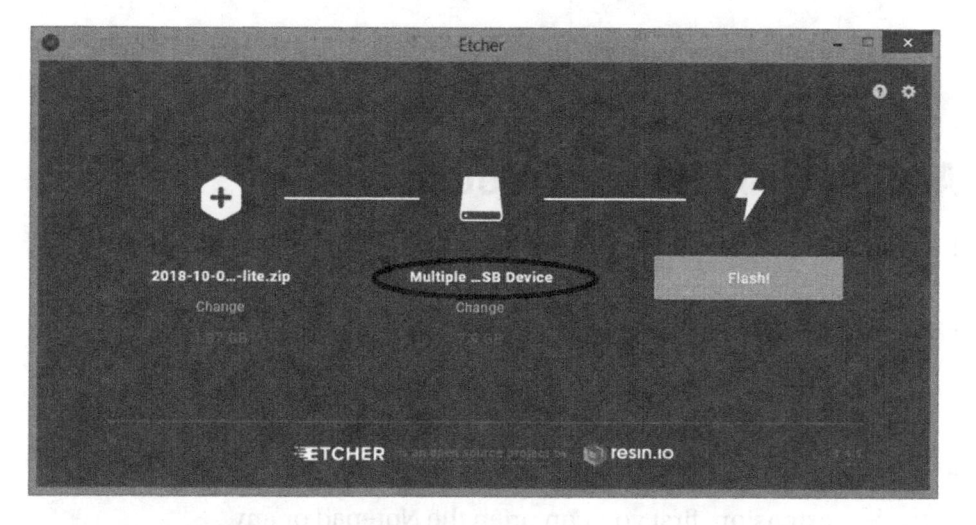

Figure 5-5. *Selecting the microSD card*

5.   Review your selections and click the Flash! button to
      begin writing data to the microSD card (Figure 5-6).

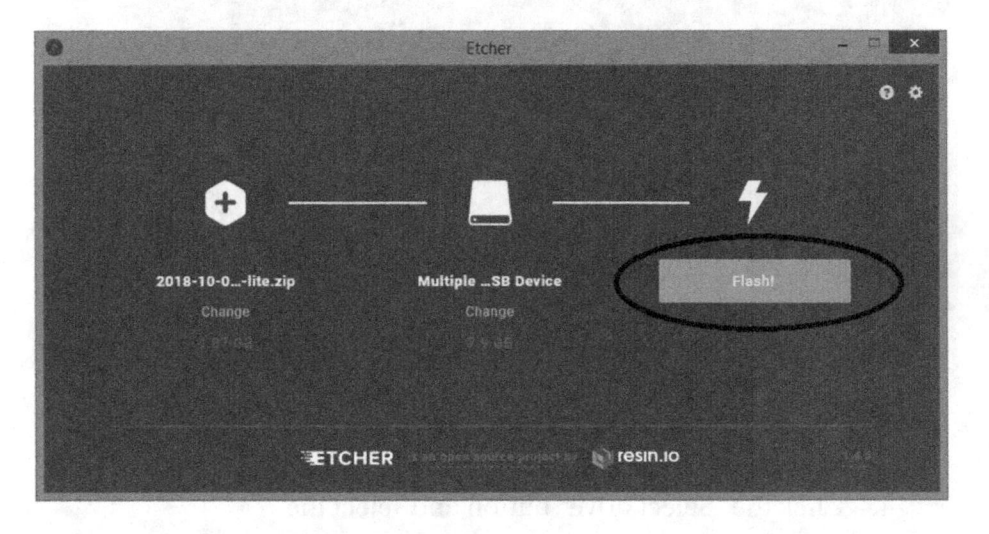

Figure 5-6. *Flashing the image*

6.   After completing the flashing process, close Etcher.
      Don't remove the microSD card yet.

Adding Wi-Fi Network Details

Raspbian Stretch Lite doesn't provide a graphical user interface to set up
Wi-Fi on the Raspberry Pi. As an option, you can create a file to store Wi-Fi
configuration settings for your preferred Wi-Fi network.

1.   WWith the SD card connected, in the root of the SD
      card (boot partition), create a new file named
      wpa_supplicant.conf. To create the file with .conf
      extension, first you can open the Notepad or any
      text editor and save it as "wpa_supplicant.conf",
      including the quotation marks, in the Save As
      dialog box.

2. In the file you should add the following
   configuration script:

```
ctrl_interface=DIR=/var/run/wpa_supplicant GROUP=netdev
network={
    ssid="YOUR_SSID"
    psk="YOUR_WIFI_PASSWORD"
    key_mgmt=WPA-PSK
}
```

3. Replace the ssid value with the name of your
   Wi-Fi network, and replace the psk value with the
   password of your Wi-Fi network. As an example, the
   configuration file will look like this:

```
ctrl_interface=DIR=/var/run/wpa_supplicant GROUP=netdev
network={
    ssid="Dialog 4G"
    psk="E76342B148"
    key_mgmt=WPA-PSK
}
```

   You can learn about more advanced options for
   adding network details to the Raspberry Pi by visiting
   https://www.raspberrypi.org/documentation/
   configuration/wireless/wireless-cli.md.

4. Save the file again to persist the changes and then
   close the editor.

Enabling SSH

The SSH protocol can be used to connect with your Raspberry Pi from
your computer over a network (Ethernet or Wi-Fi). To accept a connection
from another computer, you should first enable the SSH protocol on the
Raspberry Pi.

1. In the root of the SD card (boot partition), create a file named ssh without any extension. To create the file without any extension, first you can open the Notepad or any text editor and save it as "ssh", including the quotation marks, in the Save As dialog box.

2. Close the editor.

Inserting the microSD Card into the Raspberry Pi

First safely remove the microSD card from your computer. Then insert the microSD card to the microSD slot that can be found on the rear side of the Raspberry Pi. Firmly push in the SD card, and you will hear a clicking sound once it is locked inside the slot.

Building the Gateway

The hardware setup for the Raspberry Pi–based LoRa gateway can be built in a few minutes with the following items:

- Raspberry Pi 3 with Raspbian Stretch LITE image written

- Wall adapter power supply, 5.1 V DC 2.5 A (USB Micro-B)

- LoRa RFM9x radio transceiver breakout

- Half-size breadboard

- Breadboard holder

- A few hook-up wires

- A few jumper wires (male-to-female)

Figure 5-7 shows the wiring diagram for the LoRa gateway. Table 5-1 shows the wiring connections between each component. You can use male-to-female jumper wires to make connections between the LoRa radio transceiver breakout and the Raspberry Pi. Use hook-up wires to connect the VIN and GND of the LoRa radio transceiver breakout with the power rails of the breadboard.

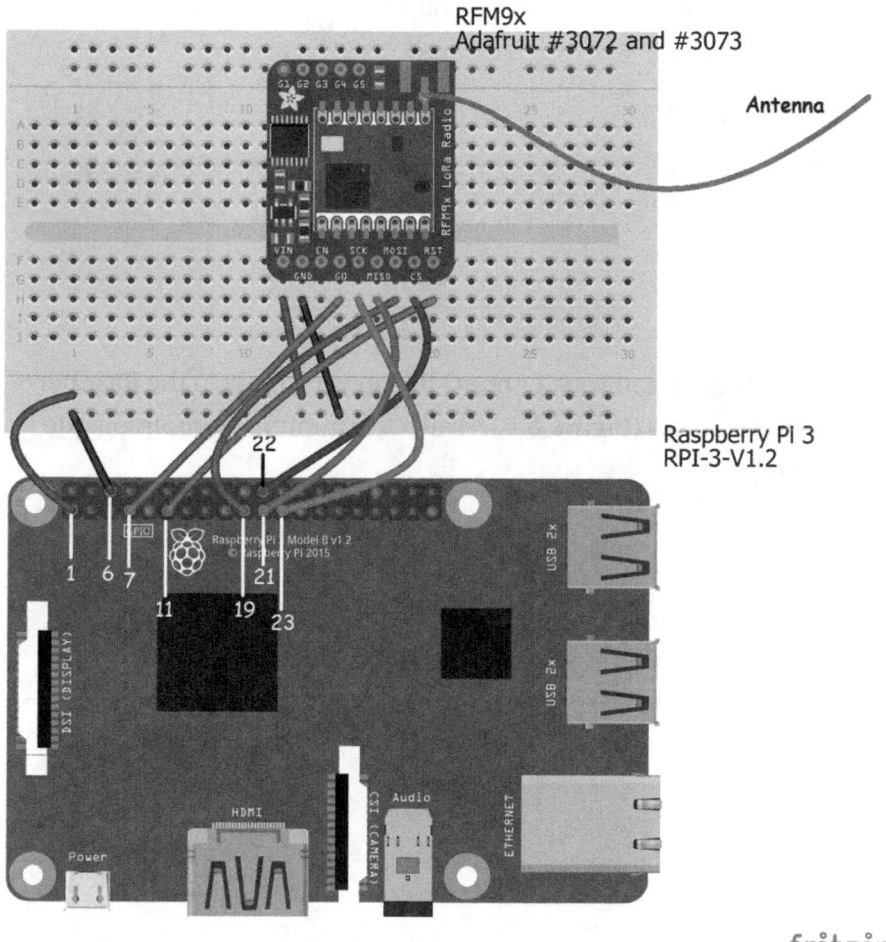

Figure 5-7. *Wiring diagram for the LoRa gateway*

Table 5-1. *Wiring Connections Between Each Component*

Raspberry Pi	RFM9x
1	VIN
6	GND
7	G0
11	RST
19	MOSI
21	MISO
22	CS
23	SCK

After building the gateway, connect the power supply to the Raspberry Pi and apply the power (Figure 5-8). Wait a few minutes to complete the first-time setup.

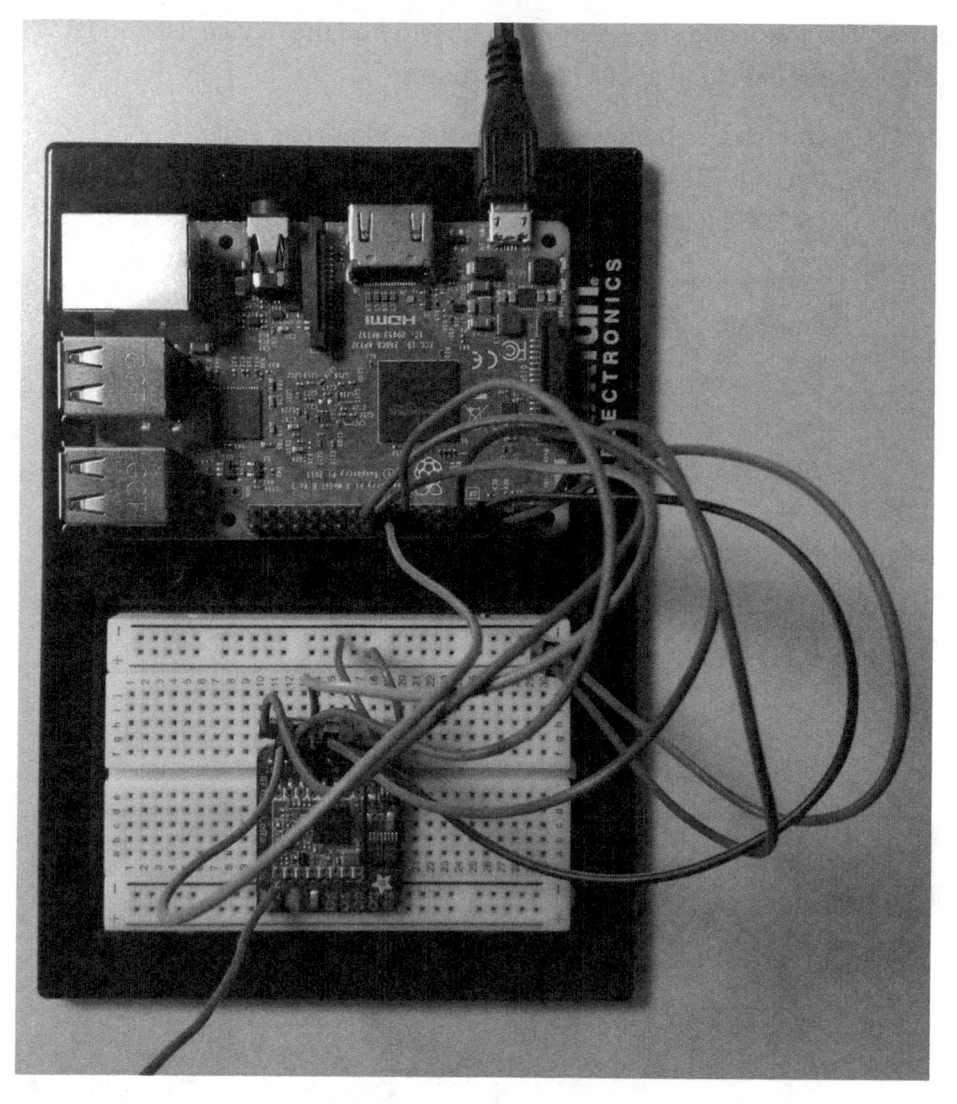

Figure 5-8. *Completed hardware setup of the LoRa gateway*

SSHing into Your Raspberry Pi

Before SSHing into your Raspberry Pi, first you should know its IP address dynamically allocated by the router. Usually the IP address of any device in your network can be found on your router's configuration portal. The following steps show you how to find the device list and IP address with the Huawei E5172s-920 router:

1. Launch a web browser, and in the address bar, enter the IP address of your router (or http://homerouter. cpe). Then click the arrow icon or press Enter.

2. In the router's configuration page, in the left navigation bar, click Product Information.

3. Scroll down the page. Under Device List, you can find the dynamically allocated IP address for each device (Figure 5-9).

Device List

Index	Computer Name	MAC Address	IP Address	Lease Time	Status	Type	Operation
1	Pradeeka	9C:2A:70:C 3:69:3F	192.168.1.2	0 days 18 hours 20 minutes 8 seconds	Active	Wi-Fi	Kick Out
2	amazon-04cfe8ca4	00:71:47:F 0:D5:AD	192.168.1.4	0 days 20 hours 59 minutes 17 seconds	Active	Wi-Fi	Kick Out
3	raspberrypi	B8:27:EB:2 F:04:80	192.168.1.6	0 days 23 hours 59 minutes 53 seconds	Active	Wi-Fi	Kick Out
4	android-f545dbea05 72d0c9	94:FE:22:6 5:B3:47	192.168.1.3	0 days 6 hours 13 minutes 16 seconds	Inactive	Ethernet	Kick Out
5	amazon-a11873fa6	FC:65:DE:2 F:0F:B4	192.168.1.5	0 days 14 hours 23 minutes 53 seconds	Inactive	Ethernet	Kick Out

Figure 5-9. *Viewing the list of connected devices*

4. Open PuTTY, and in the PuTTY Configuration window, under Host Name (or IP address), type in the IP address of your Raspberry Pi. The default port number for SSH is 22. Then click the Open button (Figure 5-10).

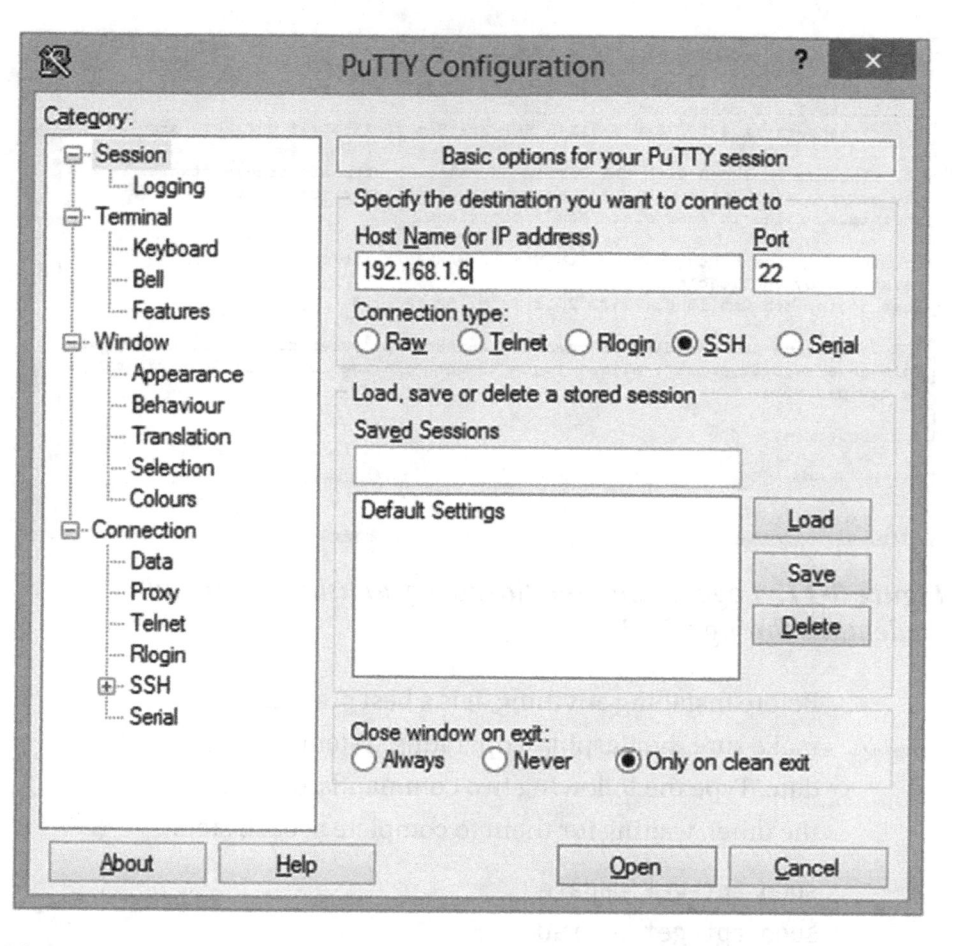

Figure 5-10. *PuTTY configuration for the SSH session*

5. The default login credentials for your Raspberry Pi
   are as follows (Figure 5-11):

```
User - pi
Password -raspberry
```

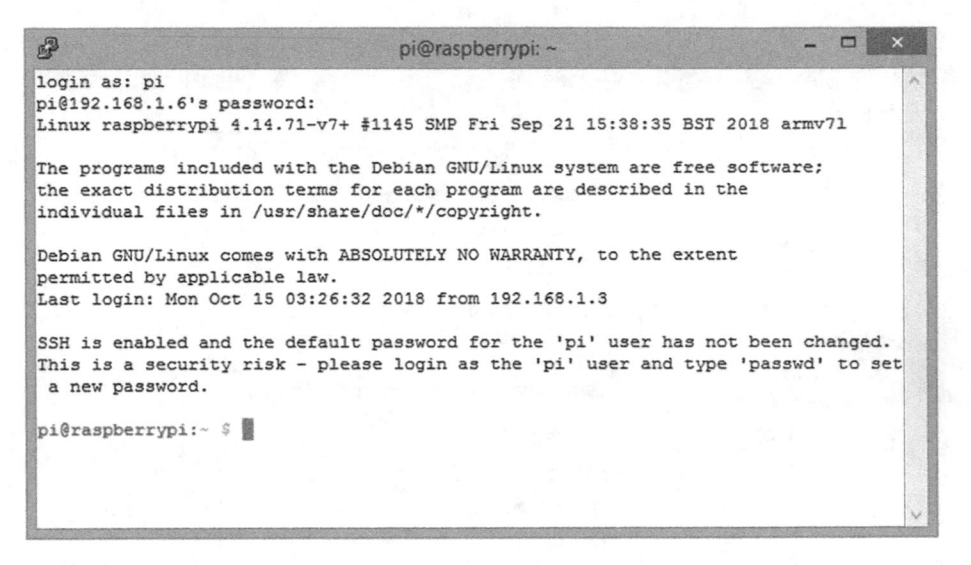

```
                                pi@raspberrypi: ~                      —  □  ×
login as: pi
pi@192.168.1.6's password:
Linux raspberrypi 4.14.71-v7+ #1145 SMP Fri Sep 21 15:38:35 BST 2018 armv71

The programs included with the Debian GNU/Linux system are free software;
the exact distribution terms for each program are described in the
individual files in /usr/share/doc/*/copyright.

Debian GNU/Linux comes with ABSOLUTELY NO WARRANTY, to the extent
permitted by applicable law.
Last login: Mon Oct 15 03:26:32 2018 from 192.168.1.3

SSH is enabled and the default password for the 'pi' user has not been changed.
This is a security risk - please login as the 'pi' user and type 'passwd' to set
 a new password.

pi@raspberrypi:~ $ █
```

Figure 5-11. *Logging into the Raspberry Pi using the default credentials through SSH*

6. Before installing anything, it is a best practice to make sure the Raspbian operating system is up-to-date. Type the following two commands, one after the other, waiting for them to complete at each step:

```
sudo apt-get update
sudo apt-get upgrade
```

```
sudo reboot
```

Enabling SPI Interface

To allow the Raspberry Pi to communicate with the LoRa radio transceiver module, you should enable the SPI interface on the Raspberry Pi.

1. Type the following command to open the Raspberry Pi Software Configuration Tool:

```
sudo raspi-config
```

2.   In the Raspberry Pi Software Configuration Tool,
     select Interfacing Options. Then press the Enter key
     on your keyboard (Figure 5-12).

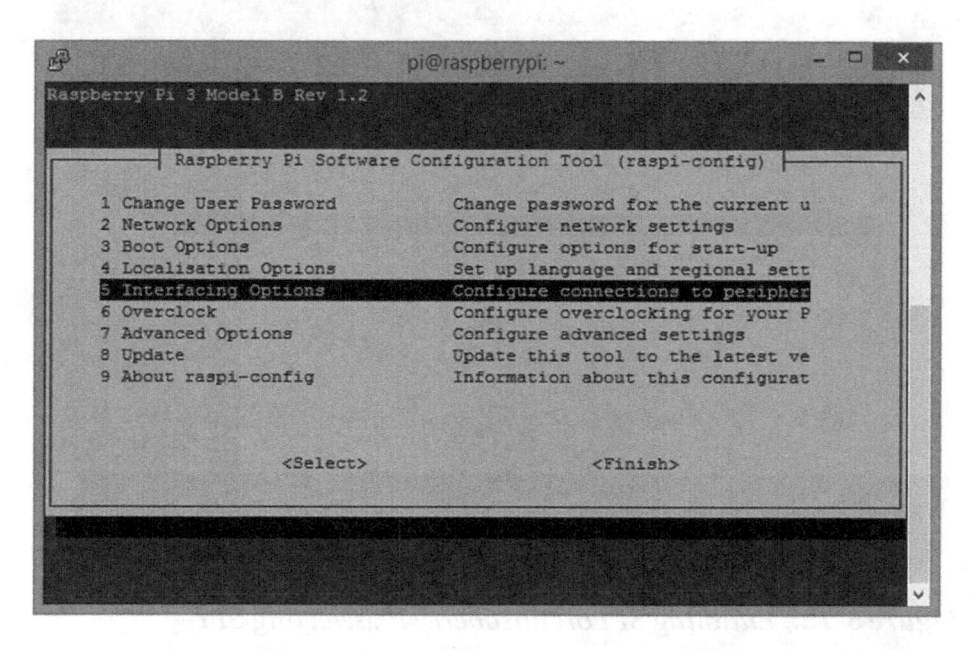

Figure 5-12.   *Enabling SPI on the Raspberry Pi, selecting Interfacing*
Options

3. Select SPI and press the Enter key on your keyboard
    (Figure 5-13).

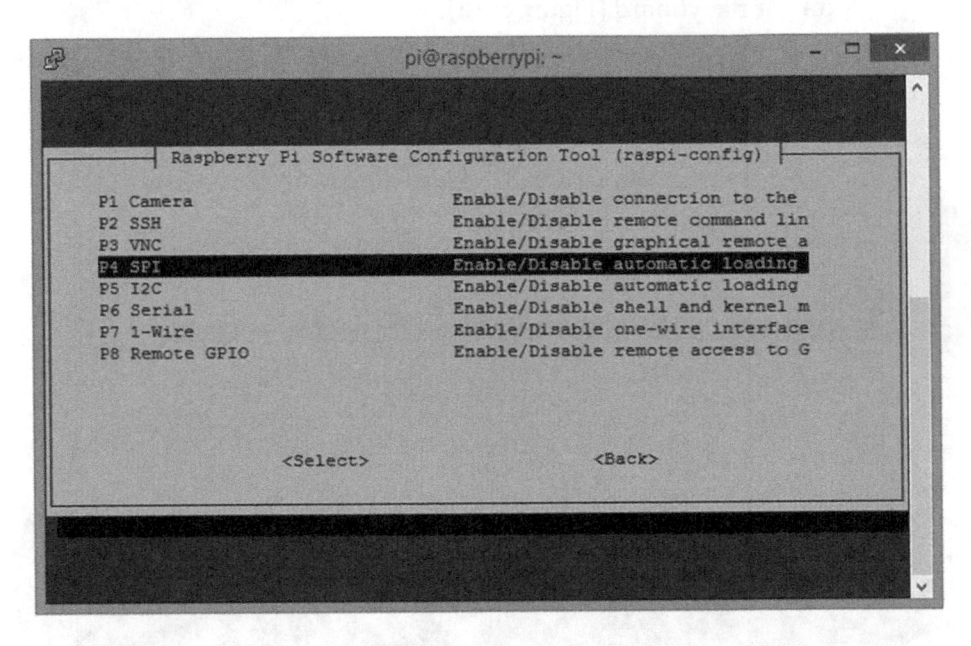

Figure 5-13. *Enabling SPI on Raspberry Pi, selecting SPI*

4. Select <Yes> and press the Enter key on your
    keyboard (Figure 5-14).

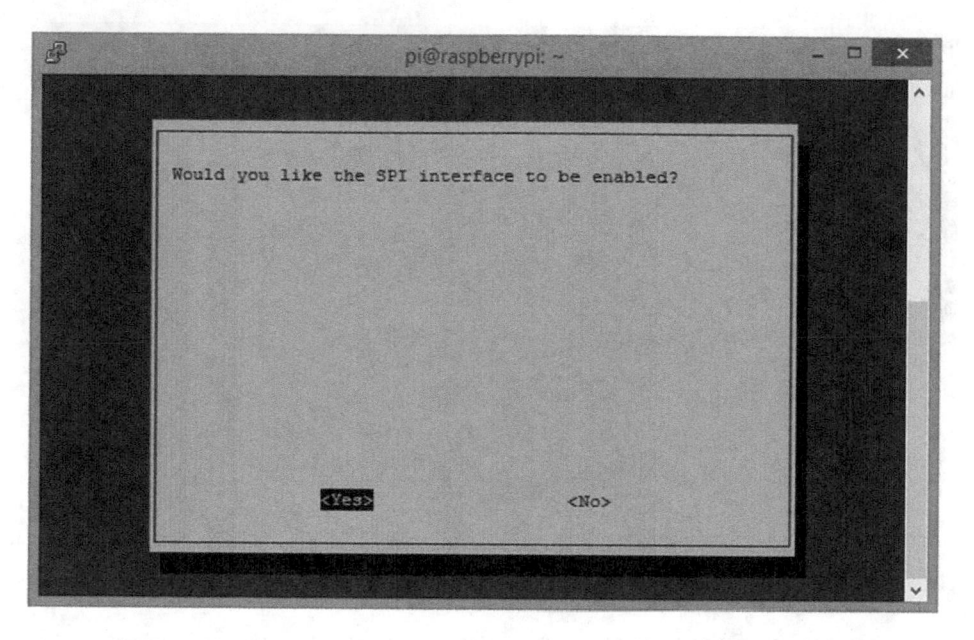

Figure 5-14. *Enabling SPI on Raspberry Pi, selecting <Yes>*

5. Press the Enter key on your keyboard to close the
    message (Figure 5-15).

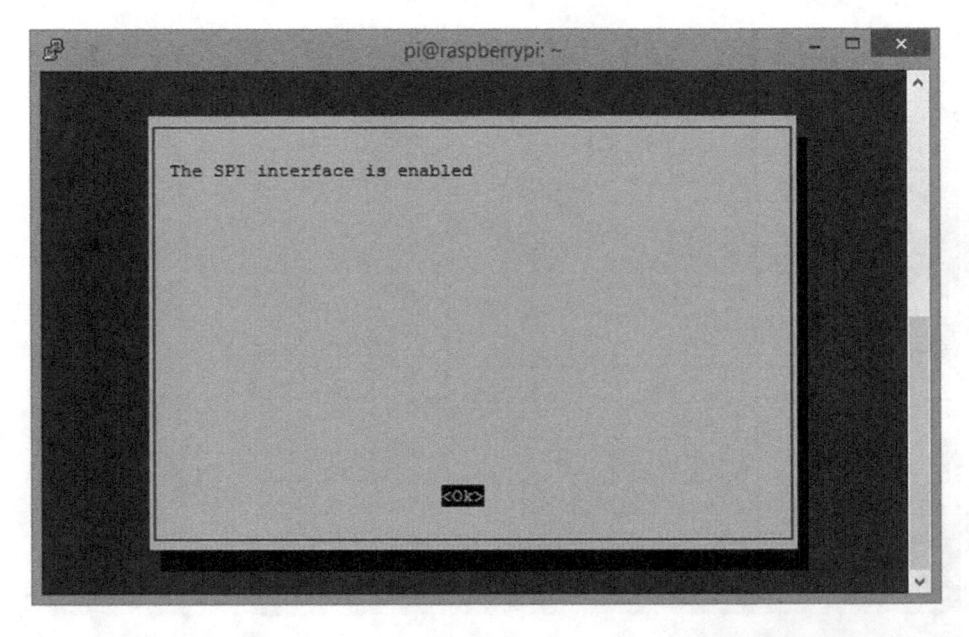

Figure 5-15. *Enabling SPI on Raspberry Pi, closing the message*

6.   Select <Finish> to exit from the Raspberry Pi
      Software Configuration Tool (Figure 5-16).

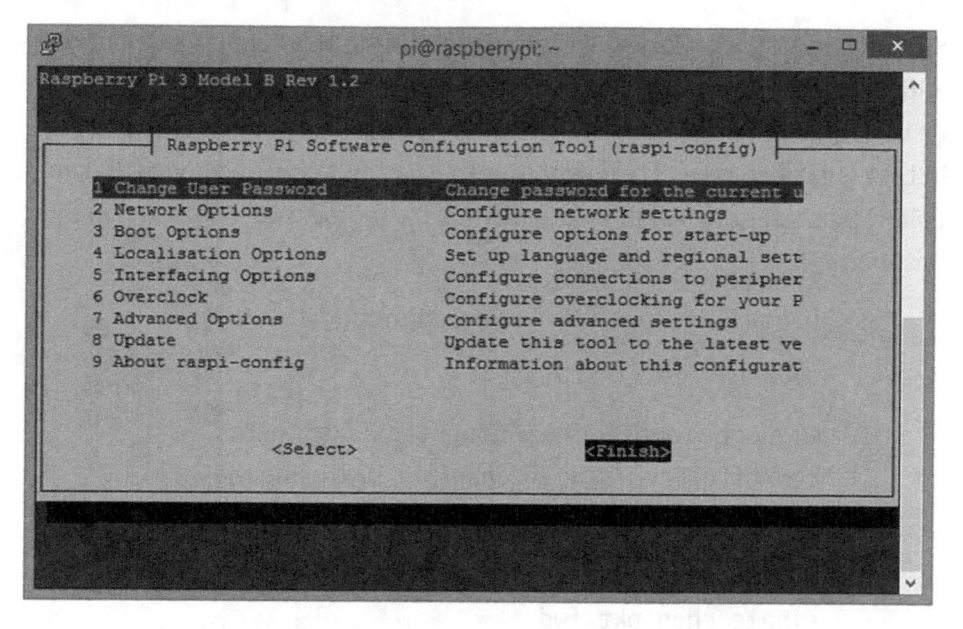

Figure 5-16.   *Enabling SPI on the Raspberry Pi, exiting*

7.   Reboot the Raspberry Pi with the following
      command:

```
sudo reboot
```

Installing Wiring

The WiringPi library allows you to easily interface with the GPIO pins of
the Raspberry Pi. It also supports I2C and SPI. You can use the following
command to install the WiringPi library on your Raspberry Pi:

```
sudo apt-get install wiringpi
```

Installing and Configuring a Single-Channel Packet Forwarder

Single-channel packet forwarder software can listen on a configurable frequency and has a spreading factor from SF7 to SF12. For this LoRa gateway, you will be installing the single-channel LoRaWAN gateway software maintained at `https://github.com/tftelkamp/single_chan_pkt_fwd` by Thomas Telkamp. Follow these steps to install single-channel packet forwarder software on the Raspberry Pi:

1. Install Git using the following command:

   ```
   sudo apt-get install git
   ```

2. Clone the repository found at `https://github.com/tftelkamp/single_chan_pkt_fwd` using the following command:

   ```
   git clone https://github.com/tftelkamp/
   single_chan_pkt_fwd
   ```

3. After cloning the repository, use the following commands to open the `main.cpp` file in the `single_chan_pkt_fwd` directory:

   ```
   cd single_chan_pkt_fwd
   nano main.cpp
   ```

4. Configure the packet forwarder for the center frequency using the following line of code:

   ```
   uint32_t freq = 868100000; // in Mhz! (868.1)
   ```

5. Modify the frequency to suit the frequency of the attached LoRa radio transceiver module. As an example, if you have a 433 MHz LoRa radio transceiver module, the center frequency will be as follows:

   ```
   uint32_t freq = 433100000; // in Mhz! (433.1)
   ```

6. Define the router address to allow the packet forwarder to connect with the Things Network by modifying the following line of code:

    ```
    #define SERVER1 "54.72.145.119" // The Things Network:
    croft.thethings.girovito.nl
    ```

    As an example, to connect with the router.eu.thethings.network, use the IP address 52.169.76.203. The modified code should look like this:

    ```
    #define SERVER1 "52.169.76.203" // The Things Network:
    router.eu.thethings.network
    ```

7. You can find the list of router addresses at https://www.thethingsnetwork.org/docs/gateways/packet-forwarder/semtech-udp.html#router-addresses. Simply use the ping command to find the IP address for any router address. As an example, to get the IP address for the router address, router.eu.thethings.network, use the following command:

    ```
    ping router.eu.thethings.network
    ```

8. This will output the IP address as follows:

    ```
    PING router.eu.thethings.network (52.169.76.203) 56(84)
    bytes of data.
    ```

9. Save the file by pressing Ctrl+X, followed by Ctrl+O.

10. Now you can compile the code using the following command:

    ```
    make
    ```

11.   After compiling the code, run the packet forwarder
using the following command:

```
./single_chan_pkt_fwd
```

12.   You will get output something similar to Figure 5-17.
This shows the status of the RFM9x LoRa radio
transceiver module as "SX1276 detected, starting."
If you get the status message "Unrecognized
transceiver," check again the wiring connections
between the RFM9x and Raspberry Pi. Also, you will
get the same message for malfunctioning or broken
radio transceivers.

13.   Note the gateway ID. The gateway ID will be
required to configure your gateway with the Things
Network. The autogenerated gateway ID for this
gateway is b8:27:eb:ff:ff:7a:51:d5.

```
pi@raspberrypi:~/single_chan_pkt_fwd $ sudo /home/pi/single_chan_pkt_fwd/single_
chan_pkt_fwd
SX1276 detected, starting.
Gateway ID: b8:27:eb:ff:ff:7a:51:d5
Listening at SF7 on 433.100000 Mhz.
------------------
stat update: {"stat":{"time":"2018-10-19 06:50:56 GMT","lati":0.00000,"long":0.0
0000,"alti":0,"rxnb":0,"rxok":0,"rxfw":0,"ackr":0.0,"dwnb":0,"txnb":0,"pfrm":"Si
ngle Channel Gateway","mail":"","desc":""}}
stat update: {"stat":{"time":"2018-10-19 06:51:26 GMT","lati":0.00000,"long":0.0
0000,"alti":0,"rxnb":0,"rxok":0,"rxfw":0,"ackr":0.0,"dwnb":0,"txnb":0,"pfrm":"Si
ngle Channel Gateway","mail":"","desc":""}}
stat update: {"stat":{"time":"2018-10-19 06:51:56 GMT","lati":0.00000,"long":0.00000,"alti":0,"
b":0,"rxok":0,"rxfw":0,"ackr":0.0,"dwnb":0,"txnb":0,"pfrm":"Single Channel Gateway","mail":"","
c":""}}
```

Figure 5-17. *Console output for the single-channel packet forwarder*

Registering Your Gateway with the Things Network

The Things Network allows you to register your LoRa gateway in no time with a few simple steps. It also allows you to build applications to decode the payloads and integrate with third-party services to further process your data.

1. Go to the Things Network (https://www.thethingsnetwork.org/) and click the Sign Up button in the top-right corner of the page (Figure 5-18).

Figure 5-18. *Signing up with the Things Network*

2. On the Create an Account page, type in a username, a valid e-mail address, and a password with at least six characters. Then click the "Create account" button (Figure 5-19).

CREATE AN ACCOUNT

Create an account for The Things Network and start exploring the world of Internet of Things with us.

USERNAME

This will be your username — pick a good one because you will **not** be able to change it.

ℒ  Type a user name

EMAIL ADDRESS

You will receive a confirmation email, as well as occasional account related emails. If this email address is managed by a third party (such as for corporate email addresses), this third party might block emails coming from The Things Network. This email address is not public.

✉  Type a valid e-mail address

PASSWORD

Use at least 6 characters.

🔒  Type a password

Create account

Figure 5-19. *Creating a new account*

3. Now go to your e-mail account's inbox and open the e-mail (the Things Network account validation). Then click the "Activate account" button.

4. After activating the account, on the welcome page, click Console at the top of the page (Figure 5-20).

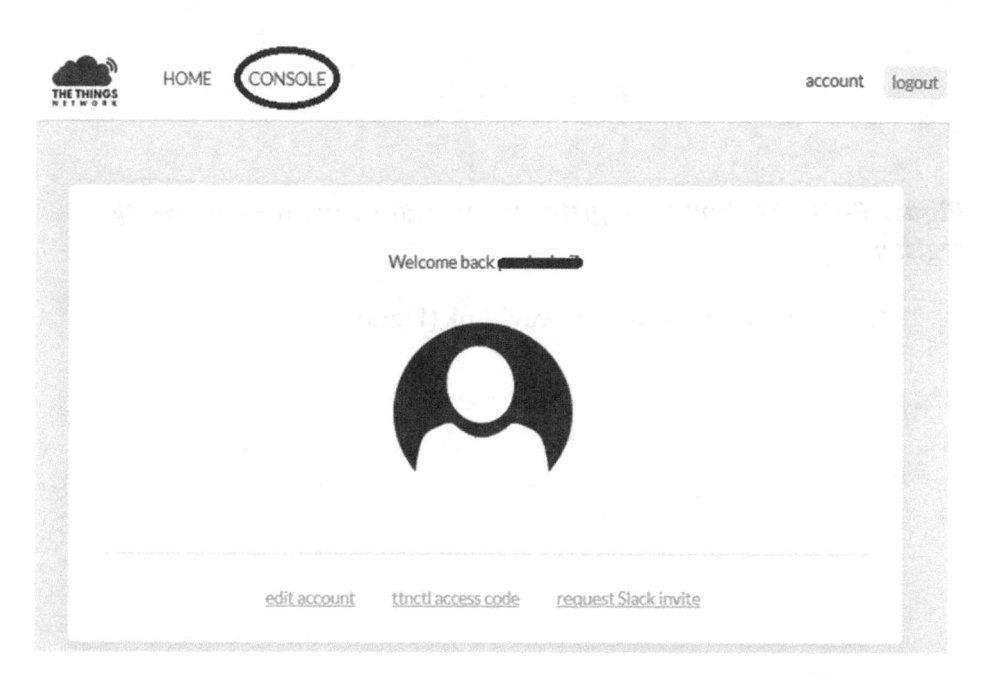

Figure 5-20. *Accessing the Things Network console*

5. This will bring you to the console at `https://console.thethingsnetwork.org/`. The console allows you to register gateways and devices, build applications, create integrations, and manage collaborators and settings.

6. On the console landing page, click Gateways (Figure 5-21).

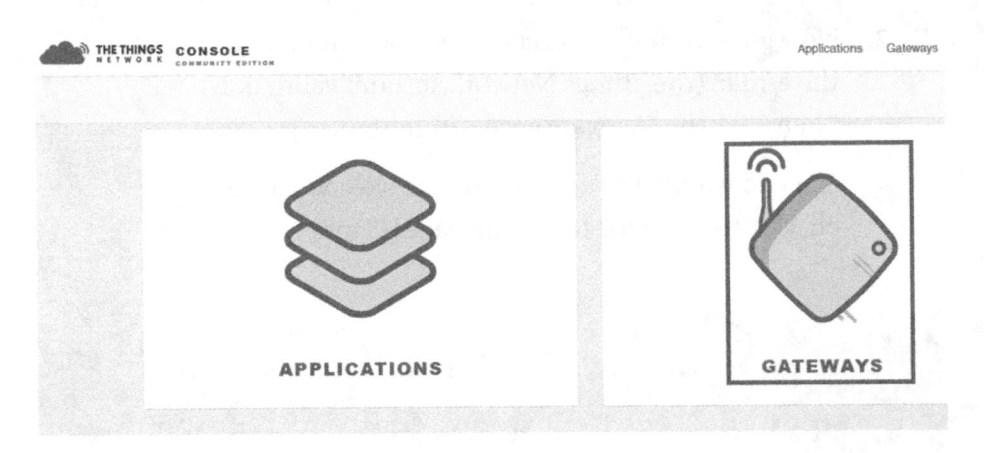

Figure 5-21. *Section for registering new gateways and accessing registered gateways*

7.   Click the "register gateway" link (Figure 5-22).

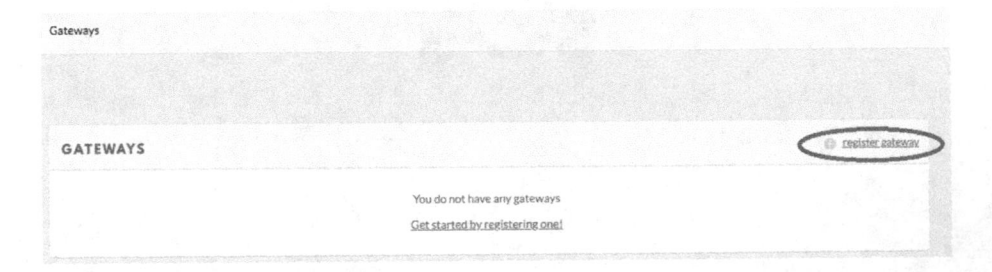

Figure 5-22. *Registering a new gateway*

8.   On the register page, under the Register Gateway section, fill out the form with the following information (Figure 5-23):

- *Gateway ID*: This is a unique human-readable identifier for your gateway. Use the gateway ID generated by the single-channel packet forwarder (see "Installing and Configuring a Single-Channel Packet Forwarder"). Type it without colons (for example, **b827ebffff7a51d5**).

- Select the "I'm using the legacy packet forwarder" check box.

- *Description*: Type in a description for your gateway (e.g., **My First Raspberry Pi Gateway**)

- *Frequency Plan*: Choose a frequency plan from the drop-down list to use with your gateway's LoRa radio transceiver module (e.g., Europe *868 MHz*).

- *Router*: Choose a router from the drop-down list to connect your gateway to the Things Network (e.g., ttn-router-eu).

- *Location*: Click the map to mark the location of your gateway.

- *Antenna Placement*: Choose Indoor.

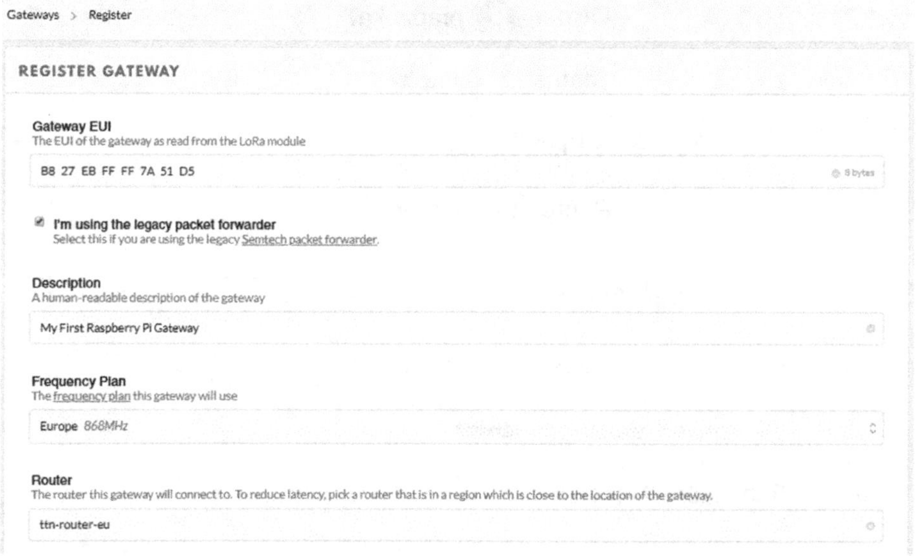

Gateways > Register

REGISTER GATEWAY

Gateway EUI
The EUI of the gateway as read from the LoRa module

B8 27 EB FF FF 7A 51 D5   8 bytes

☑ **I'm using the legacy packet forwarder**
Select this if you are using the legacy Semtech packet forwarder.

Description
A human-readable description of the gateway

My First Raspberry Pi Gateway

Frequency Plan
The frequency plan this gateway will use

Europe 868MHz

Router
The router this gateway will connect to. To reduce latency, pick a router that is in a region which is close to the location of the gateway.

ttn-router-eu

Figure 5-23. *Registering a gateway*

9. Click the Register Gateway button to complete the registration. You will be navigated to the gateway page.

10. On the gateway page, under the Gateway Overview section, you can view the status of your Raspberry Pi gateway (Figure 5-24). The status should be connected if the packet forwarding software is still running on the Raspberry Pi. If not, run the packet forwarding software and wait for the status to update.

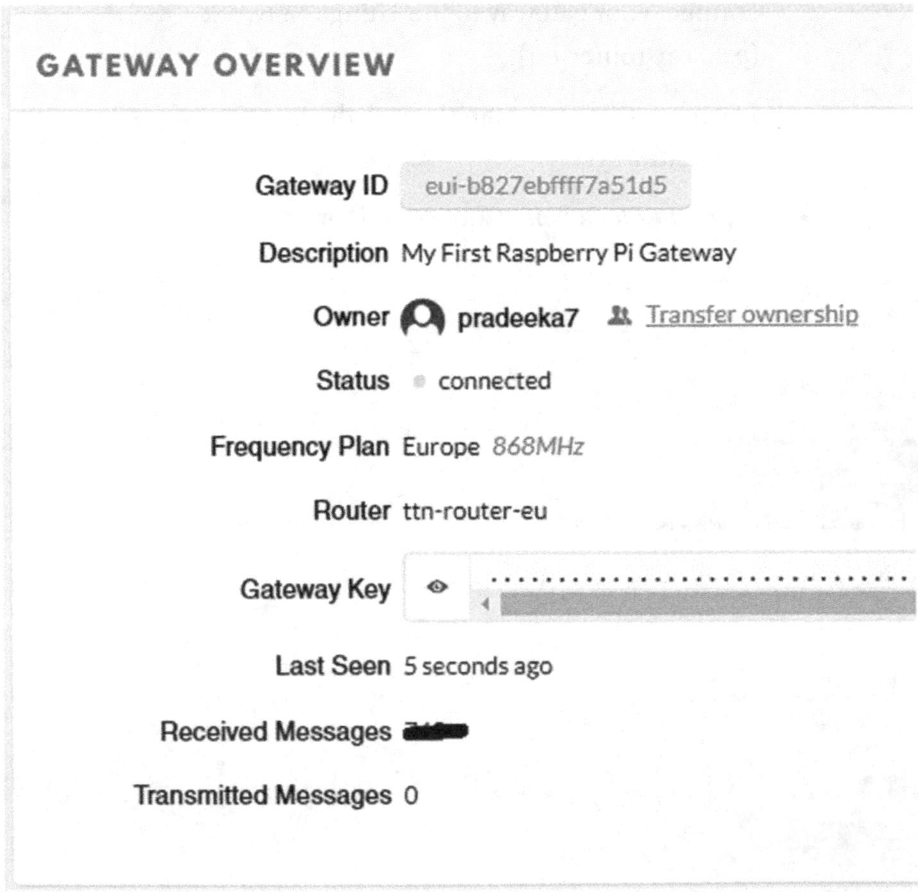

GATEWAY OVERVIEW

Gateway ID	eui-b827ebffff7a51d5
Description	My First Raspberry Pi Gateway
Owner	○ pradeeka7 ⁀ Transfer ownership
Status	● connected
Frequency Plan	Europe 868MHz
Router	ttn-router-eu
Gateway Key	◉ ....
Last Seen	5 seconds ago
Received Messages	
Transmitted Messages	0

Figure 5-24. *Overview of the registered gateway*

11. If you want to change the settings for your gateway, click the Settings tab. On the Settings page, under Gateway Settings section, modify the fields and click the Update Gateway button.

Creating an Application

The LoRa gateway receives raw data packets. These data packets include payloads and other information related to the transmitter. You should decode the payloads to extract the data from the data packets.

1. In the Things Network console, click Applications.

2. On the Applications page, click the "add application" link.

3. On the Add Application page, in the Add Application section, fill out the form (Figure 5-25).

    • *Application ID*: Enter the unique identifier of your application on the network (e.g., b827ebffff7a51d51).

    • *Description*: This is a human-readable description of your new application (e.g., My sensor network application).

    • *Handler registration*: Select the handler you want to register this application to (e.g., ttn-handler-eu).

Applications > Add Application

ADD APPLICATION

Application ID
The unique identifier of your application on the network

b827ebffff7a51d51

Description
A human readable description of your new app

My sensor network application

Application EUI
An application EUI will be issued for The Things Network block for convenience, you can add your own in the application settings page.

EUI issued by The Things Network

Handler registration
Select the handler you want to register this application to

ttn-handler-eu

Figure 5-25. *Adding an appication*

4. Click the "Add application" button to create the
    application. You will be navigated to the application page.
    Scroll down the page and locate the Devices section.
    Then, click the "register device" link (Figure 5-26).

Applications > b827ebffff7a51d51

DEVICES   register device   manage devices

0   registered devices

Figure 5-26. *Registering a device*

5. On the Devices page, in the Register Device section,
    fill out the form (Figure 5-27).

- *Device ID*: This is the unique identifier for the device in this application (e.g., 12346789). The device ID will be immutable.

- *Device EUI*: The device EUI is the unique identifier for this device on the network (e.g., 827ebffff7a51d5). The device EUI must consist of exactly 8 bytes.

- *App Key*: The app key will be used to secure the communication between your device and the network. This is an autogenerated key.

- *App EUI*: This is an autogenerated identifier.

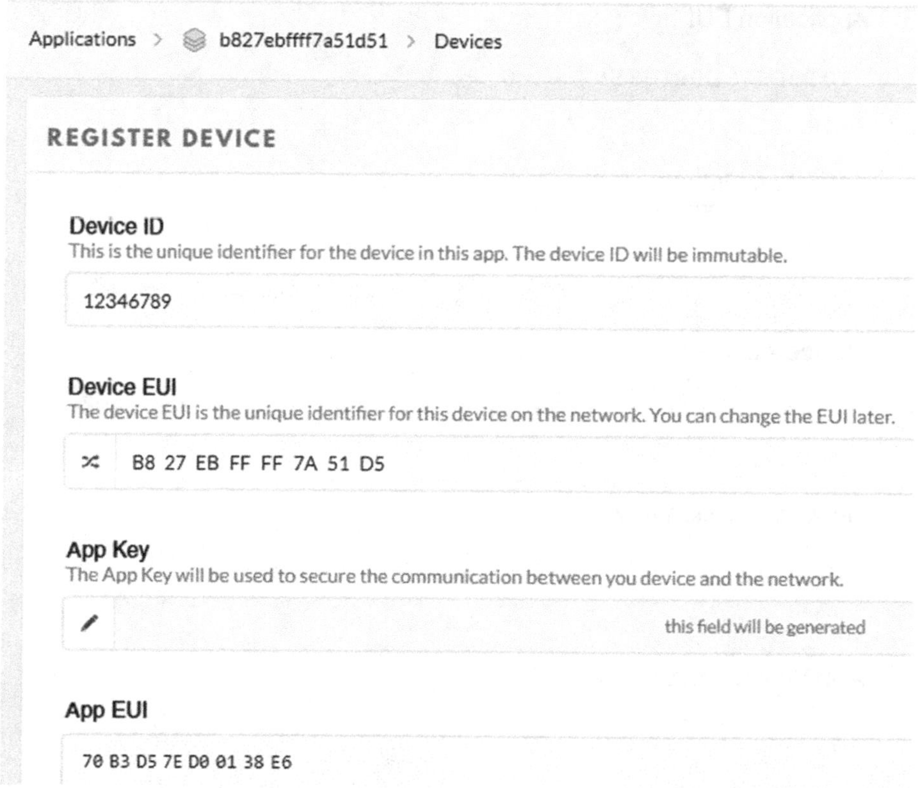

Applications > 🟦 b827ebffff7a51d51 > Devices

REGISTER DEVICE

Device ID
This is the unique identifier for the device in this app. The device ID will be immutable.

12346789

Device EUI
The device EUI is the unique identifier for this device on the network. You can change the EUI later.

⤭   B8 27 EB FF FF 7A 51 D5

App Key
The App Key will be used to secure the communication between you device and the network.

✏   this field will be generated

App EUI

70 B3 D5 7E D0 01 38 E6

Figure 5-27. *Device registering form*

6. Click the Register button to register the device. You will be navigated to the device page.

7. On the device page, click the Settings tab.

8. On the Settings page, in the Settings section, choose ABP as the activation method. This means activating a device by personalization. Then click the Save button. This will generate the device address, network session key, and app session key (Figure 5-28).

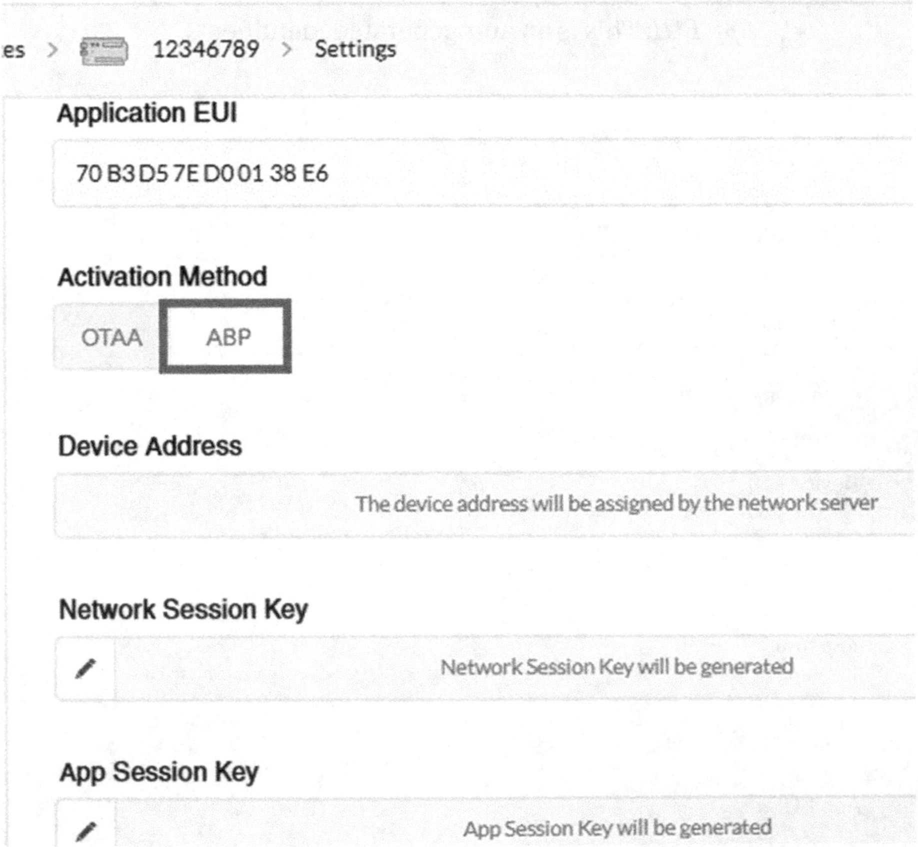

Figure 5-28. *Setting the activation method to activation by personalization (ABP)*

9. Now you can view the autogenerated device address, network session key, and app session key on the device page, in the Device Overview section (Figure 5-29).

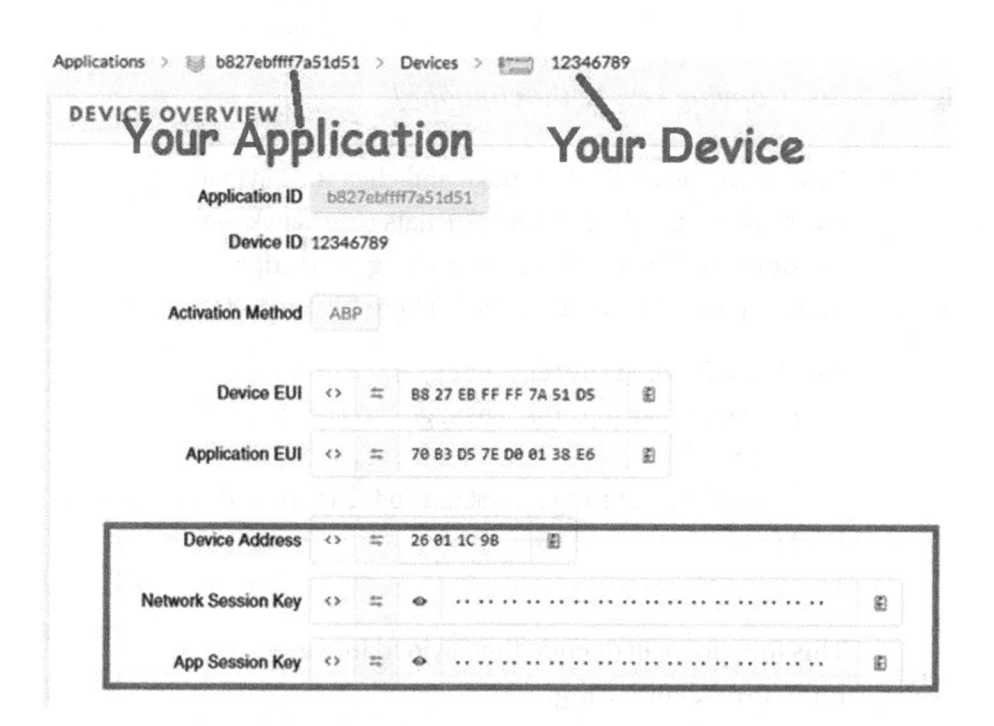

Figure 5-29. *Device address, network session key, and app session key*

10. For the Network Session Key and App Session Key fields, click hex/C-style buttons to view them in C-style. The Copy to Clipboard button can be used to copy them to the clipboard (Figure 5-30).

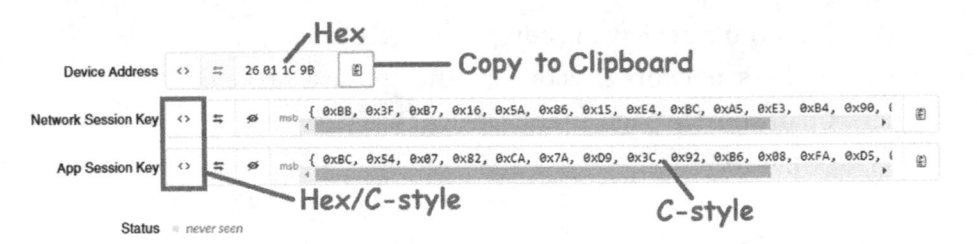

Figure 5-30. *Copying keys to the clipboard*

11. Now go to the application page and click the Payload
     Formats tab. On the Payload Formats page, click the
     Decoder tab. Then replace the existing JavaScript
     function with the function shown here (Figure 5-31):

```
function Decoder(bytes, port) {
    // Decode an uplink message from a buffer
    return {
       message: String.fromCharCode.apply(null,bytes)
    };
}
```

This function will decode the payload into a
human-readable string.

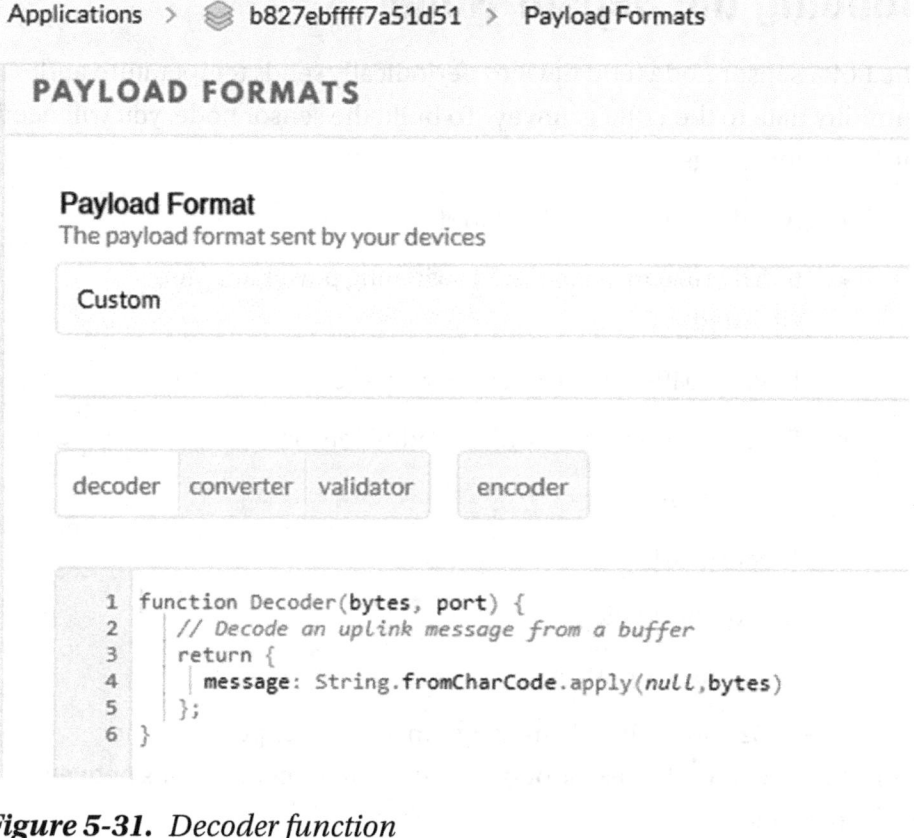

Applications > b827ebffff7a51d51 > Payload Formats

PAYLOAD FORMATS

Payload Format
The payload format sent by your devices

Custom

decoder | converter | validator | encoder

```
1  function Decoder(bytes, port) {
2      // Decode an uplink message from a buffer
3      return {
4        message: String.fromCharCode.apply(null,bytes)
5      };
6  }
```

Figure 5-31. *Decoder function*

12. Finally, click the "save payload functions" button to save the changes.

Building the Sensor Node

The LoRa sensor node (end device) periodically sends temperature and humidity data to the LoRa gateway. To build the sensor node, you will need the following things:

- Arduino Uno or Adafruit Metro

- 9 VDC 1000 mA–regulated switching power adapter, UL listed

- LoRa RFM9x radio transceiver breakout

- DHT11 temperature and humidity sensor

- 10 K ohm resistor

- Breadboard

- Breadboard holder

- A few hook-up wires

Figure 5-32 shows the wiring diagram for the temperature and humidity sensor node. Use hook-up wires to make connections between each component.

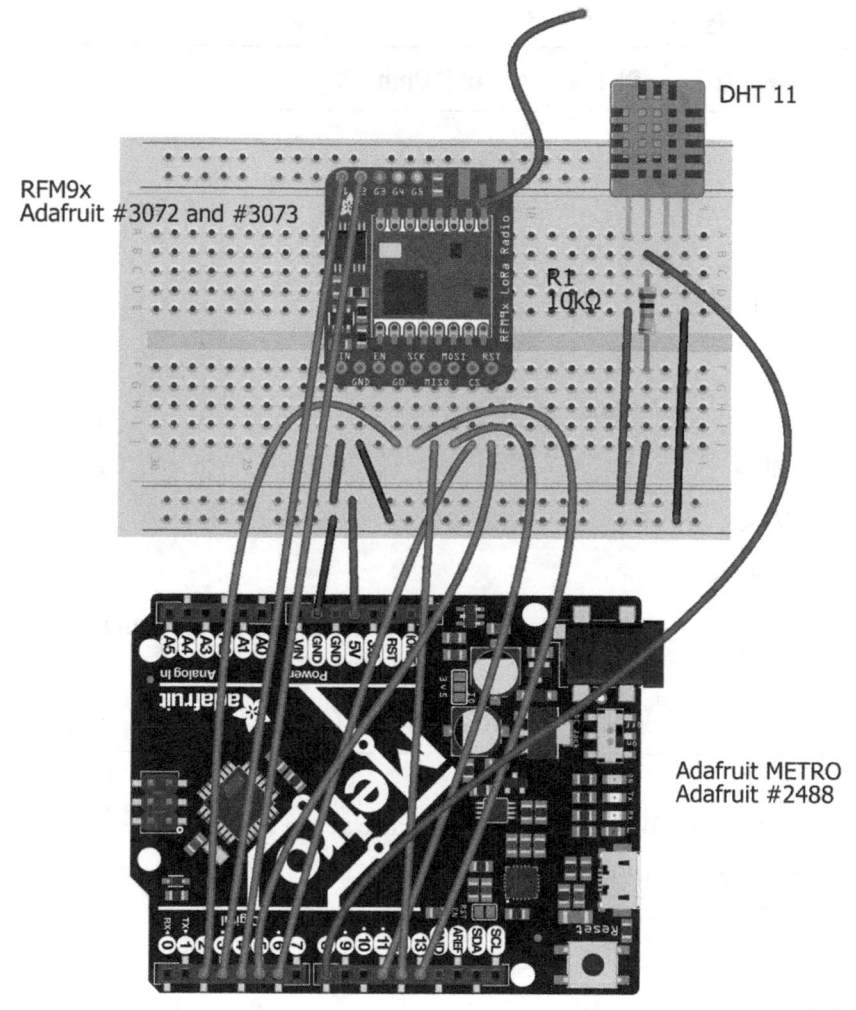

Figure 5-32. *Wiring diagram for the temperature and humidity sensor node*

Table 5-2 shows the wiring connection between each component of the sensor node.

Table 5-2. *Wiring Connections*

Arduino	RFM9x	DHT11	10 K Ohm
2	G0		
3	G1		
4	G2		
5	RST		
6	CS		
8		DATA	
11	MOSI		
12	MISO		
13	SCK		
5V		VCC	Connects between Arduino (5V) and DHT11 (VCC)
GND		GND	

Figure 5-33 shows the completed hardware setup with all the previously mentioned components.

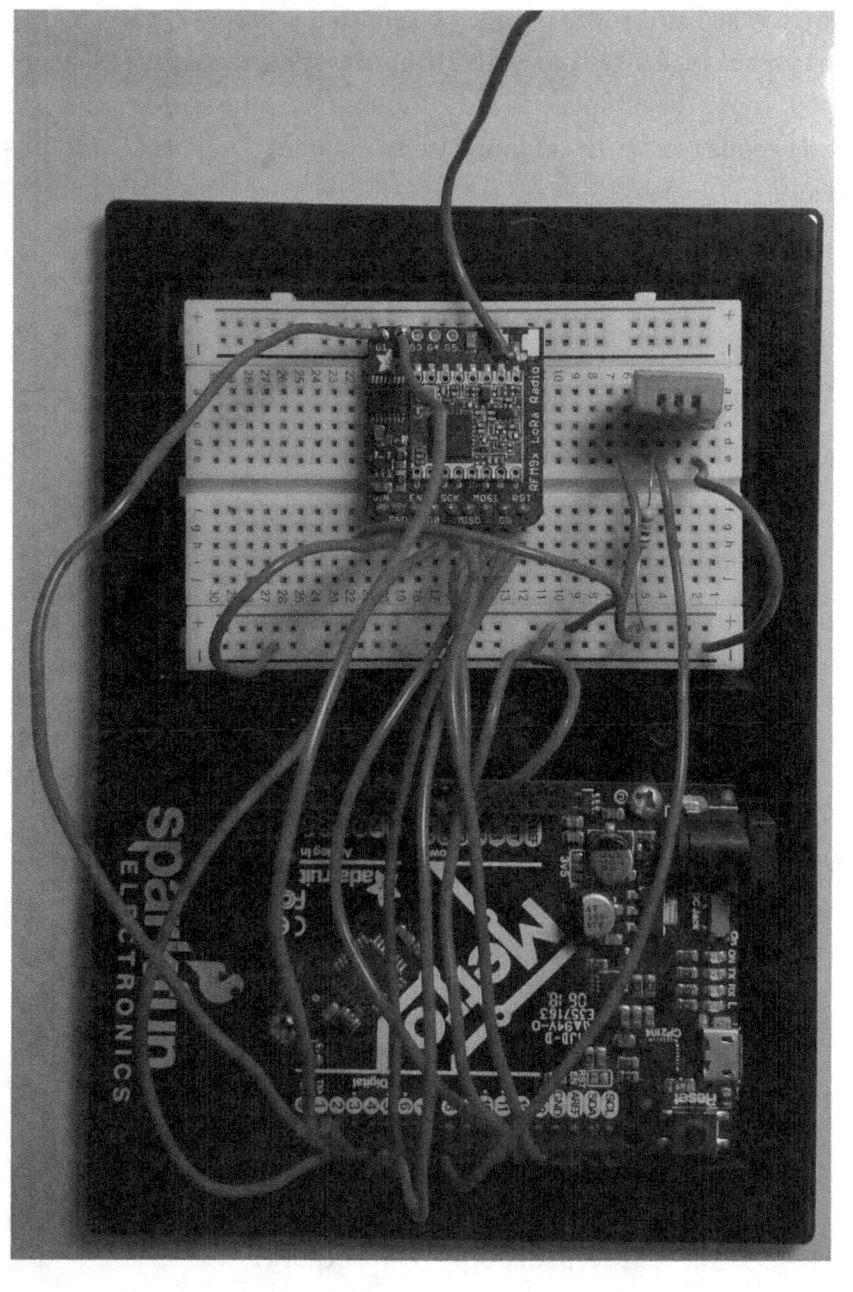

Figure 5-33. *Completed hardware setup of the LoRa sensor node*

You will be using some sample code hosted at https://github.com/matthijskooijman/arduino-lmic/blob/master/examples/ttn-abp/ttn-abp.ino as the template to write the sketch for the sensor node. The same code can be downloaded from Chapter 5/Original Source/ttn-abp.ino.

1. Open the Arduino IDE and paste the code from https://github.com/matthijskooijman/arduino-lmic/blob/master/examples/ttn-abp/ttn-abp.ino.

2. Save the file to your local drive as ttn-abp.ino.

3. Add following code snippets just below the line #include <SPI.h>:

    ```
    #define DHTPIN 8
    #define DHTTYPE DHT11
    DHT dht(DHTPIN, DHTTYPE);
    ```

4. Comment the following line of code:

    ```
    static uint8_t mydata[] = "Hello, world!";
    ```

    as follows:

    ```
    //static uint8_t mydata[] = "Hello, world!";
    ```

5. Replace the network session key, application session key, and end-device address with the Network Session Key, App Session Key, and Device Address values, respectively, that can be found on the Things Network Console's device page.

    ```
    // LoRaWAN NwkSKey, network session key
    // This is the default Semtech key, which is used by
    // the early prototype TTN network.
    ```

```
static const PROGMEM u1_t NWKSKEY[16] = { 0xBB, 0x3F,
0xB7, 0x16, 0x5A, 0x86, 0x15, 0xE4, 0xBC, 0xA5, 0xE3,
0xB4, 0x90, 0xC3, 0x26, 0xF0 };

// LoRaWAN AppSKey, application session key
// This is the default Semtech key, which is used by
// the early prototype TTN network.
static const u1_t PROGMEM APPSKEY[16] = { 0xBC, 0x54,
0x07, 0x82, 0xCA, 0x7A, 0xD9, 0x3C, 0x92, 0xB6, 0x08,
0xFA, 0xD5, 0xE6, 0xAC, 0x22 };

// LoRaWAN end-device address (DevAddr)
static const u4_t DEVADDR = 0x26011C9B ;
// <-- Change this address for every node!
```

6. Modify the pin mapping function (Figure 5-34) if
    your hardware setup has different connections than
    the wiring diagram shown previously.

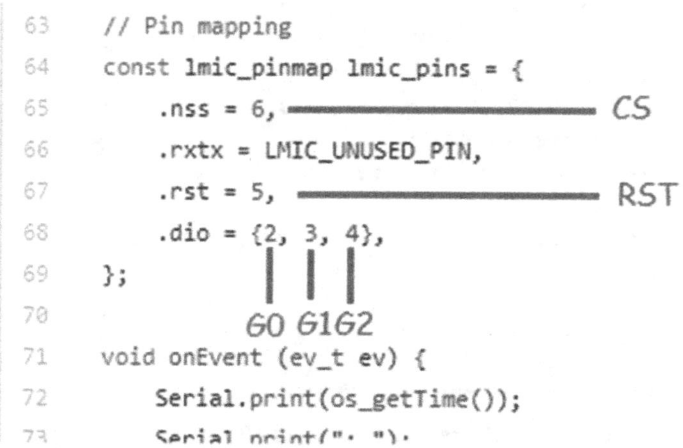

Figure 5-34. *Pin mapping function for the RFM9x LoRa radio transceiver module*

7. Add the following code snippets to the do_
    send(osjob_t* j) function (Figure 5-35):

```
byte buffer[8];
    float t = dht.readTemperature();
    float h = dht.readHumidity();
    dtostrf(t, 2, 1, buffer);
    dtostrf(h, 2, 1, &buffer[4]);
    String res = buffer;
    res.getBytes(buffer, res.length() + 1);
    Serial.println("");
    Serial.print("Sending - temperature: ");
    Serial.print(t);
    Serial.print(", humidity: ");
    Serial.print(h);
    Serial.println("");
```

```
void do_send(osjob_t* j){
    byte buffer[8];
    float t = dht.readTemperature();
    float h = dht.readHumidity();
    dtostrf(t, 2, 1, buffer);
    dtostrf(h, 2, 1, &buffer[4]);
    String res = buffer;
    res.getBytes(buffer, res.length() + 1);
    Serial.println("");
    Serial.print("Sending - temperature: ");
    Serial.print(t);
    Serial.print(", humidity: ");
    Serial.print(h);
    Serial.println("");

    // Check if there is not a current TX/RX job running
    if (LMIC.opmode & OP_TXRXPEND) {
        Serial.println(F("OP_TXRXPEND, not sending"));
    } else {
```

Figure 5-35. *Modified do_send() function*

8. In the `setup()` function, add the following code just after `Serial.println(F("Starting"));`:

    `dht.begin();`

9. In the `setup()` function, define the frequency for the sensor node as follows by commenting all the unnecessary center frequencies (Figure 5-36). Also, the center frequency should be matched with the center frequency you defined in the Things Network Console for the gateway. As an example, the line of code for the center frequency, 433.1 MHz, is as follows:

    `LMIC_setupChannel(0, 433100000, DR_RANGE_MAP(DR_SF12, DR_SF7),  BAND_CENTI);        // g-band`

```
// works, so it is good for debugging, but can overload those            First channel starts
// frequencies, so be sure to configure the full frequency range of      with 0
// your network here (unless your network autoconfigures them).
// Setting up channels should happen after LMIC_setSession, as that
// configures the minimal channel set.                                   Center Frequency:
// NA-US channels 0-71 are configured automatically                      433.1 MHz
  LMIC_setupChannel(0, 433100000, DR_RANGE_MAP(DR_SF12, DR_SF7),  BAND_CENTI);    // g-band
//LMIC_setupChannel(1, 868300000, DR_RANGE_MAP(DR_SF12, DR_SF7B), BAND_CENTI);    // g-band
//LMIC_setupChannel(2, 868500000, DR_RANGE_MAP(DR_SF12, DR_SF7),  BAND_CENTI);    // g-band
//LMIC_setupChannel(3, 867100000, DR_RANGE_MAP(DR_SF12, DR_SF7),  BAND_CENTI);    // g-band
//LMIC_setupChannel(4, 867300000, DR_RANGE_MAP(DR_SF12, DR_SF7),  BAND_CENTI);    // g-band
//LMIC_setupChannel(5, 867500000, DR_RANGE_MAP(DR_SF12, DR_SF7),  BAND_CENTI);    // g-band
//LMIC_setupChannel(6, 867700000, DR_RANGE_MAP(DR_SF12, DR_SF7),  BAND_CENTI);    // g-band
//LMIC_setupChannel(7, 867900000, DR_RANGE_MAP(DR_SF12, DR_SF7),  BAND_CENTI);    // g-band
//LMIC_setupChannel(8, 868800000, DR_RANGE_MAP(DR_FSK,  DR_FSK),  BAND_MILLI);    // g2-band
// TTN defines an additional channel at 869.525Mhz using SF9 for class B
// devices' ping slots. LMIC does not have an easy way to define set this
// frequency and support for class B is spotty and untested, so this
// frequency is not configured here.|
#elif defined(CFG_us915)
// NA-US channels 0-71 are configured automatically
// but only one group of 8 should (a subband) should be active
```

Comment all unnecessary frequencies

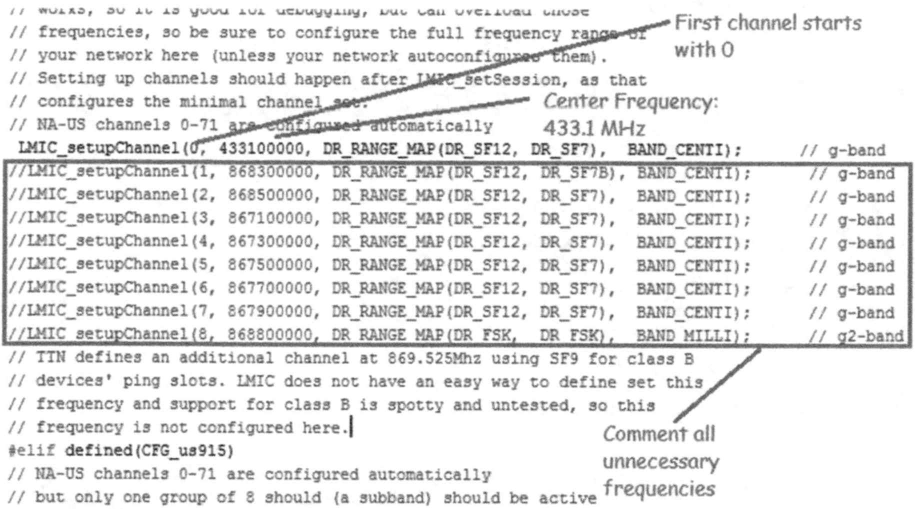

Figure 5-36. *Defining the center frequency for the sensor node to match with the gateway's frequency*

10. Save the sketch again by clicking File ➤ Save. The modified source code can be found at Chapter 5/ ttn-abp.ino.

11. Connect the Arduino board to your computer using a USB cable.

12. Click Tools ➤ Board ➤ Arduino/Genuino Uno.

13. Click Tools ➤ Port and select the correct COM port for your Arduino board.

14. Upload the sketch into the Arduino board by clicking the Upload button.

15. After completing the upload, open the serial monitor by clicking Tools ➤ Serial Monitor (Figure 5-37).

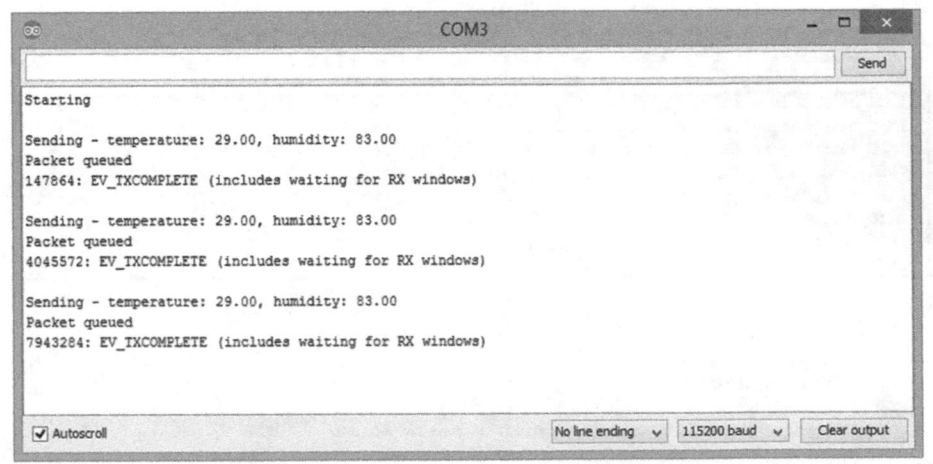

Figure 5-37. *Serial monitor output of the sensor node*

Viewing Decoded Payload Data

Now you are ready to view the decoded payload on the Things Network Console.

1. On the application page, click the Data tab (Figure 5-38). Then in the Application Data section, click the Uplink tab. You can see all the incoming (uplink) data packets in the list view.

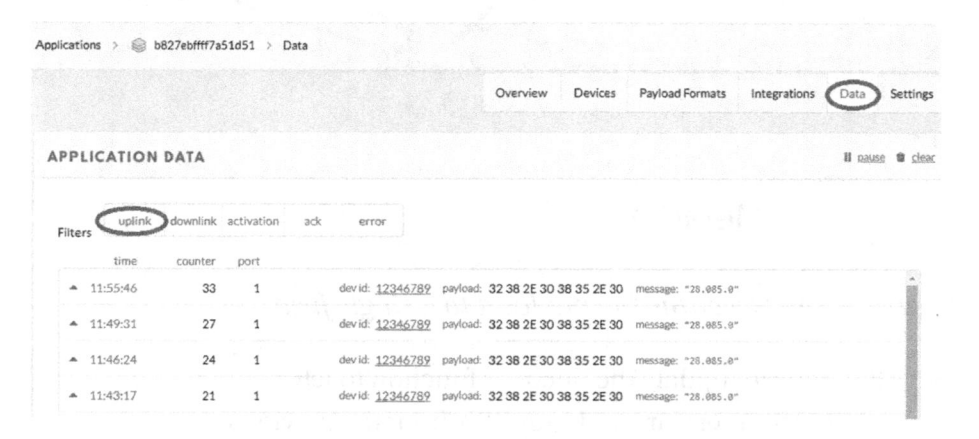

Figure 5-38. *Uplink data captured by the application*

2. Click one of the list items to expand (Figure 5-39). In the Fields section, you can view the decoded payload as a readable string containing the temperature and humidity.

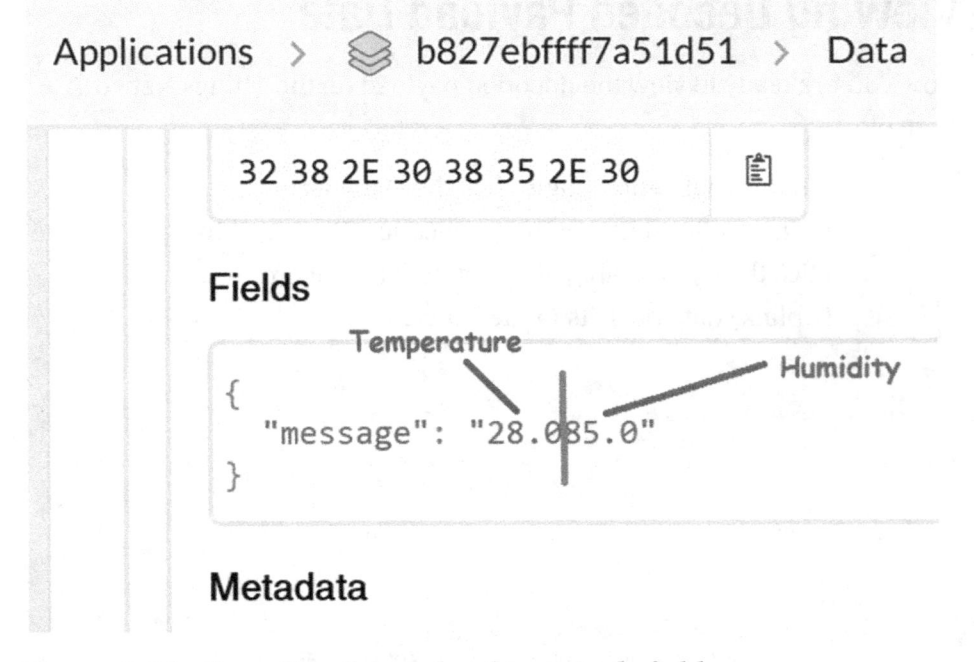

Figure 5-39. *Decoding the payload to a single field*

3. You can update the decoder function to fetch
    the temperature and humidity from the previous
    message. Here is the modified JavaScript function:

```
function Decoder(bytes, port) {
    // Decode an uplink message from a buffer
    return {
      temperature:
String.fromCharCode.apply(null,bytes).substring(0,4),
      humidity:
String.fromCharCode.apply(null,bytes).substring(4,8)
    };
}
```

Figure 5-40 shows the result for the updated decoder function. Now
you can easily read the temperature and humidity data under Fields.

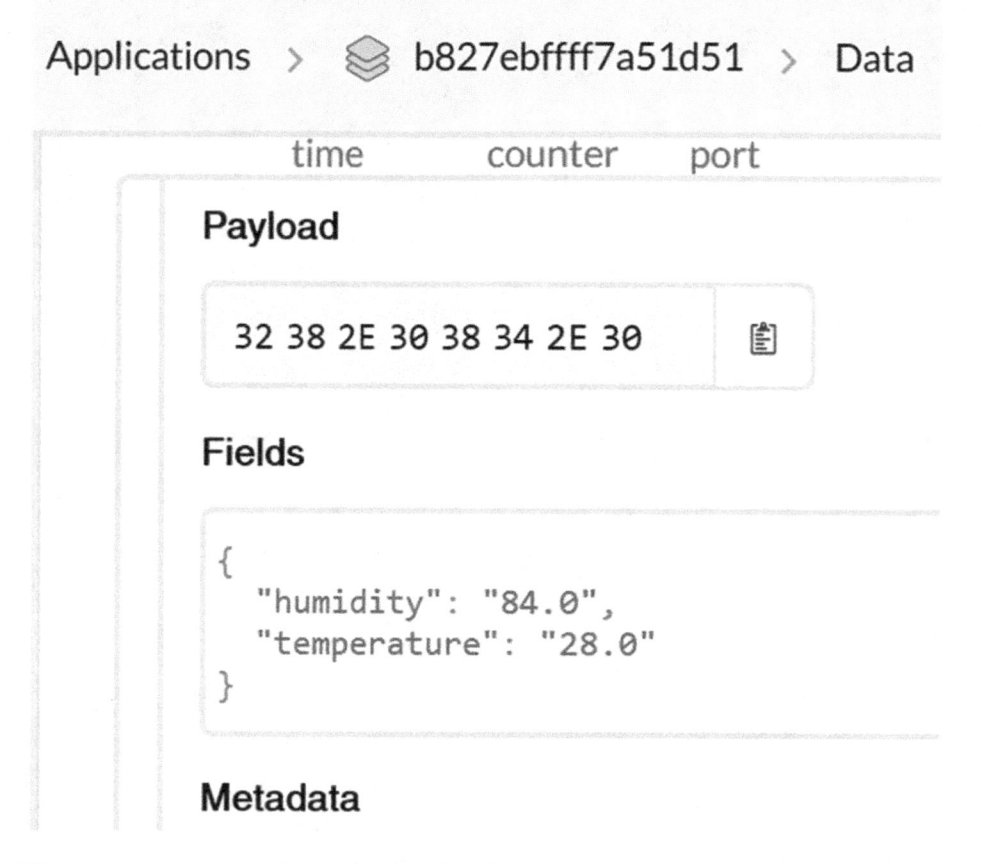

Figure 5-40. *Decoding the payload to extract individual data fields*

Summary

In this chapter, you built a single-channel LoRa gateway using the Raspberry Pi and connected it to the Things Network. Then you built a simple LoRa sensor node (end device) to send humidity and temperature data to the LoRa gateway. Finally, you developed an application to decode the payload to extract humidity and temperature data from the payload.

In the next chapter, you will learn about how to send data to the ThingSpeak IoT server using the RESTful API.

CHAPTER 6

Connecting with IoT Servers Using a RESTful API

In this chapter, you'll learn how to send data to an IoT server using a RESTful API. A RESTful API is an application program interface (API) that uses HTTP requests to GET, PUT, POST, and DELETE data. The ThingSpeak IoT platform enables clients to update and receive updates from channel feeds through the ThingSpeak RESTful API.

The network you'll build consists of a LoRa end node, LoRa gateway, and the ThingSpeak IoT. The LoRa end node will periodically send temperature and humidity data to the LoRa gateway. Once the data is received, the LoRa gateway forwards the data to ThingSpeak via the HTTP GET method using a RESTful API.

Technical Requirements

To complete the project discussed in this chapter, you will need following hardware and software:

- Arduino Uno or Adafruit Metro

- RFM9x radio transceiver breakout

© Pradeeka Seneviratne 2019
P. Seneviratne, *Beginning LoRa Radio Networks with Arduino*,
https://doi.org/10.1007/978-1-4842-4357-2_6

- DHT11 temperature and humidity sensor

- Dragino LG01 LoRa gateway

- ThingSpeak account

Using ThingSpeak as the IoT Server

The ThingSpeak IoT server allows you to store and display sensor data. You can use a RESTful API to update a channel feed on the ThingSpeak IoT server using the HTTP GET method. First, create a free user account on the ThingSpeak server.

1. Go to ThingSpeak (`https://thingspeak.com/`) and sign up for a new free account. Usually, the Sign Up link can be found in the top-right corner of the page.

2. Fill out the form with all the required information and click the Continue button to create a MathWorks account.

Creating a New Channel

A channel stores all the data that a ThingSpeak application collects. Each channel can have up to eight fields that can hold any type of data, three fields for location data, and one field for status data. Follow these steps to create a new channel on the Thing Speak IoT server:

1. In the top navigation menu, select Channels ➤ My Channels (Figure 6-1).

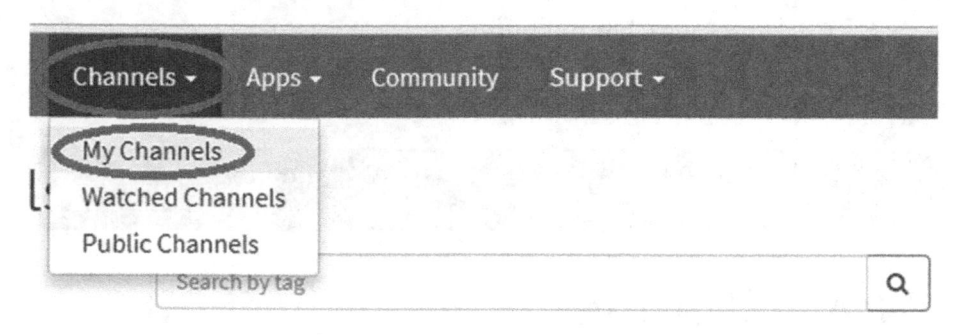

Figure 6-1. *Menu command for accessing the My Channels page*

    2.   On the My Channels page, click the New Channel
            button (Figure 6-2).

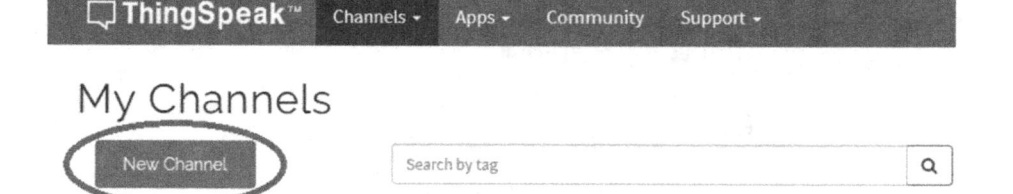

Figure 6-2. *Creating a new channel*

    3.   On the New Channel page, fill out the form fields as
            follows (Figure 6-3):

- *Channel Name*: Type in a unique name for the
  ThingSpeak channel (e.g., **My RESTful Channel**).

- *Description*: Type in a description for the ThingSpeak
  channel (e.g., **Testing with RESTful API**).

- *Field #*: Use only two fields to store data. First, enable the
  Field 1 text box by clicking the check box next to it, and
  type in **temperature**. Then, enable the Field 2 text box by
  clicking the check box next to it, and type in **humidity**.

- Select the Show Status check box.

173

4. Click the Save Channel button.

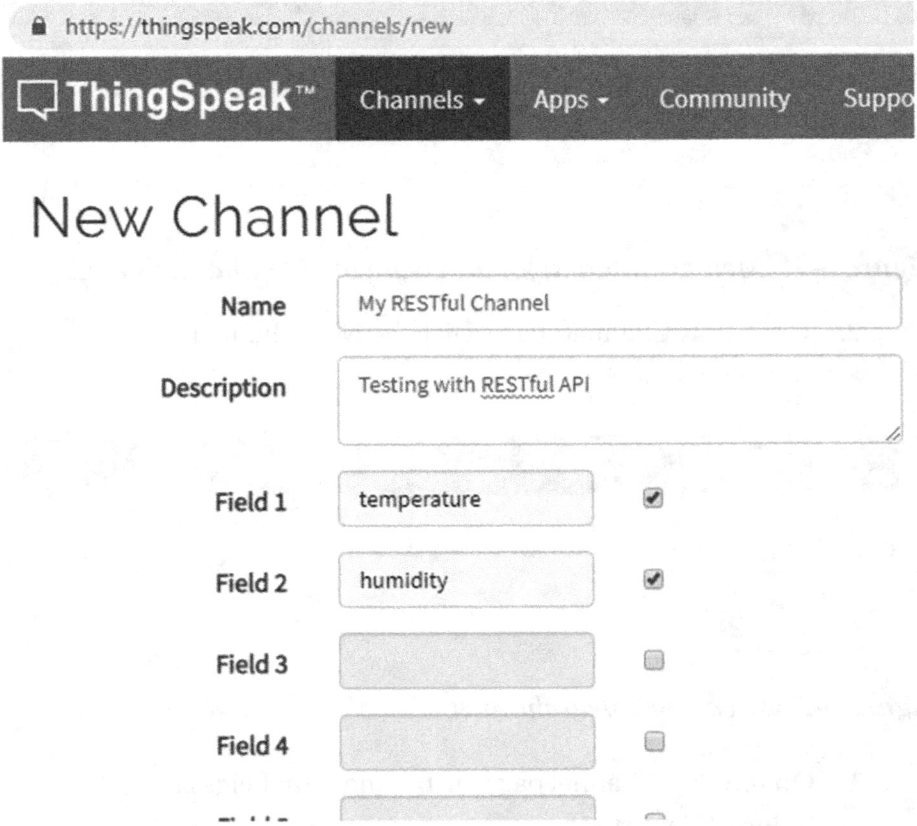

Figure 6-3. *Channel settings*

5. Once created, you will get the page titled My RESTful Channel. It shows the channel ID, description, author, access level, charts for each data field, channel settings, and API keys (Figure 6-4).

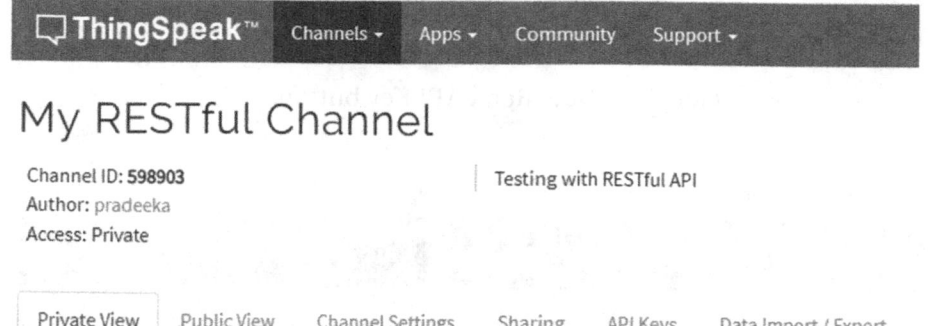

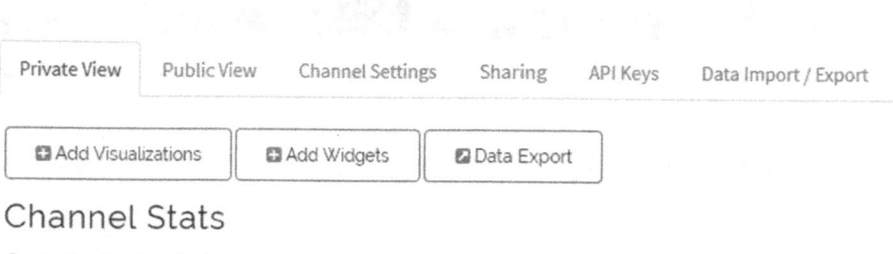

Figure 6-4. *My RESTful Channel page*

Getting the API Keys

ThingSpeak provides two types of API keys. You need these keys to write to a channel and read data from a private channel. API keys are autogenerated when you create a new channel.

1. In the My RESTful Channel page, click the API Keys tab. It shows the autogenerated Write API key and the Read API key (Figure 6-5).

   • The Write API key allows you to write data to a channel. If you want, you can generate a new Write API key by clicking the Generate New Write API Key button.

- The Read API key allows you to read data from a private channel. If you want, you can generate an additional Read API key for the channel by clicking the Generate New Read API Key button.

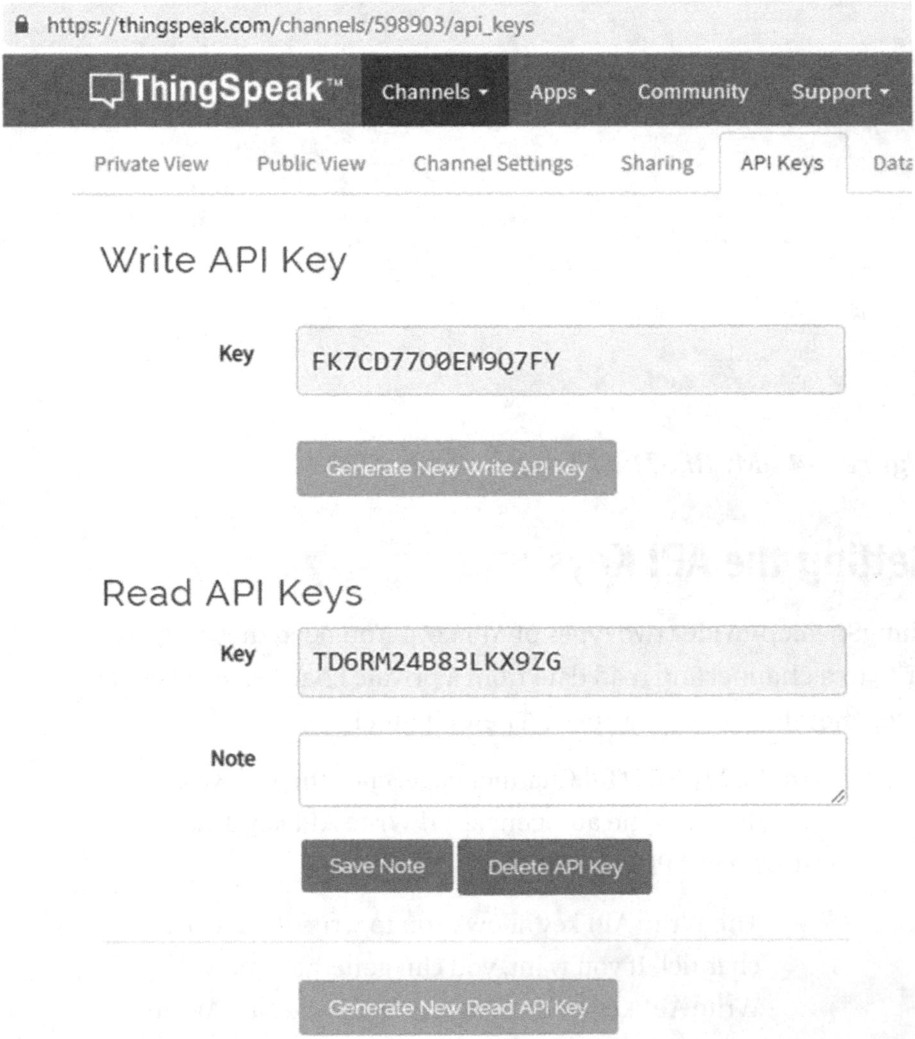

Figure 6-5. Write API key and Read API key

Testing Your Channel with a Web Browser

You can use the HTTP GET method to update a channel feed. Follow these steps to send some sample data to the Thing Speak channel:

1. The URL syntax for the channel update using the HTTP GET method will be as follows:

   ```
   https://api.thingspeak.com/update?api_key=WRITE_
   API_KEY&field1=value1&field2=value2
   ```

2. Using a web browser, copy and paste the following URLs into the address bar and press the Enter key:

   ```
   https://api.thingspeak.com/update?api_key=FK7CD
   7700EM9Q7FY&field1=15&field2=79
   https://api.thingspeak.com/update?api_key=FK7CD
   7700EM9Q7FY&field1=17&field2=80
   https://api.thingspeak.com/update?api_key=FK7CD
   7700EM9Q7FY&field1=20&field2=78
   https://api.thingspeak.com/update?api_key=FK7CD
   7700EM9Q7FY&field1=18&field2=81
   https://api.thingspeak.com/update?api_key=FK7CD
   7700EM9Q7FY&field1=23&field2=80
   ```

3. For each successful update for a channel feed, the browser will display an entry ID starting from 1 (Figure 6-6). 0 indicates an unsuccessful update for the channel feed.

Figure 6-6. *Updating a channel feed*

4. The entry ID is a unique identification number for
    updating a channel feed. If you want to reset the entry
    counter, you can do it by clearing all the feed data from
    the channel. To clear all the data feed from a channel,
    click the Channel Settings tab and then scroll down the
    page and click the Clear Channel button. To delete a
    channel, click the Delete Channel button (Figure 6-7).

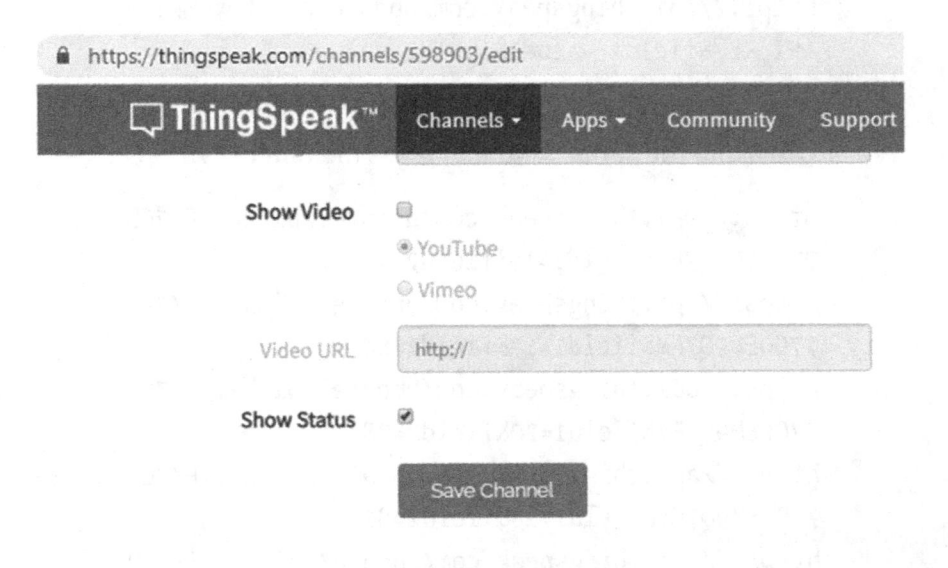

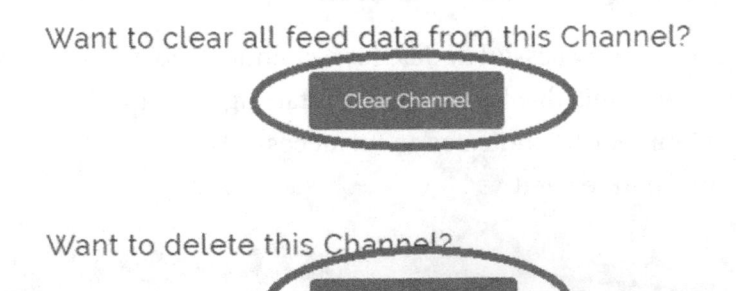

Figure 6-7. *Clearing all the feed data from a channel and deleting a channel*

5.   On the Private View tab, you can view the Field 1
      Chart and Field 2 Chart graphs with the submitted
      data through the channel feed (Figure 6-8).

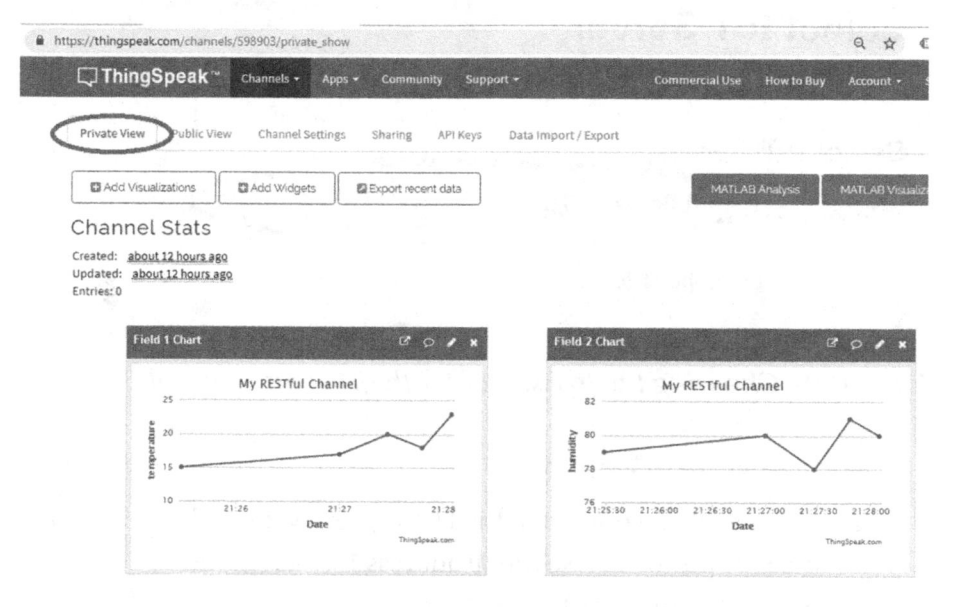

Figure 6-8. *Field 1 Chart shows temperature data over time, and
Field 2 Chart shows humidity data over time*

Testing Your Channel with the LG01 Console

You can send HTTP GET requests to the ThingSpeak server using the LG01
console. It uses a tool known as curl to transfer data from or to a server.

1.   Log in to the LG01 configuration interface by
      providing the default credentials, which are *root* (the
      username) and *dragino* (the password).

2.   In the configuration interface, select Sensor
      ➤ IoT Server. On the Select IoT Server page, from
      the IoT Server drop-down list, choose TCP/IP
      Protocol (Figure 6-9).

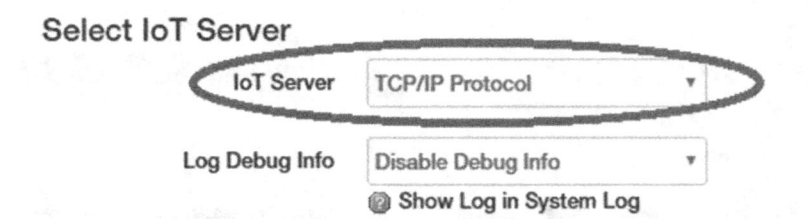

Figure 6-9. *Choosing the IoT server for the TCP/IP protocol*

3. Click the Save & Apply button.

4. Using PuTTY, connect to the LG01 gateway through the SSH protocol. Use the IP address 10.130.1.1 and port 22 (Figure 6-10).

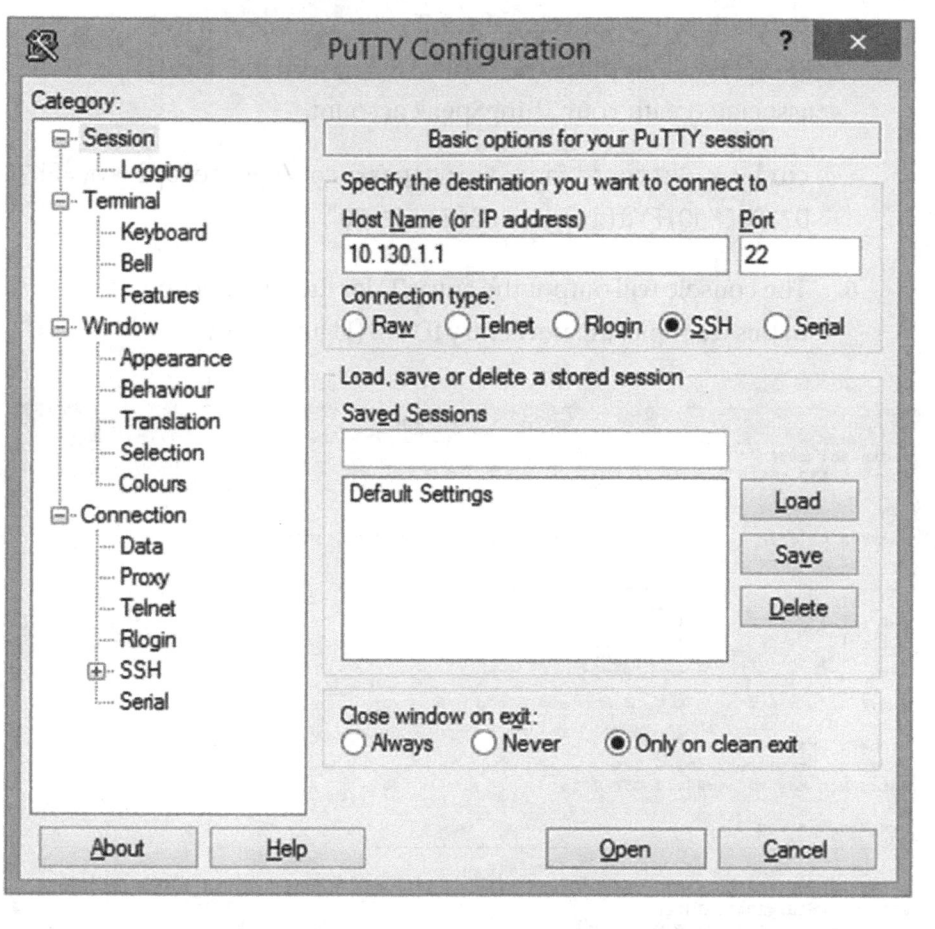

Figure 6-10. *PuTTY configuration to specify the destination LG01 console to connect with LG01*

5. Log in to the LG01 console using the default user name, *root*, and the password, *dragino*.

6. The syntax for the curl command is as follows:

```
curl -k "https://api.thingspeak.com/update?api_
key=WRITE_API_KEY&field1=value1&field2=value2"
```

7. To test the channel, issue the following `curl` command. Remember to replace the Write API key with the one associated with your ThingSpeak account.

```
curl -k "https://api.thingspeak.com/update?api_key=FK7C
D7700EM9Q7FY&field1=28&field2=80"
```

8. The console will output the entry ID for the channel update. In this example, the new entry ID is 6 (Figure 6-11).

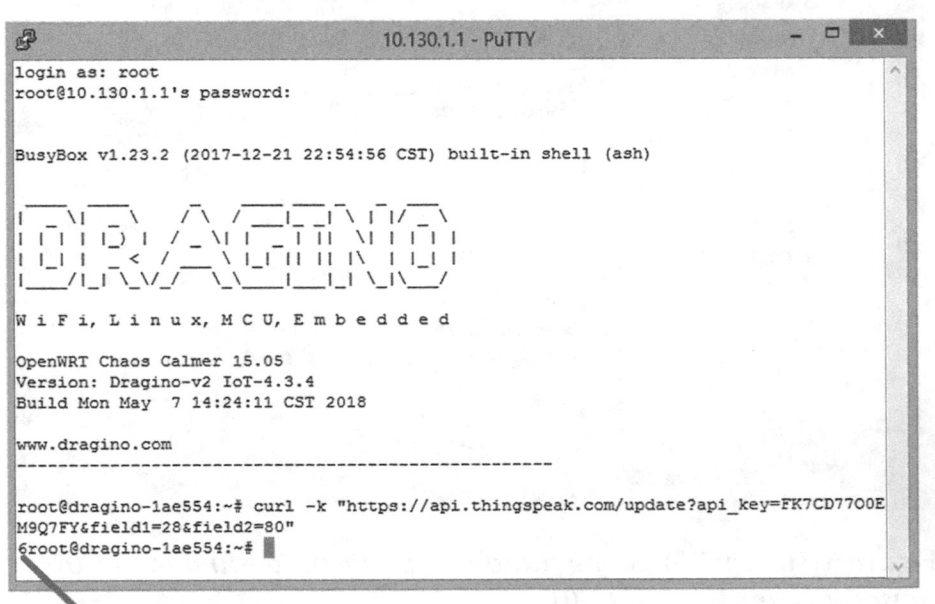

New Entry ID

Figure 6-11. *Issuing the curl command from the LG01 gateway console*

9. Figure 6-12 shows the charts with the newly updated data points.

Channel Stats

Created: about 23 hours ago
Updated: about 23 hours ago
Last entry: 2 minutes ago
Entries: 6

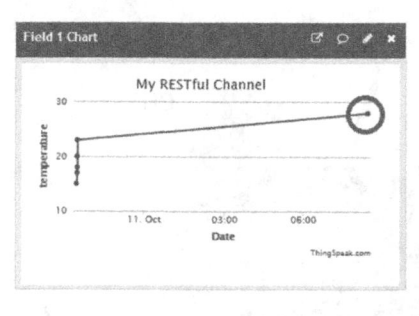
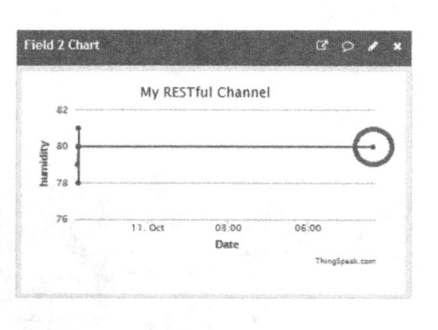

Figure 6-12. *New data points for temperature and humidity*

Now you should be ready to update the ThingSpeak channel feed with a LoRa wireless network by building a simple sensor node and using the LG01 LoRa gateway.

Building the Sensor Node

The LoRa sensor node (end device) periodically collects temperature and humidity data from the environment. You will need the following things to build the sensor node:

- Arduino Uno or Adafruit Metro

- RFM9x LoRa radio transceiver breakout

- DHT11 temperature and humidity sensor

- 10 kiloohm resistor (usually Adafruit provides a free resistor with a DHT11 sensor)

- Solid core hook-up wires

- Half-size breadboard

- Breadboard holder

183

Figure 6-13 shows the wiring diagram for the sensor node. Using hook-up wires, make connections between all the electronic components.

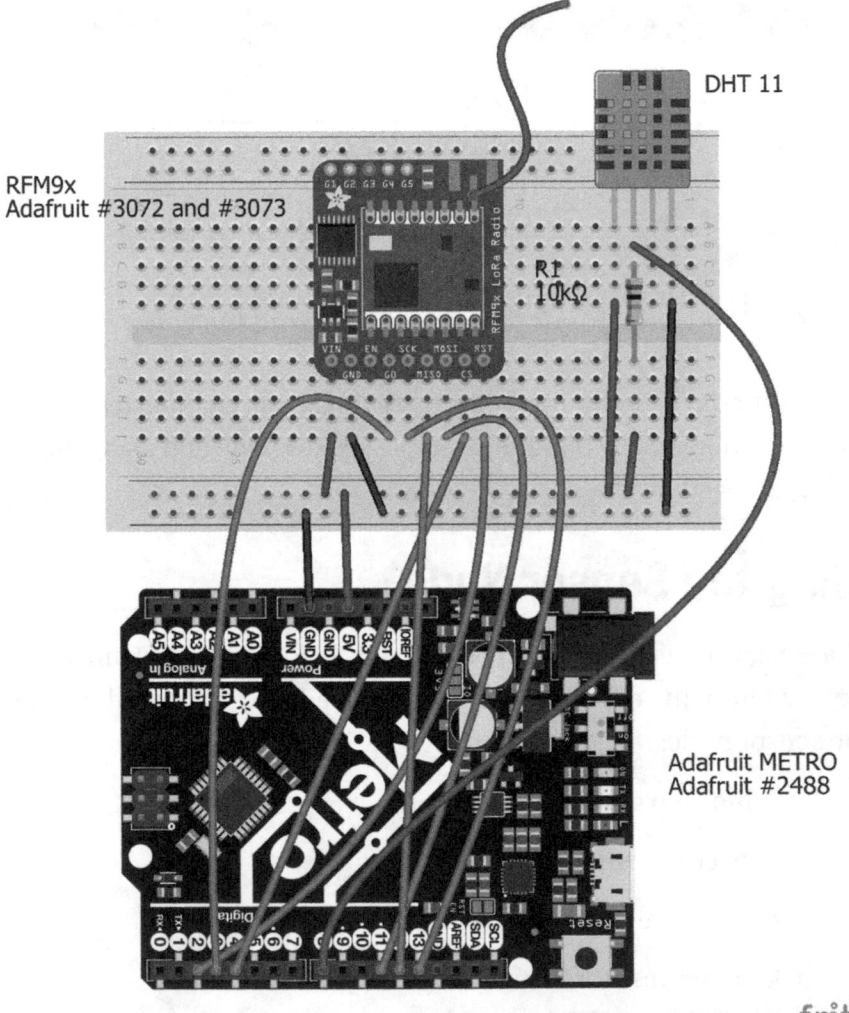

Figure 6-13. *Wiring diagram for the LoRa end device (sensor node)*

Table 6-1 shows the connections between the Arduino/Metro, radio transceiver, and DHT11 sensor.

Table 6-1. *Wiring Connections for Sensor Node*

Arduino/Metro	Radio Transceiver	DHT11
VIN	VIN	VIN
GND	GND	GND
2	RST	
3	G0	
4	CS	
8		DATA
11	MOSI	
12	MISO	
13	SCK	

Make sure to keep the antenna wire perpendicular to the LoRa radio transceiver module. Figure 6-14 shows the completed sensor node.

Figure 6-14. *Completed LoRa end device (sensor node)*

Uploading Sketch to the Sensor Node

Follow these steps to upload the sample sketch to the LoRa sensor node:

1. Go to `https://github.com/dragino/Arduino-Profile-Examples/blob/master/libraries/Dragino/examples/IoTServer/ThingSpeak/dht11_client/` and download the sample Arduino sketch, `dht11_client.ino`. The same source code can be found at Chapter 6/Original Source/dht11_client.ino.

2. Open `dht11_client.ino` with your Arduino integrated development environment.

3. Find the following line:

   ```
   RH_RF95 rf95;
   ```

4. Modify it as shown here by passing G0 and CS pins, where G0 is connected to the Arduino digital pin 4 and CS is connected to the Arduino digital pin 3:

   ```
   RH_RF95 rf95(4, 3);
   ```

5. Then, find the following line:

   ```
   #define dht_dpin A0 // Use A0 pin as Data pin for DHT11.
   ```

6. The sample code uses Arduino analog pin A0 to connect with the data pin of the DHT11 sensor.

   ```
   #define dht_dpin 8 // Use digital pin 8 as
   Data pin for DHT11.
   ```

7. Find the following line:

   ```
   float frequency = 868.0;
   ```

187

8. Change it to match with your frequency. For example, if you're using a LoRa radio transceiver with a frequency of 433 MHz, the code can be modified as follows:

```
float frequency = 433.0;
```

9. Save the file by clicking File ➤ Save.

10. Connect the Arduino with your computer using a USB cable.

11. In the Arduino IDE, make sure to choose the correct board type and the COM port. The board type should be Arduino/Genuine Uno. Also, the programmer should be AVRISP mkll (Figure 6-15).

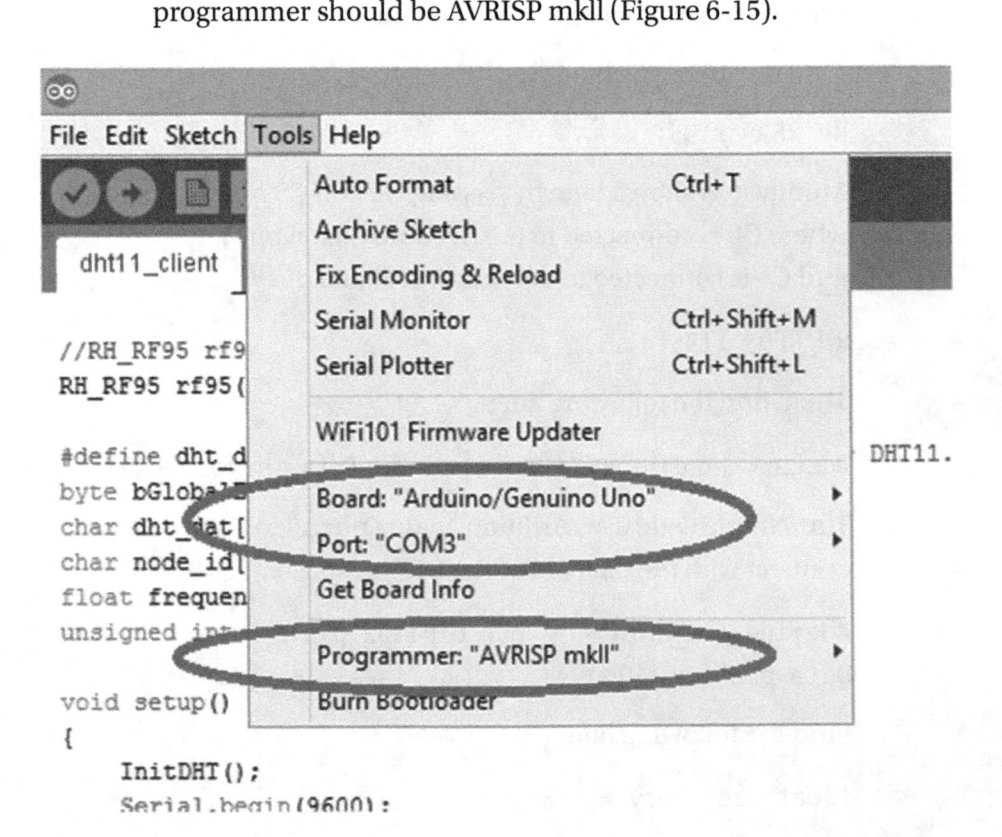

Figure 6-15. *Choosing the board type, port, and programmer for the sensor node*

12.   Verify and upload the code into the Arduino board.

After uploading the sketch, select Tools ➤ Serial Monitor (Figure 6-16). You can see the node is periodically sending data packets to the LG01 gateway. Note that your sensor node ID is 111 and can be configured with the Arduino sketch.

```
char node_id[3] = {1,1,1}; //LoRa End Node ID
```

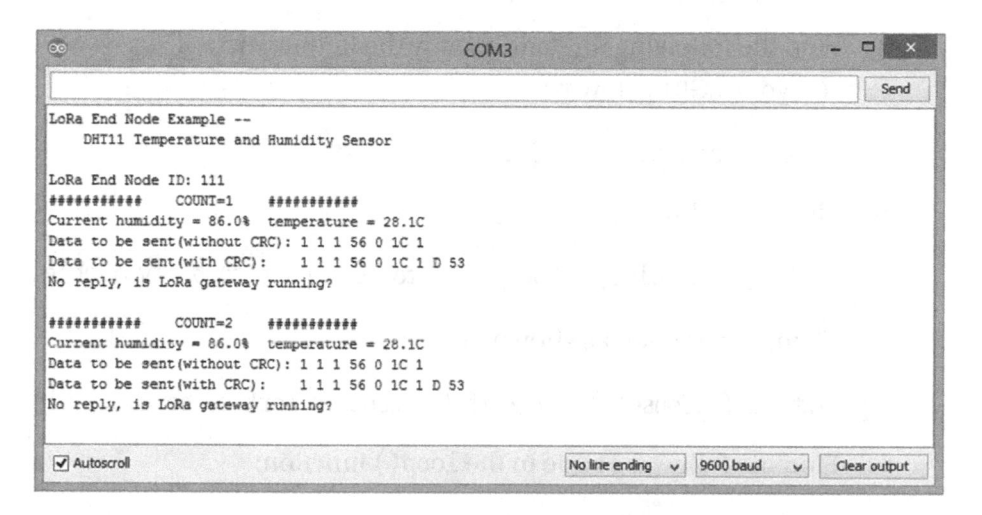

Figure 6-16. *Serial monitor output for the LoRa sensor node*

Uploading Arduino Sketch to the LG01

Now you should upload the sample Arduino sketch to the LG01 gateway. This allows the LG01 gateway to receive, process, and send data to the ThingSpeak IoT through the HTTP GET protocol.

1.   Download the sample Arduino sketch, LG01_
    ThingSpeak_RESTful_Single_Data.ino, from
    https://github.com/dragino/Arduino-
    Profile-Examples/tree/master/libraries/

189

Dragino/examples/IoTServer/ThingSpeak/LG01_
ThingSpeak_RESTful_Single_Data/. The same source
code can be found at Chapter 6/Original Source/
LG01_ThingSpeak_RESTful_Single_Data.ino.

2. Open the sketch with a new instance of the Arduino IDE.

3. Find and modify the following lines with your Write
    API key:

    ```
    String myWriteAPIString = "B9ZOR25QNVEBKIFY";
    ```

4. Find the following line and modify the frequency to
    suit your LG01 gateway:

    ```
    float frequency = 868.0;
    ```

5. Find the following line:

    ```
    while (! Console); // Wait for console port to be available
    ```

    Then, comment it as shown here:

    ```
    //while (! Console); // Wait for console port to be available
    ```

6. Find the following code in the loop() function:

    ```
    //dataString ="field2=";
    //dataString += h;
    ```
    Uncomment the two lines and add another two lines to
    append the humidity data to the HTTP GET request.

    ```
    dataString ="field2=";
    dataString += hh;
    dataString +=".";
    dataString += hl;
    ```

7. Save the file by clicking File ➤ Save.

8. Click Tools ➤ Board and choose Dragino Yun + Uno or LG01/OLG01 (Figure 6-17).

9. Click Tools ➤ Port and choose the correct network port for the LG01 (e.g., dragino-1ae554 at 10.130.1.1 (Arduino Yun)).

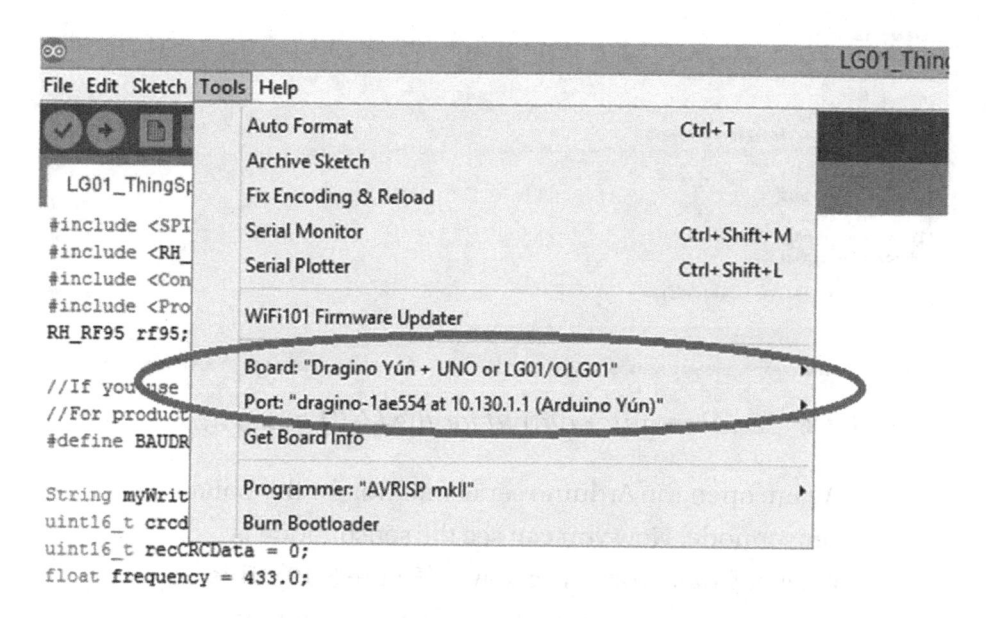

Figure 6-17. *Sketch upload settings for the LG01 gateway*

10. Verify the sketch by clicking the Verify button.

11. Click the Upload button to upload the sketch into the LG01.

12. If prompted, type **dragino** for the board password. Then click the Upload button.

13. After uploading the sketch, press the Reset (toggle) button. You can use a paper clip to access the reset button resides inside the enclosure.

14.   In the Arduino IDE, select Tools ➤ Serial Monitor. You can see the details for each data packet received by the gateway and the status of the `curl` (Linux) command (Figure 6-18).

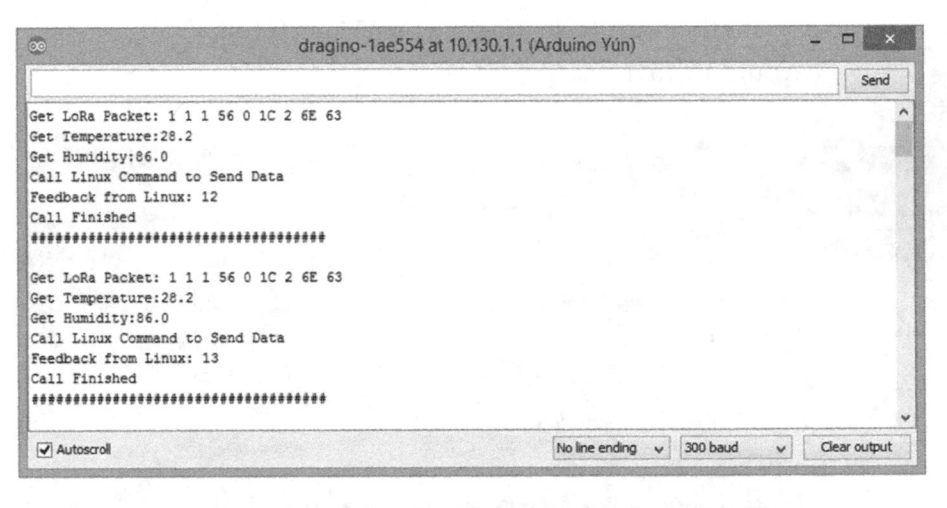

Figure 6-18. *Serial monitor output for the LG01 gateway*

15.   Again, open the Arduino serial monitor for the LoRa sensor node. Now you can see the sensor node is receiving data from the gateway (Figure 6-19). This means your LoRa network is working properly and performing two-way data transmission.

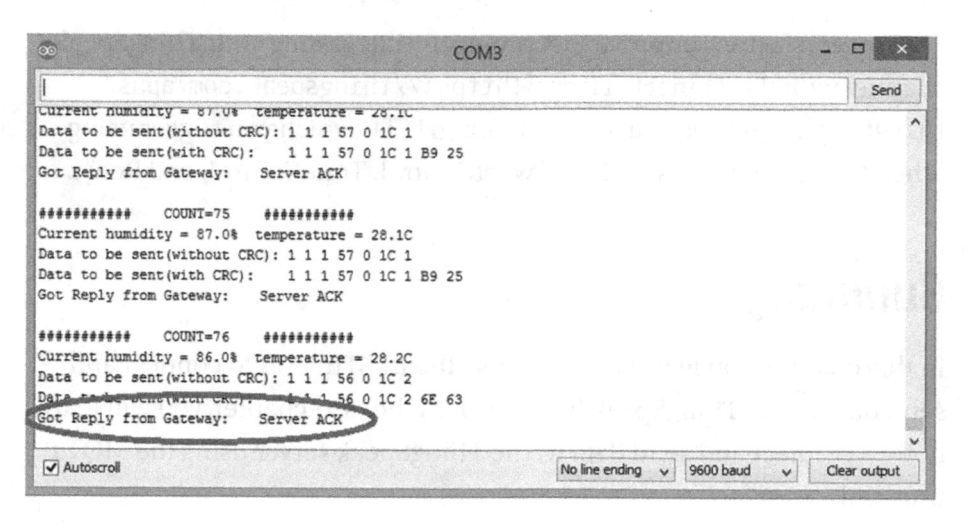

Figure 6-19. *Serial monitor output for the sensor node*

16. Now, go to your ThingSpeak account and open the
My RESTful Channel page. Figure 6-20 shows the
two charts updated by the LoRa gateway.

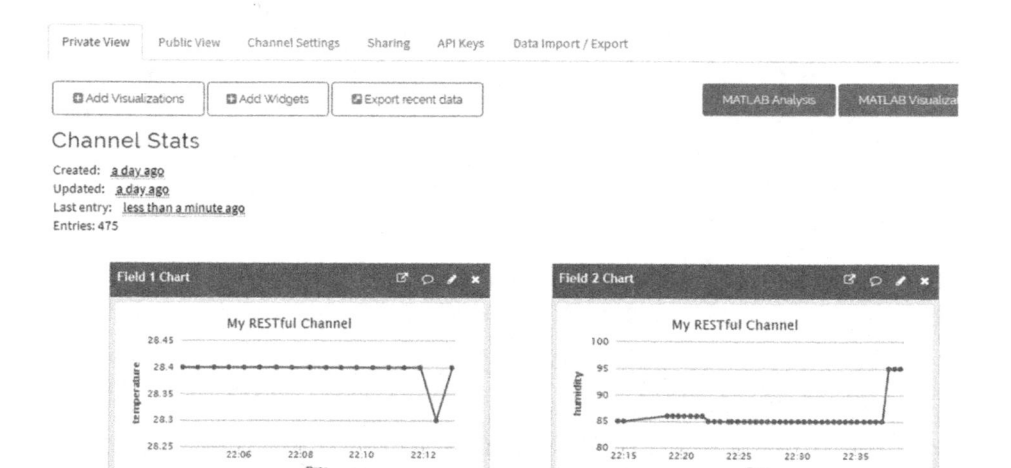

Figure 6-20. *Updating charts through the LoRa gateway*

You can further improve this project by integrating your ThingSpeak channel with the ThingHTTP app (`https://thingspeak.com/apps/thinghttp`). You specify actions in ThingHTTP, which you trigger using other ThingSpeak apps such as TweetControl, TimeControl, and React.

Summary

In this chapter, you learned how to use the RESTful API to connect and send data to the ThingSpeak IoT server. In the next chapter, you will learn how to connect and send data to the ThingSpeak server using the MQTT protocol.

CHAPTER 7

Connecting with IoT Servers Using MQTT

In this chapter, you will learn how to send data to an IoT server using the MQTT protocol with a LoRa wireless network. The ThingSpeak IoT platform enables clients to update and receive updates from channel feeds through the ThingSpeak MQTT broker. MQTT is a publish/subscribe communication protocol that uses TCP/IP sockets or WebSockets. MQTT over WebSockets can be secured with SSL. A client device connects to the MQTT broker and can publish to a channel or subscribe to updates from that channel.

The network you'll build consists of a LoRa end node (sensor node), a LoRa gateway, and the ThingSpeak IoT server. The LoRa end node will periodically send temperature and humidity data to the LoRa gateway. Once received, the LoRa gateway forwards the data to the ThingSpeak IoT server using the MQTT protocol.

Technical Requirements

In this chapter, you will need the following hardware and software prerequisites to build the LoRa wireless sensor network:

- Arduino Uno or Adafruit Metro (`https://www.sparkfun.com/products/11224` or `https://www.adafruit.com/product/2488`)

© Pradeeka Seneviratne 2019
P. Seneviratne, *Beginning LoRa Radio Networks with Arduino,*
https://doi.org/10.1007/978-1-4842-4357-2_7

- RFM9x radio transceiver breakout
  (https://www.adafruit.com/product/3072 or
  https://www.adafruit.com/product/3073)

- DHT11 temperature and humidity sensor
  (https://www.adafruit.com/product/386)

- Dragino LG01 LoRa gateway
  (https://www.tindie.com/products/edwin/
  lg01-lora-openwrt-iot-gateway/)

- Breadboard, self-adhesive (white)
  (https://www.sparkfun.com/products/12002)

- Arduino and breadboard holder
  (https://www.sparkfun.com/products/11235)

- Hook-up wire, assortment (solid core, 22 AWG)
  (https://www.sparkfun.com/products/11367)

- MQTT.fx
  (https://mqttfx.jensd.de/index.php/download)

- ThingSpeak account
  (https://thingspeak.com/)

Using ThingSpeak as the IoT Server

The ThingSpeak IoT service now supports MQTT subscriptions to receive instant updates when a ThingSpeak channel gets updated. MQTT is a powerful standard for IoT systems. ThingSpeak enables clients to update and receive updates from channel feeds via the ThingSpeak MQTT broker. MQTT is a publish/subscribe communication protocol that uses TCP/IP sockets or WebSockets. MQTT over WebSockets can be secured with SSL. A client device connects to the MQTT broker and can publish to a channel or subscribe to updates from that channel.

Follow these steps to create a new user account on the ThingSpeak IoT server:

1. Go to ThingSpeak (`https://thingspeak.com/`) and sign up for a free new account. Usually, the Sign Up link is at the top-right corner of the page.

2. Fill out the form with all the required information and click the Continue button to create a MathWorks account.

3. You will receive an e-mail to verify your address. In the e-mail body, click the verify button to complete the registration.

Creating a New Channel

Follow these steps:

1. In the top navigation menu, select Channels ➤ My Channels (Figure 7-1).

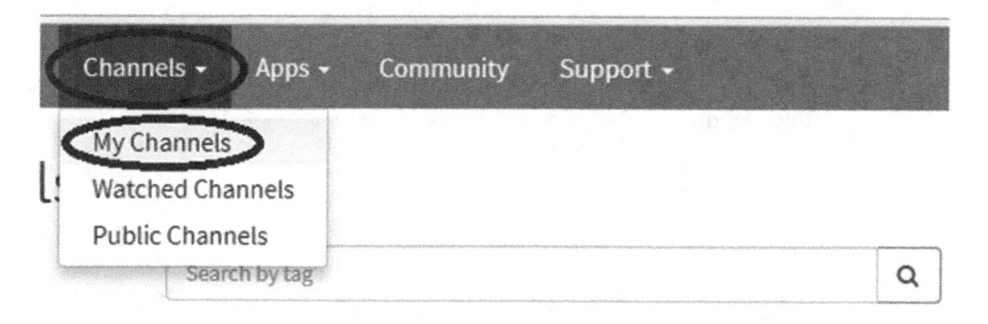

Figure 7-1. *Menu command for accessing all the channels associated with your account*

2. Under My Channels, click the New Channel button (Figure 7-2).

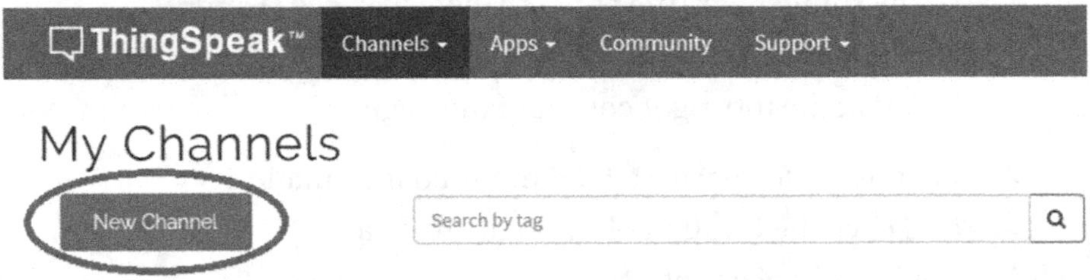

Figure 7-2. *Creating a new channel*

3. Fill out these form fields to create a new channel (Figure 7-3):

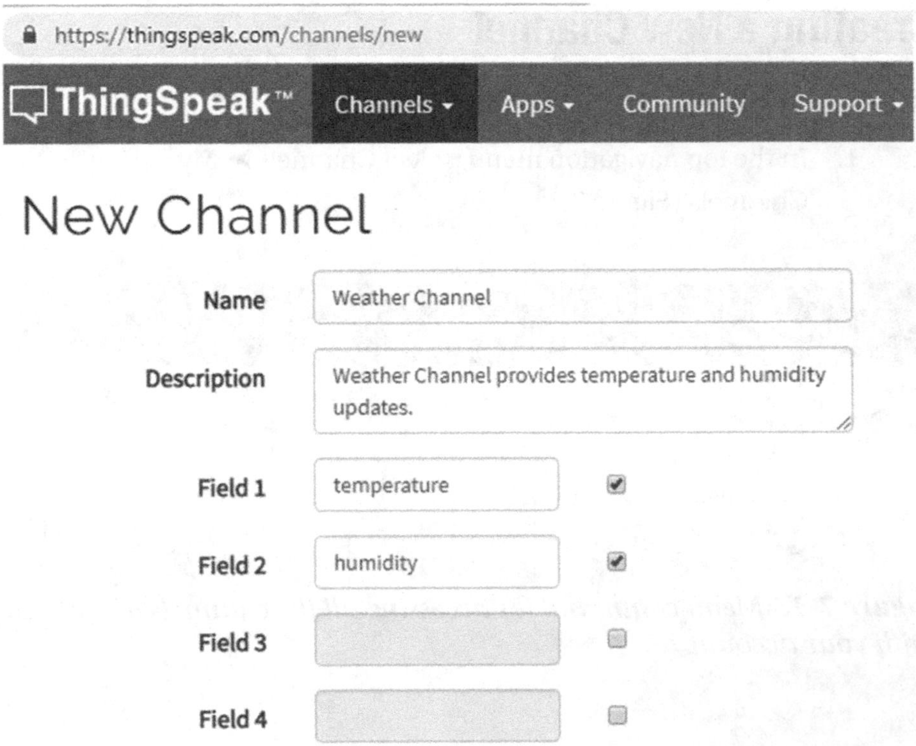

Figure 7-3. *Channel settings for Weather Channel*

- *Channel Name*: Type in a unique name for the
  ThingSpeak channel (e.g., **Weather Channel**).

- *Description*: Type in a description for the
  ThingSpeak channel (e.g., **Weather Channel
  provides temperature and humidity updates.**).

- *Field #*: Each ThingSpeak channel can have up to
  eight fields. Click the first check box to enable Field
  1 and type in **temperature**. Click the second check
  box to enable Field 2 and type in **humidity**.

4. Click the Save Channel button.

5. After creating the channel, you will get a page titled
   Weather Channel with channel settings, sharing
   options, API keys, import and export options, and
   charts for each data field (Figure 7-4).

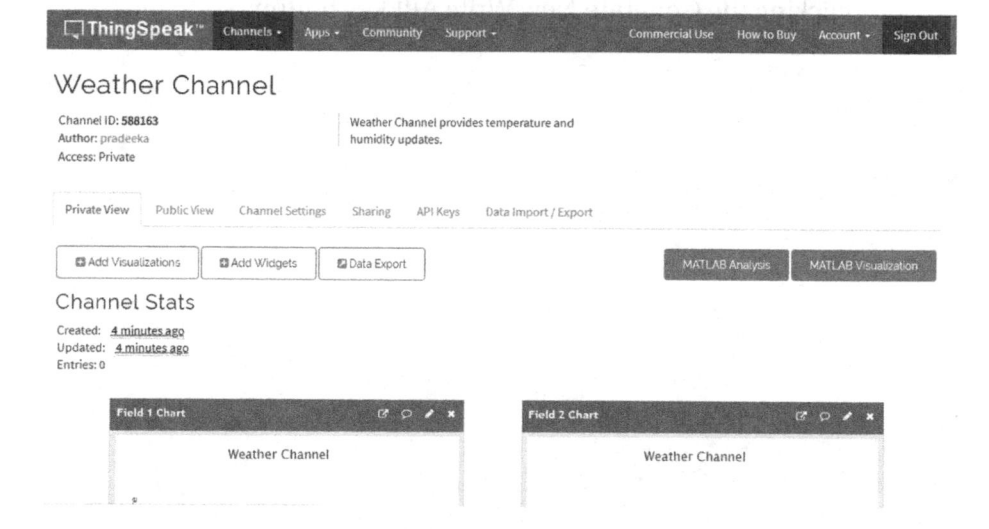

Figure 7-4. *Page for the Weather Channel*

Getting the API Keys

ThingSpeak provides two types of API keys. You need these keys to write to a channel and read data from a private channel. API keys are autogenerated when you create a new channel.

1. On the Weather Channel page, click API Keys tab. It shows the autogenerated Write API key and Read API key (Figure 7-5).

2. The Write API key allows you to write data to a channel. If you want, you can generate a new Write API key by clicking the Generate New Write API Key button.

3. The Read API key allows you to read data from a private channel. If you want, you can generate an additional Read API key from the channel by clicking the Generate New Write API Key button.

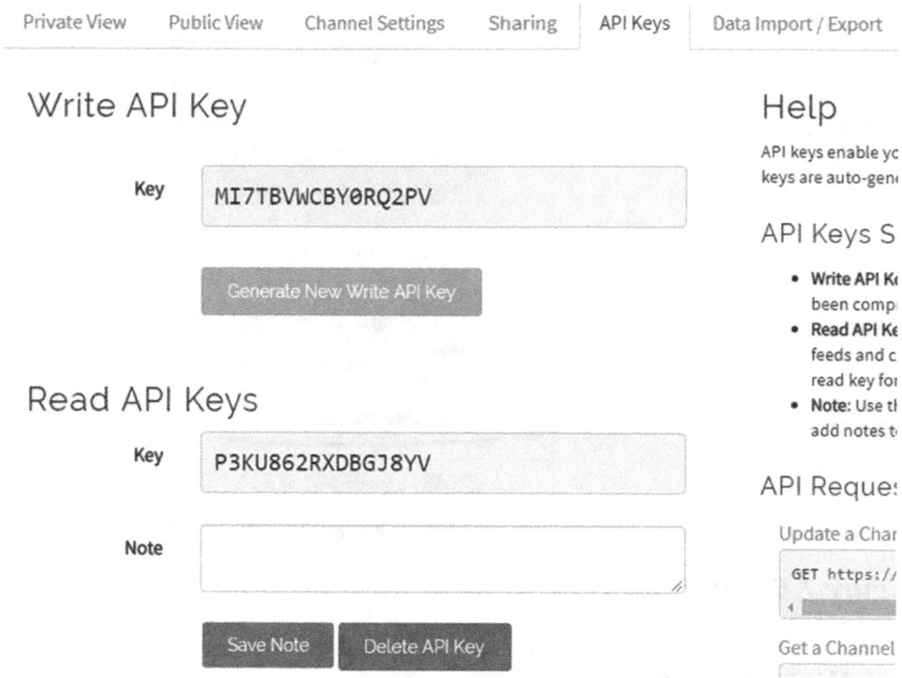

Private View	Public View	Channel Settings	Sharing	API Keys	Data Import / Export

Write API Key

Key   `MI7TBVWCBY0RQ2PV`

Generate New Write API Key

Read API Keys

Key   `P3KU862RXDBGJ8YV`

Note

Save Note   Delete API Key

Help

API keys enable yc
keys are auto-gen(

API Keys S

- **Write API Ke**
  been comp
- **Read API Ke**
  feeds and c
  read key for
- **Note:** Use tl
  add notes t(

API Reque:

Update a Char

`GET https://`

Get a Channel

Figure 7-5. *Write and Read API keys*

Finding Your MQTT API Key

The MQTT API key is required to subscribe to channel topics using the
MQTT API. The MQTT API Key can be found on your profile page.

1. Select Account ➤ My Profile.

2. Scroll down the page. Under ThingSpeak Settings, in
   the MQTT API Key section, click the Generate New
   MQTT API Key button to generate a new MQTT API
   key (Figure 7-6).

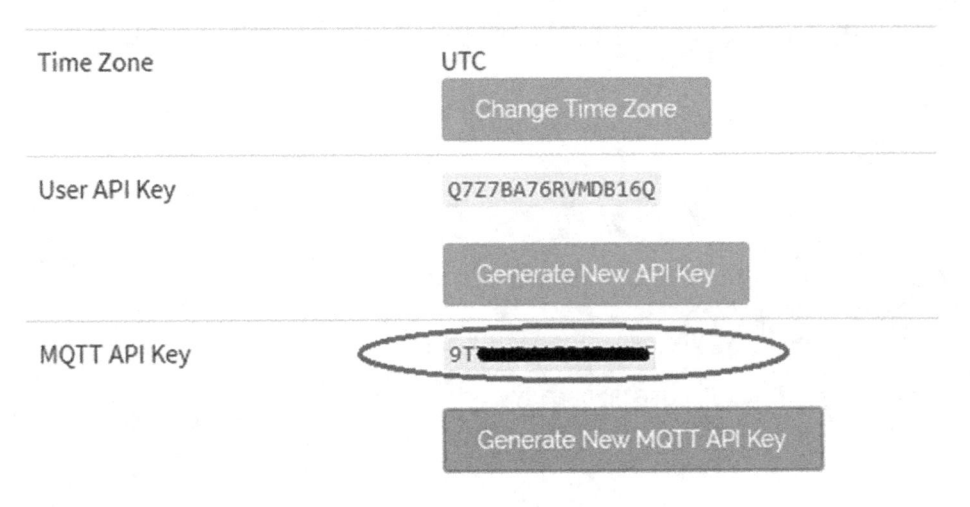

Figure 7-6. *MQTT API key*

Testing Your Channel

You can use your LG01 gateway console to send direct MQTT messages to the ThingSpeak server using the built-in command `mosquitto_pub`.

1. Using PuTTY, log in to your LG01 gateway through SSH. The default username is *root,* and the password is *dragino.*

2. You can use the following command to update the Weather Channel with temperature and humidity data:

```
mosquitto_pub -h mqtt.thingspeak.com -p 1883 -u user_id
-P mqtt_api_key -i client_id -t channels/channel_id/
publish/write_api_key -m "field1=value1&field2=value2&s
tatus=MQTTPUBLISH"
```

3. By replacing user_id, mqtt_api_key, client_id,
    channel_id, write_api_key, value1, and value2 with
    the parameters associated with the ThingSpeak account,
    the command will look something like this (Figure 7-7):

    ```
    mosquitto_pub -h mqtt.thingspeak.com -p 1883 -u
    pradeeka -P 9TTLYB4AERCZ4MWF -i weather_client -t
    channels/588163/publish/4ELVID1N7KLD8LG2 -m "field1=23.
    5&field2=57.5&status=MQTTPUBLISH"
    ```

4. client_id is a unique ID and can be anything.

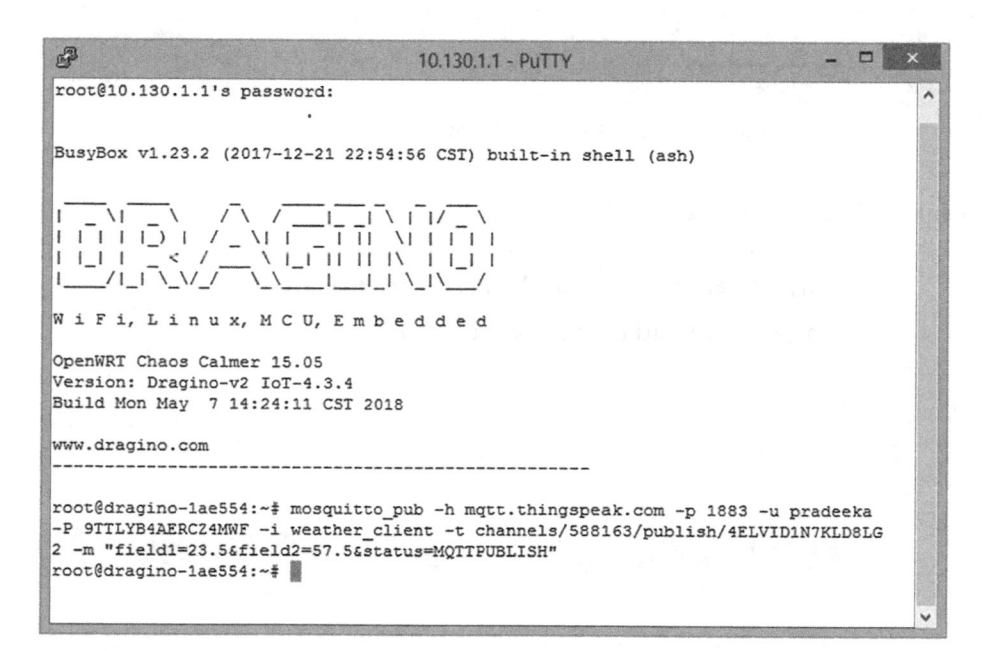

Figure 7-7. *Sending data to ThingSpeak using the mosquitto_pub command*

1. In the ThingSpeak, click Channels ➤ My Channels.

2. On the My Channels page, under Name, click Weather Channel (Figure 7-8).

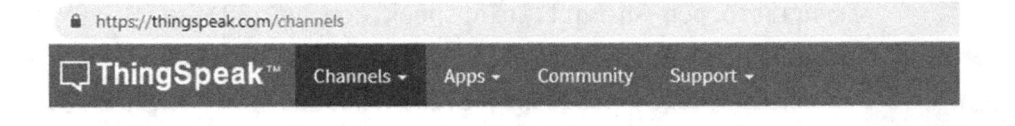

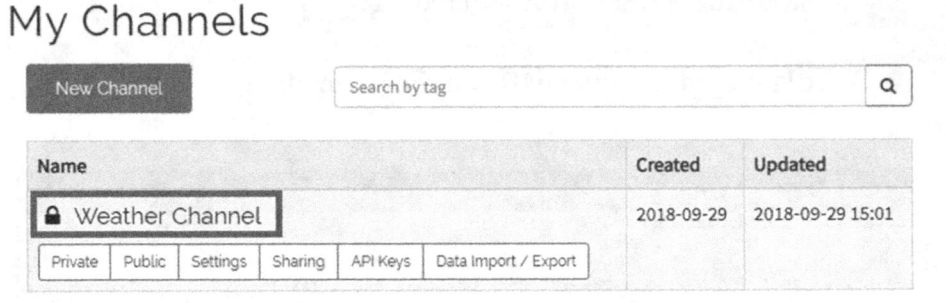

Figure 7-8. *List of channels*

3. Scroll down the page, and you can see two charts for temperature and humidity (Figure 7-9).

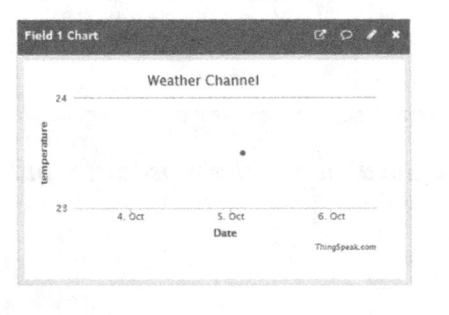

Figure 7-9. *Charts for temperature and humidity*

Building the Sensor Node

The LoRa sensor node (end device) periodically collects temperature and humidity data from the environment. You will need the following things to build the sensor node:

- Arduino Uno or Adafruit Metro

- RFM9x LoRa radio transceiver breakout

- DHT11 temperature and humidity sensor

- 10 kiloohm resistor (usually Adafruit provides a free resistor with the DHT11 sensor)

- Solid-core hook-up wires

- Half-size breadboard

- Breadboard holder

Figure 7-10 shows the wiring diagram for the sensor node. Using hook-up wires, make connections between all the electronic components.

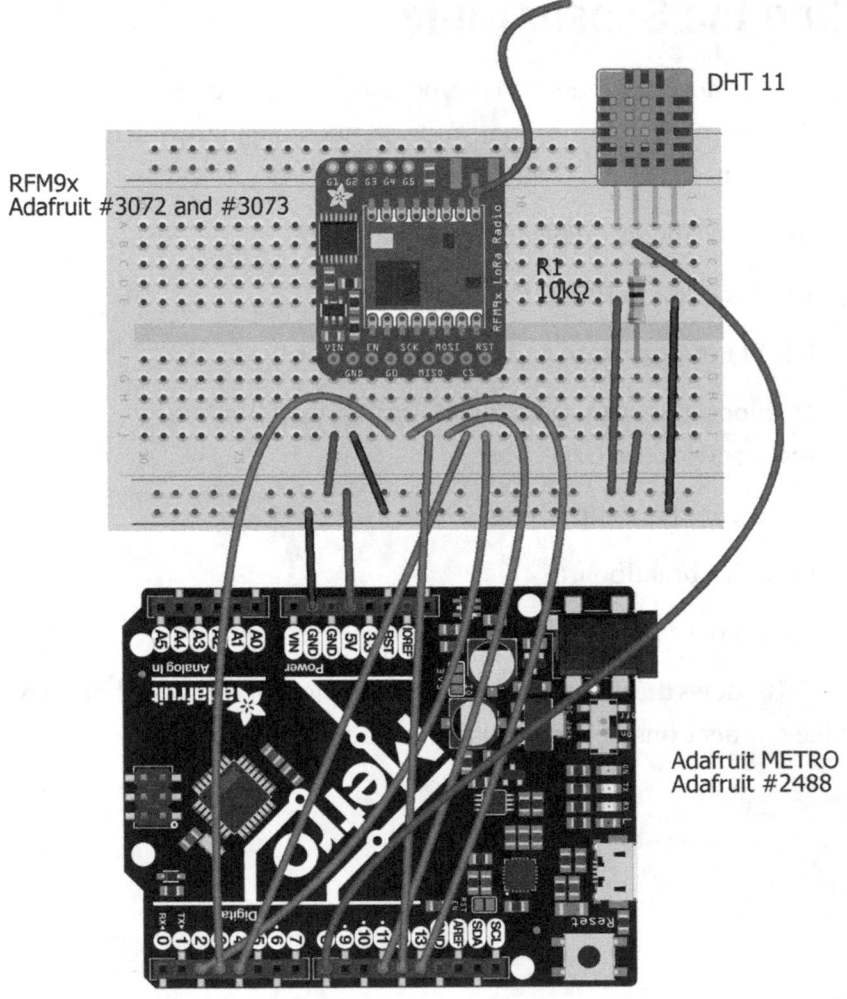

Figure 7-10. *Wiring diagram for the LoRa end node*

Table 7-1 shows the connections between the Arduino/Metro, radio transceiver, and DHT11 sensor.

Table 7-1. *Wiring Connections for Sensor Node*

Arduino/Metro	Radio Transceiver	DHT11
VIN	VIN	VIN
GND	GND	GND
2	RST	
3	G0	
4	CS	
8		DATA
11	MOSI	
12	MISO	
13	SCK	

Make sure to keep the antenna wire perpendicular to the LoRa radio transceiver module. Figure 7-11 shows the completed sensor node.

Figure 7-11. *Completed LoRa sensor node*

Uploading the Sketch to the Sensor Node

The sensor node will periodically send temperature and humidity data as a bundle to the LG01 LoRa gateway using a simple Arduino sketch.

1. Download the sample Arduino sketch, MQTT_ DHT11_Client_updata_to_ThingSpeak_.ino, from https://github.com/dragino/Arduino-Profile-Examples/blob/master/libraries/Dragino/ examples/IoTServer/ThingSpeak/MQTT_Client/ MQTT_DHT11_Client_updata_to_ThingSpeak_/.

The same sketch can be downloaded from Chapter 7/Original Source/MQTT_DHT11_Client_updata_to_ThingSpeak_.ino.

2. Open MQTT_DHT11_Client_updata_to_ ThingSpeak_.ino with your Arduino integrated development environment.

3. Find this line:

   ```
   RH_RF95 rf95;
   ```

4. Modify it as shown here by passing the G0 and CS pins where G0 is connected to the Arduino digital pin 4 and CS is connected to the Arduino digital pin 3.

   ```
   RH_RF95 rf95(4, 3);
   ```

5. Find the following line:

   ```
   #define DHT11_PIN A0
   ```

6. The sample code uses Arduino analog pin A0 to connect with the data pin of the DHT11 sensor. Replace it with digital pin 8 as per your hardware setup. The modified line should be as follows:

```
#define DHT11_PIN 8 // Use digital pin 8 as
Data pin for DHT11.
```

7. Find the following line:

```
float frequency = 868.0; //frequency settings
```

8. Change it to match with your frequency. For example, if you're using a LoRa radio transceiver with frequency 433 MHz, the code can be modified as follows:

```
float frequency = 433.0; //frequency settings
```

9. In the dhtWrite() function, find the following code block:

```
strcat(data,"field1=");
    strcat(data,hum_1);
    strcat(data,"&field2=");
    strcat(data,tem_1);
    strcpy((char *)datasend,data);
```

10. Modify it by swapping the tem_1 and hum_1 variables as shown here:

```
strcat(data,"field1=");
    strcat(data,tem_1);
    strcat(data,"&field2=");
    strcat(data,hum_1);
    strcpy((char *)datasend,data);
```

11. Find the following line to update the node_id value:

     ```
     char *node_id = "<12345>";   //From LG01 via web Local
     Channel settings on MQTT.Please refer <> dataformat in here.
     ```

12. The node_id value should be match with the
     local channel in /var/iot/channels/ on the
     LG01 gateway's MQTT Server Settings page (see
     "Configuring the LG01 Gateway").

13. If you haven't yet, download and install the
     modified version of the DHT library from https://
     github.com/goodcheney/Lora/blob/patch-1/
     Lora%20Shield/Examples/DHTlib.zip.

14. Connect the Arduino with your computer using a
     USB cable. (For the Adafruit Metro, use USB-A to
     Micro-B. For the Arduino Uno, use USB A-to-B.)

15. Make sure to choose the correct board type and
     the COM port. The board type should be Arduino/
     Genuino Uno. Also, the programmer should be
     AVRISP mkll (Figure 7-12).

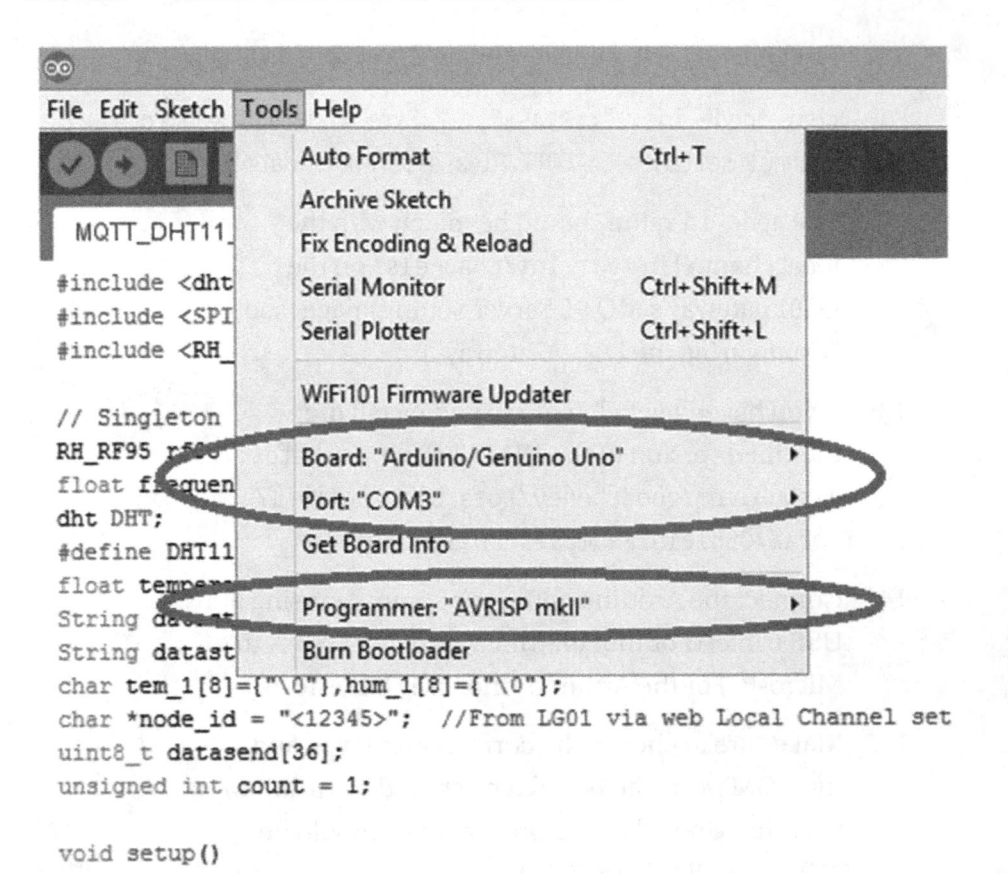

Figure 7-12. *Upload settings for Arduino board*

16. Verify and upload the code to the Arduino board.

17. After uploading the sketch, in the Arduino IDE, select Tools ➤ Serial Monitor. You should see something like that shown in Figure 7-13.

```
Start MQTT Example
###########    COUNT=1    ###########
The temperature and humidity:
[28.00°C,85.00%]
Sending data to LG01
No reply, is LoRa server running?
###########    COUNT=2    ###########
The temperature and humidity:
[28.00°C,85.00%]
Sending data to LG01
No reply, is LoRa server running?
###########    COUNT=3    ###########
The temperature and humidity:
[28.00°C,85.00%]
Sending data to LG01
No reply, is LoRa server running?
###########    COUNT=4    ###########
The temperature and humidity:
[28.00°C,85.00%]
Sending data to LG01
No reply, is LoRa server running?
###########    COUNT=5    ###########
The temperature and humidity:
[28.00°C,85.00%]
Sending data to LG01
No reply, is LoRa server running?
```
☐ Autoscroll

Figure 7-13. *Serial monitor output for the sensor node*

18.   Close the serial monitor.

Configuring the LG01 Gateway

The LG01 gateway should be configured to receive and forward data to the ThingSpeak IoT server. Follow these steps to configure it for MQTT and radio settings:

1. Using your web browser, log in to the configuration interface of the LG01 gateway. The default username is *root*, and the default password is *dragino*.

2. In the configuration interface, select Sensor ➤ IoT Server. On the Select IoT Server page, from the IoT Server drop-down list, choose MQTT Server (Figure 7-14).

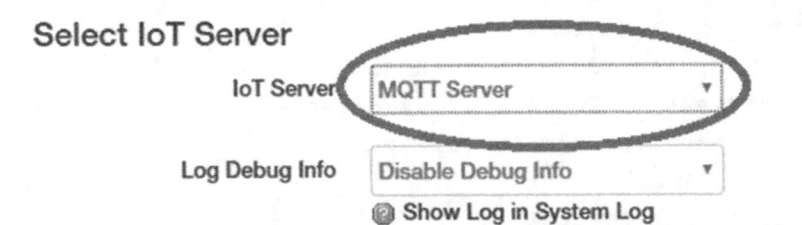

| re | 10.130.1.1/cgi-bin/luci//admin/sensor/iotserver |

dragino-1ae554   Status ▾   Sensor ▾   System ▾   Network ▾   Logout

Select IoT Server

Select the IoT Server type to connect

Select IoT Server

IoT Server | MQTT Server   ▾ |

Log Debug Info | Disable Debug Info   ▾ |
                  🔘 Show Log in System Log

Figure 7-14. *Choosing the MQTT server as the IoT server*

3. Select Sensor ➤ MQTT. On the MQTT Server Settings page, fill out the form to configure the LG01 to communicate with the MQTT server (ThingSpeak) (Figure 7-15).

- *Select Server*: Choose ThingSpeak MQTT from the drop-down list.

- *User Name [-u]*: Enter your ThingSpeak account's username.

- *Password [-p]*: Enter your MQTT API key.

- *Client ID [-i]*: Enter your any unique ID (e.g., **weather_client**).

4.   Click the Save & Apply button.

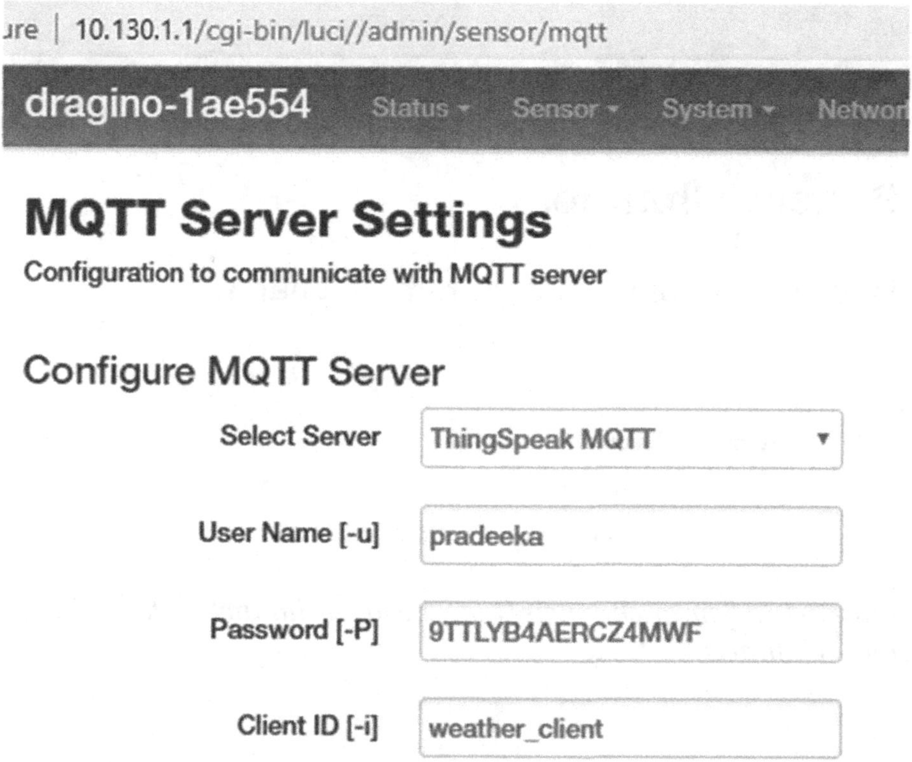

Figure 7-15. *MQTT server settings*

5. Under MQTT Channel, click the Add button. On the
    Sensor Channels page, fill out the form (Figure 7-16).

    - *Local Channel ID*: Enter a unique ID with a
      combination of digits.

    - *Remote Channel ID*: Enter the channel ID in your
      ThingSpeak account.

    - *Write API Key*: Enter the Write API key in your
      ThingSpeak account.

Figure 7-16. *Sensor channels (how the local channel matches the
remote channel)*

6. Click the Save & Apply button. Now your MQTT
    Server Settings page should look like Figure 7-17.

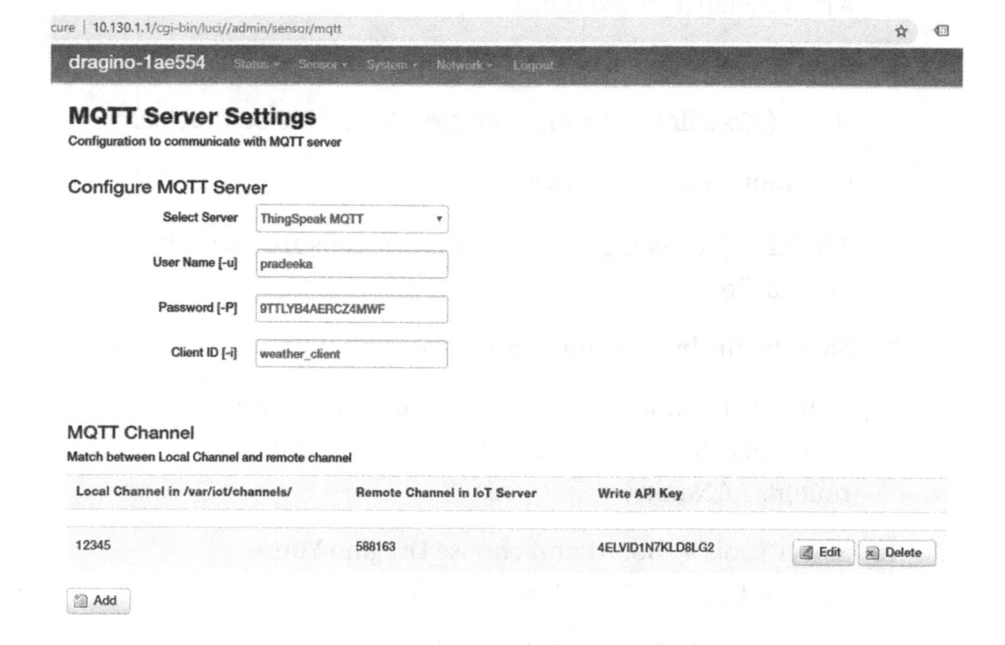

Figure 7-17. *Completed MQTT Server Settings page*

Uploading the Sketch to the LG01 Gateway

The LG01 gateway uses a simple Arduino sketch to process incoming data
packets and extract temperature and humidity values from the payload.

1. Download the sample Arduino sketch, `MQTT_Simple_`
    `Server.ino`, from `https://github.com/dragino/`
    `Arduino-Profile-Examples/tree/master/libraries/`
    `Dragino/examples/LoRa/MQTT_Simple_Server`.

    The same sketch can be downloaded from Chapter 7/
    Original Source/MQTT_Simple_Server.ino.

2. Open `MQTT_Simple_Server.ino` with your Arduino integrated development environment. (Open it with a new instance of the IDE.)

3. Find the following line:

    `while (!Console) ; // Wait for console port to be available`

4. Comment it as shown here:

    `//while (!Console) ; // Wait for console port to be available`

5. Save the file by clicking File ➤ Save.

6. Connect the LG01 gateway with your router using an Ethernet cable (connect LG01's WAN port with the router's LAN port).

7. Select Tools ➤ Board and choose Dragino Yun + UNO or LG01/OLG01 (Figure 7-18).

8. Select Tools ➤ Port and choose the correct network port for the LG01 (e.g., dragino-1ae554 at 10.130.1.1 (Arduino Yun)).

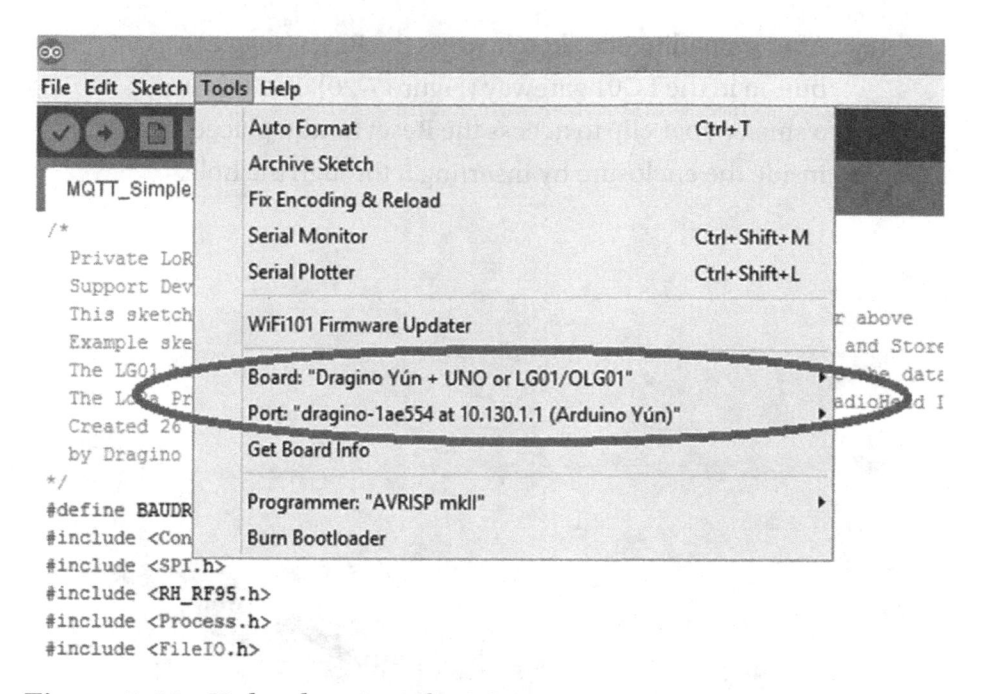

Figure 7-18. *Upload options for LG01 gateway*

9. Verify the sketch for errors and then click the
    Upload button to upload the sketch into the LG01. If
    prompted, type the board password as **dragino** and
    click the Upload button (Figure 7-19).

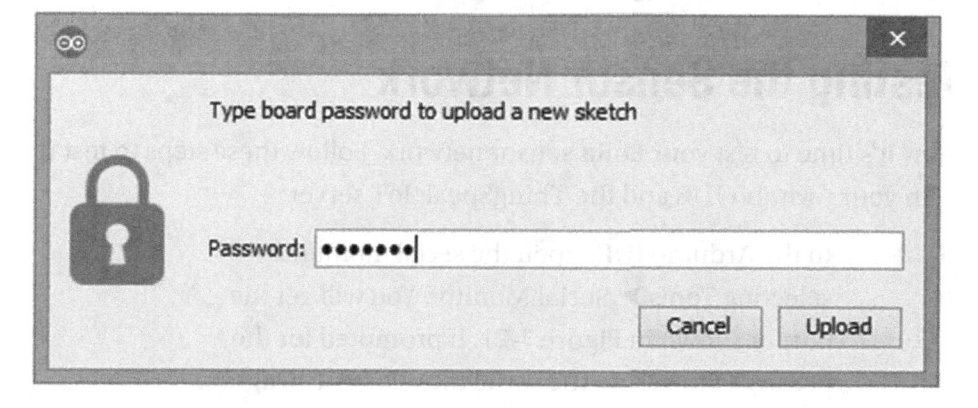

Figure 7-19. *Providing the board password*

10. After uploading the sketch, press the Reset (toggle) button in the LG01 gateway (Figure 7-20). You can use a small paper clip to access the Reset button placed inside the enclosure by inserting it through the hole.

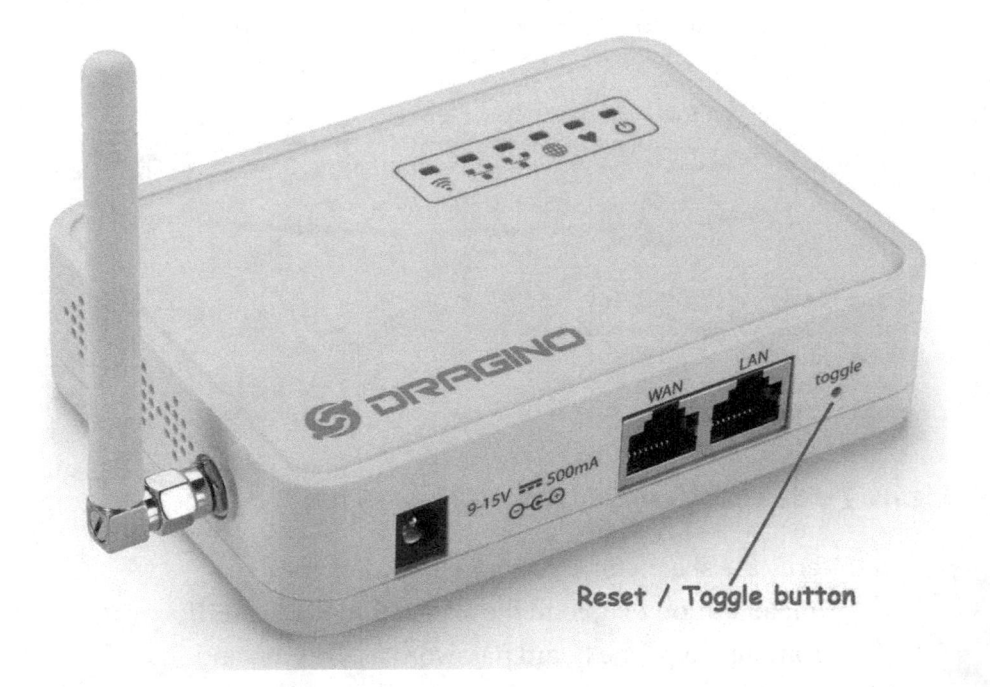

Figure 7-20. *Reset/Toggle button*

Testing the Sensor Network

Now it's time to test your LoRa sensor network. Follow these steps to test it with your Arduino IDE and the ThingSpeak IoT server:

1. In the Arduino IDE, open the serial monitor by selecting Tools ➤ Serial Monitor. You will get the output shown in Figure 7-21. If prompted for the password to access the serial monitor, use **dragino**.

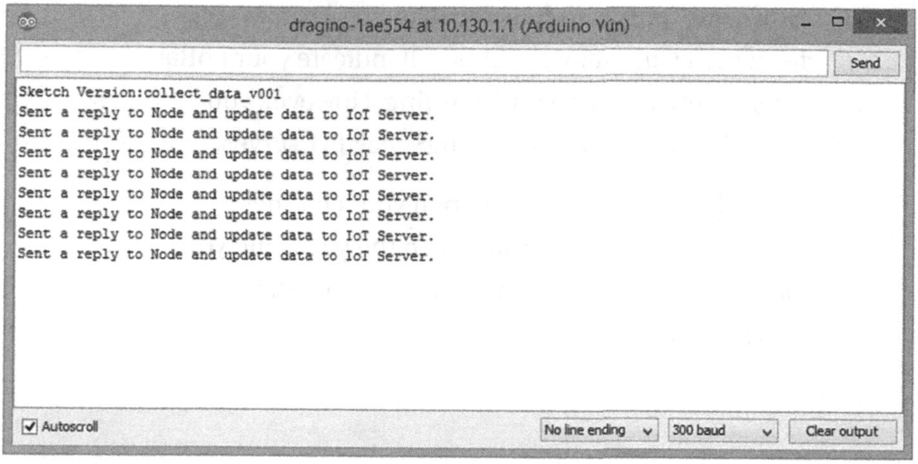

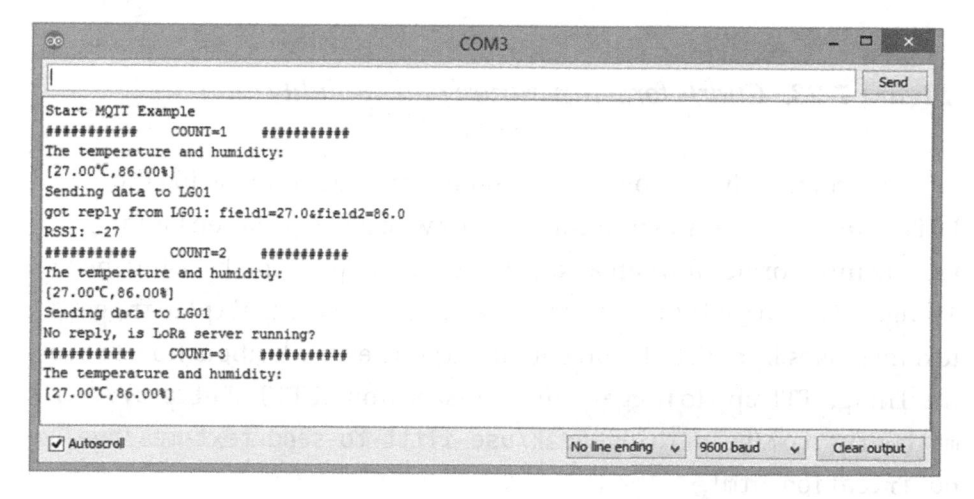

Figure 7-21. *Output on serial monitor for LG01 gateway*

2. In the MQTT_DHT11_Client_updata_to_
   ThingSpeak_.ino sketch, open the serial monitor.
   This should be a new instance of the Arduino
   IDE. You will get the output shown in Figure 7-22.

Figure 7-22. *Serial monitor output for the sensor node*

3. Now your sensor node is receiving replay messages from the LG01 gateway. This will indicate your LoRa sensor network is up and running. However, you should confirm with the ThingSpeak IoT server.

4. Go to the ThingSpeak and open your channel (Weather Channel). Scroll down the page, and you can see your charts are populated with temperature and humidity data (Figure 7-23).

Channel Stats

Created: 8 days ago
Updated: a day ago
Last entry: about a minute ago
Entries: 326

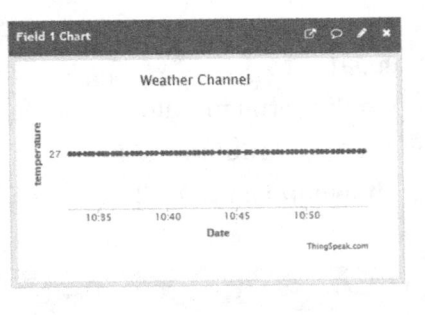
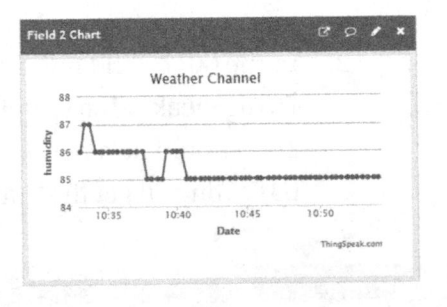

Figure 7-23. *Charts for temperature and humidity data*

You can modify the LoRa sensor node hardware by replacing the DHT11 temperature and humidity sensor with any type of sensor for remote monitoring. You can also enhance this application by using the ThingHTTP app (`https://thingspeak.com/apps/thinghttp`) to trigger text messages from IFTTT. You can find a good example about how to use the ThingHTTP app to trigger a text message from IFTTT at `https://www.mathworks.com/help/thingspeak/use-ifttt-to-send-text-message-notification.html`.

Summary

In this chapter, you learned how to connect and send data to the ThingSpeak IoT server using the MQTT protocol. The next chapter will explain how to build a GPS tracker to send data through LoRa wireless to a LoRa gateway and display real-time tracking with the Traccar server.

CHAPTER 8

GPS Tracking

The Global Position System (GPS) is a satellite-based navigation system that provides continuous positioning and timing information anywhere in the world under any weather condition.

In this chapter, you will learn how to build a GPS tracker to use real-time location tracking. The LoRa end node will parse GPS data and send it to the LoRa gateway using LoRa wireless. The LoRa gateway will encode the data and send it to GPS tracking software.

GPS satellite signals can be processed with a GPS tracker. Usually, a GPS tracker consists of a GPS module, a processing unit, and a cellular module. The GPS module receives GPS signals and outputs raw GPS NMEA sentences. These NMEA sentences can be further processed using a processing unit to take out information such as the time, date, latitude, longitude, altitude, estimated land speed, and fix type. Finally, these coordinates are sent to GPS tracking software to display the current location of the device. A cellular data connection is needed to send the location data to the GPS tracking software.

With LoRa wireless, you can replace some parts of the cellular network. With the LoRa-based GPS tracking system, only an Internet connection is needed for the gateway. GPS trackers can send data to the gateway using LoRa wireless without the aid of a cellular network.

© Pradeeka Seneviratne 2019
P. Seneviratne, *Beginning LoRa Radio Networks with Arduino*,
https://doi.org/10.1007/978-1-4842-4357-2_8

Prerequisites

You need the following hardware, software, and user accounts to build the LoRa-based GPS tracking network.

Hardware

Here is the hardware needed:

- Arduino Uno or Adafruit Metro

- Adafruit RFM9x LoRa radio transceiver (three frequency options are available)

    - Adafruit RFM95W LoRa Radio transceiver breakout, 868 or 915 MHz, Radio Fruit

    - Adafruit RFM96W LoRa Radio transceiver breakout, 433 MHz, Radio Fruit

- Adafruit Ultimate GPS breakout, 66 channel with10 Hz updates, version 3, `https://www.adafruit.com/product/746`

- GPS external active antenna, 3 to 5 V 28 dB 5 meter SMA (optional), `https://www.adafruit.com/product/960`

- SMA to full/U.FL/IPX/IPEX RF adapter cable (optional), `https://www.adafruit.com/product/851`

- 9 V alkaline battery (`https://www.sparkfun.com/products/10218`)

- 9 V to barrel jack adapter (`https://www.sparkfun.com/products/9518`)

- Dragino LG01 gateway (three frequency options)
  https://www.tindie.com/products/edwin/lg01-
  lora-openwrt-iot-gateway/

  - *LG01-P 868*: LoRa gateway, best tuned at 868 MHz
    frequency

  - *LG01-P 915*: LoRa gateway, best tuned at 915 MHz
    frequency

  - *LG01-P 433*: LoRa gateway, best tuned at 433 MHz
    frequency

Software

You should install the following Arduino libraries in the Arduino IDE to
compile and upload sketches to the Arduino Uno:

- RadioHead library modified by Dragino, https://
  github.com/dragino/RadioHead/archive/master.zip

- TinyGPS, https://github.com/mikalhart/TinyGPS/
  releases/tag/v13

- Arduino LMIC library, https://github.com/
  matthijskooijman/arduino-lmic

User Accounts

You'll need these user accounts:

- Create a free account at https://www.traccar.org/ to
  visualize the real-time location of the GPS tracker on a map.

- Create a free account on the Things Network (https://
  www.thethingsnetwork.org).

- Create a free account on IFTTT (https://ifttt.com/).

Configuring the Gateway

You can use the Dragino LG01 single-channel gateway (Figure 8-1) to forward any incoming data packet from the GPS tracker to the Things Network (https://www.thethingsnetwork.org/).

Figure 8-1. *Dragino LG01 LoRa single-channel gateway*

The same gateway can be built with a Raspberry Pi by installing the single-channel packet forwarder software (refer to Chapter 5 for a detailed explanation).

Follow these steps to configure the LG01 gateway to forward the data packets to the Things Network:

1. Download the hex file for the single-channel packet forwarder from www.dragino.com/downloads/index.php?dir=motherboards/lg01/sketch/. Make sure to download the latest file (Figure 8-2). At the time of this writing, the latest version is v004.

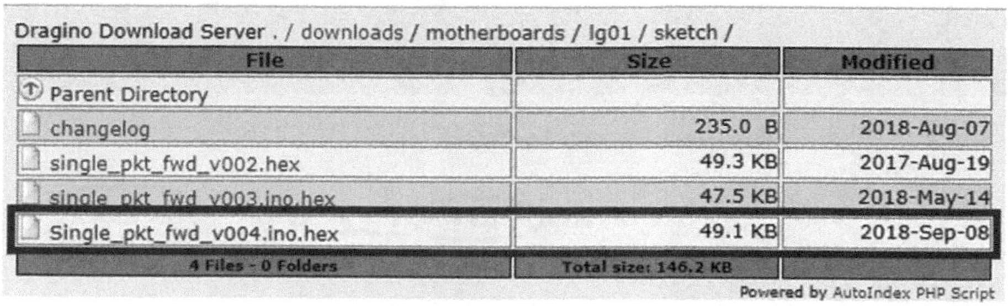

File	Size	Modified
⬆ Parent Directory		
🗋 changelog	235.0 B	2018-Aug-07
🗋 single_pkt_fwd_v002.hex	49.3 KB	2017-Aug-19
🗋 single_pkt_fwd_v003.ino.hex	47.5 KB	2018-May-14
🗋 Single_pkt_fwd_v004.ino.hex	49.1 KB	2018-Sep-08
4 Files - 0 Folders	Total size: 146.2 KB	

Powered by AutoIndex PHP Script

Figure 8-2. *Single-channel packet forwarder software for LG01*

2. Connect the LG01 gateway to the Internet (connect
   LG01's WAN port to your router's LAN port using an
   Ethernet cable). In the LG01 configuration interface
   (http://10.130.1.1), choose Sensor ➤ Flash MCU
   (Figure 8-3).

Figure 8-3. *Menu command for uploading an MCU image*

3. On the Upload Image to MCU page, click the Choose
   File button to browse and locate the downloaded
   hex file (Single_pkt_fwd_v004.ino.hex). Then
   click the Flash Image button to start uploading it to
   the LG01 gateway (Figure 8-4).

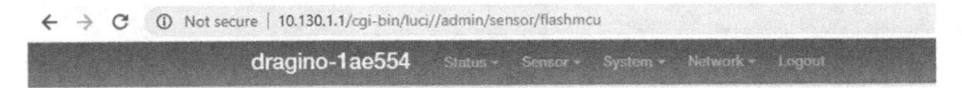

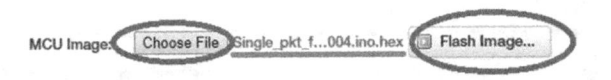

Figure 8-4. *Uploading image to MCU*

4.   Once uploaded, reboot the LG01 gateway.

5.   After rebooting the LG01 gateway, in the configuration interface, select Sensor ➤ Microcontroller to verify the flashed hex file (Figure 8-5).

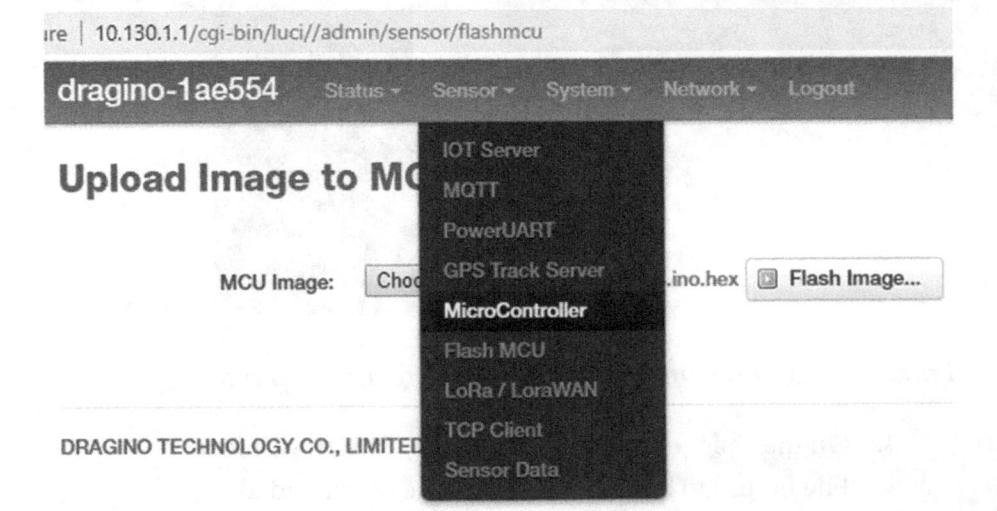

Figure 8-5. *Menu command for accessing microcontroller settings*

6. On the "Micro-controller settings" page, under MCU Upload Profile, you should see the file name of the uploaded hex file next to the MCU version (Figure 8-6).

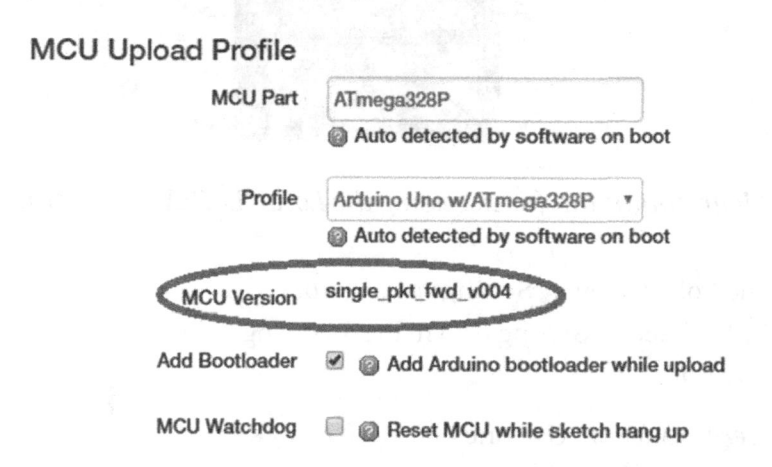

Figure 8-6. *Finding the MCU version. The MCU version is equivalent to the version of the single-channel packet forwarder software.*

7. In the configuration interface, select Sensor ➤ LoRa/LoRaWAN (Figure 8-7).

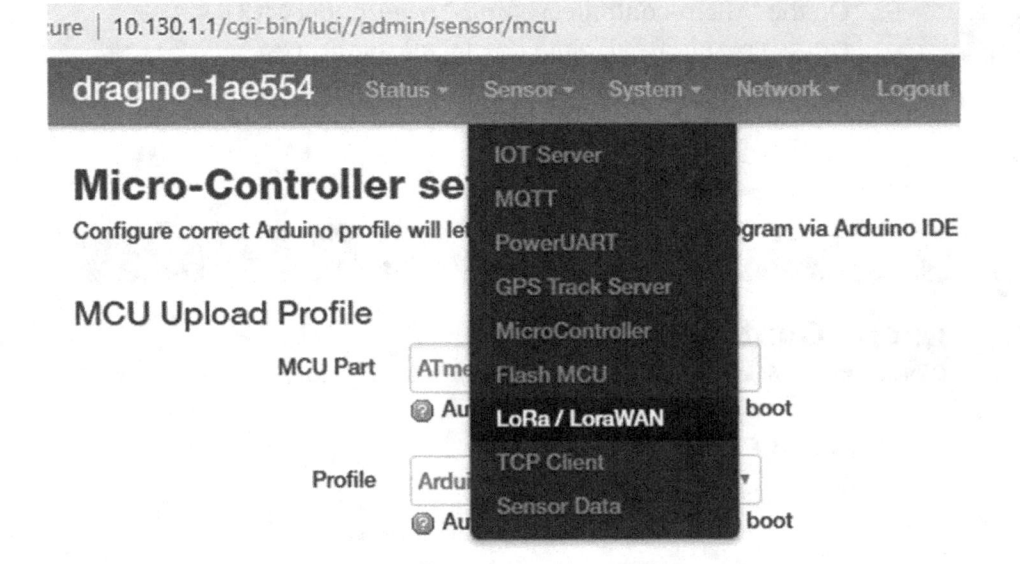

Figure 8-7. *Menu command for accessing the LoRa/LoRaWAN settings*

8. On the LoRa Gateway Settings page, under LoRaWAN Server Settings, fill in the following fields (Figure 8-8):

   • *Server Address*: Use one of the following server addresses from the Things Network:

      • `router.eu.thethings.network` (EU 433 and EU 863-870)

      • `router.us.thethings.network` (US 902-928)

      • `router.cn.thethings.network` (China 470-510 and 779-787)

      • `router.au.thethings.network` (Australia 915 to 928 MHz)

   • *Server Port*: Use the port number1700 for all the servers.

- *Gateway ID*: Use the Media Access Control (MAC) address of your LG01 gateway by appending FFFF to the end. As an example, if you have an LG01 gateway with the MAC address A840411AE554, the resulting gateway ID would be A840411AE554FFFF.

- *Mail Address*: Provide a valid e-mail address.

- *Latitude and Longitude*: Provide the geographical coordinates of your gateway. This assumes you have mounted your gateway in a fixed location.

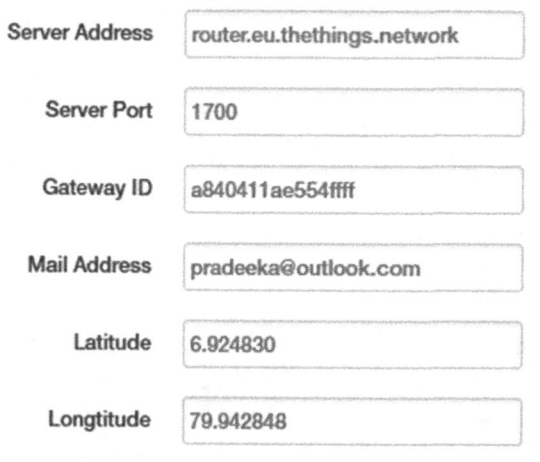

Figure 8-8. *LoRaWAN server settings*

9. Scroll down the page and find the Radio Settings section (Figure 8-9). Type the frequency in hertz for TX Frequency and RX Frequency. Use the same frequency for both input boxes. Figure 8-1 shows the radio settings for EU-433 LoRaWAN 433.175 MHz.

10. Don't provide an encryption key.

11. For Spreading Factor, Transmit Spreading Factor, Coding Rate, Signal Bandwidth, and Preamble Length, use the default values.

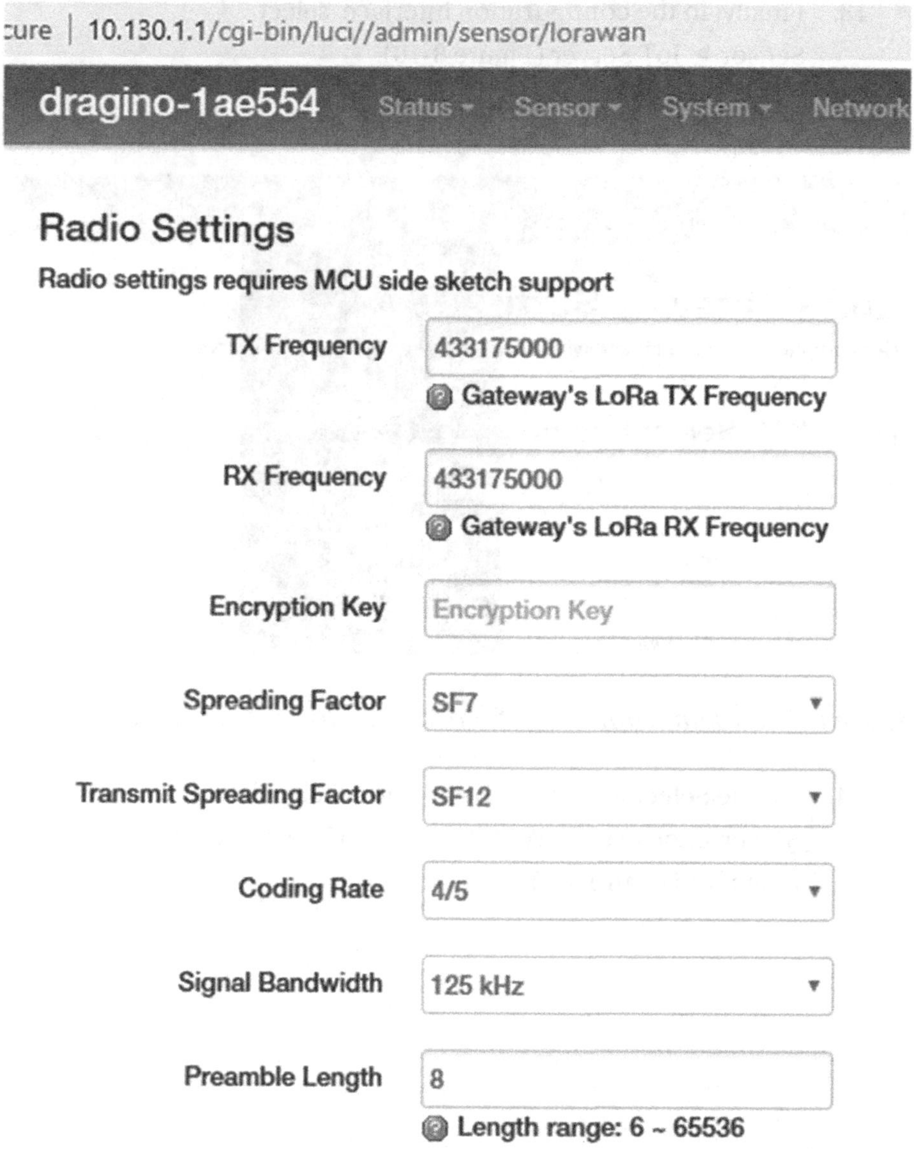

cure | 10.130.1.1/cgi-bin/luci//admin/sensor/lorawan

dragino-1ae554   Status ▾   Sensor ▾   System ▾   Network

Radio Settings

Radio settings requires MCU side sketch support

TX Frequency	433175000
	ⓘ Gateway's LoRa TX Frequency
RX Frequency	433175000
	ⓘ Gateway's LoRa RX Frequency
Encryption Key	Encryption Key
Spreading Factor	SF7 ▾
Transmit Spreading Factor	SF12 ▾
Coding Rate	4/5 ▾
Signal Bandwidth	125 kHz ▾
Preamble Length	8
	ⓘ Length range: 6 ~ 65536

Figure 8-9. *Radio settings*

12. Click the Save & Apply button to save the configuration settings.

13. Finally, in the configuration interface, select
    Sensor ➤ IoT Server (Figure 8-10).

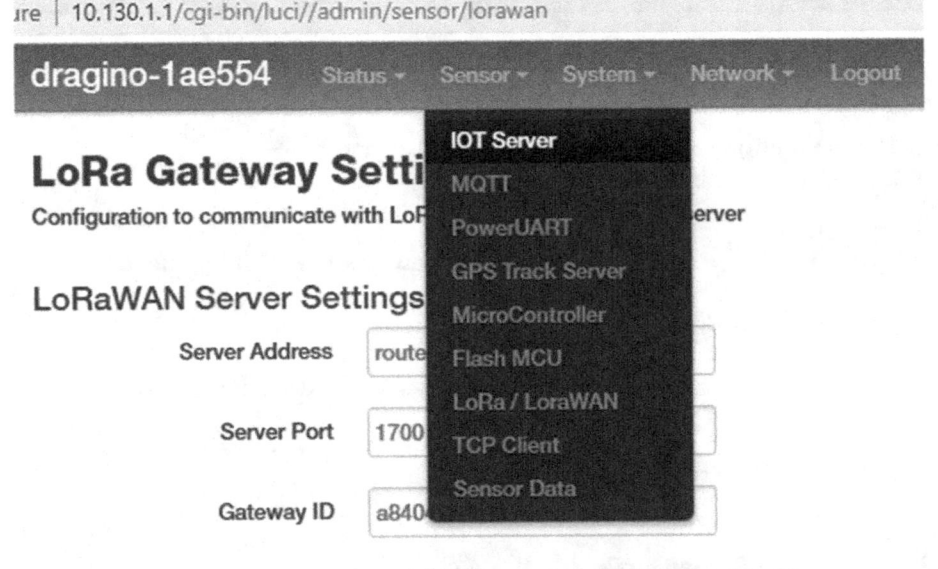

Figure 8-10. *Menu command for accessing IoT Server settings*

14. On the Select IoT Server page, under Select IoT
    Server, choose LoRaWAN from the IoT Server drop-
    down list (Figure 8-11).

ure | 10.130.1.1/cgi-bin/luci/admin/sensor/iotserver

dragino-1ae554   Status ▾   Sensor ▾   System ▾   Network ▾   Logout

Select IoT Server

Select the IoT Server type to connect

Select IoT Server

IoT Server   LoRaWAN   ▾

Log Debug Info   Level 2   ▾

                   ⓘ Show Log in System Log

Figure 8-11. *Selecting the IoT server*

15.   Click the Save & Apply button.

Registering Your Gateway with the Things Network

Before forwarding any data packets to the Things Network, you should register your LG01 gateway with the Things Network Console. In Chapter 5, you created an account with the Things Network. You can use the same credentials with the Things Network Console.

1.   Log in to the Things Network using your credentials (https://account.thethingsnetwork.org/users/login/).

2.   After you successfully logged in, click the Console link (Figure 8-12).

237

Figure 8-12. *Accessing the Things Network Console*

3. Click Gateways (Figure 8-13).

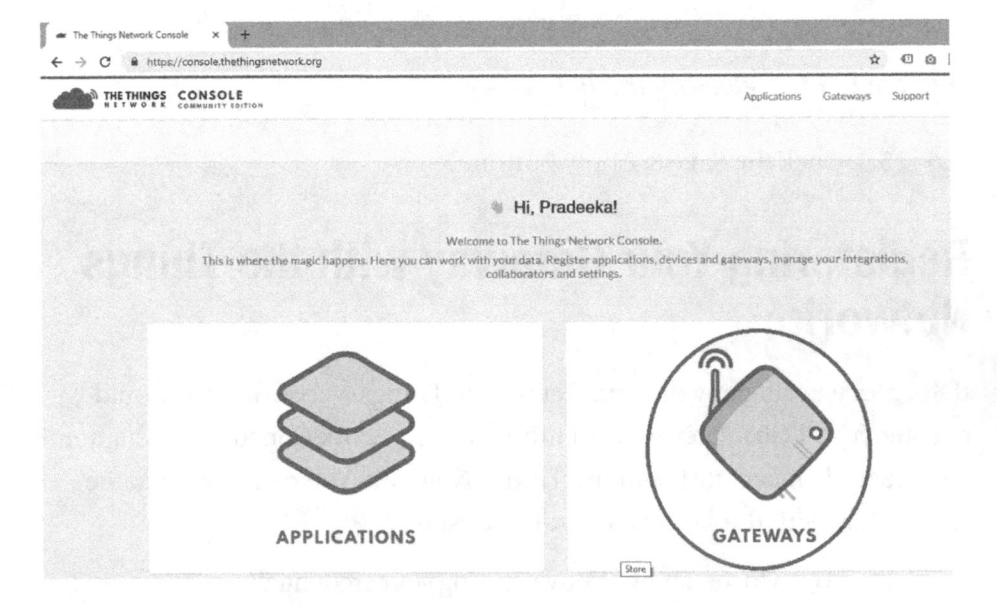

Figure 8-13. *Accessing gateways*

4. On the Gateways page, click the "register gateway" link.

5. In the Register Gateway page, fill out the form with the following technical details:

- *GATEWAY EUI*: Type in the MAC address of the LG01 gateway (Figure 8-14) by appending FFFF to the end. As an example, if you have an LG01 gateway with the MAC address A840411AE554, the resulting gateway ID would be A8 40 41 1A E5 54 FF FF.

Figure 8-14. *MAC address of the LG01 gateway*

- Select the "I'm using the legacy packet forwarder" check box.

- *Description*: Type in a human-readable description for the gateway (e.g., **Dragino LoRa Gateway**).

- *Frequency Plan*: Choose a frequency plan from the list (e.g., Europe 868MHz) to match your gateway's frequency. It doesn't show a frequency plan for EU433. However, if your gateway supports 433 MHz, you can use any frequency plan from the list. This will not affect the correct operation of your gateway (Figure 8-15).

Frequency Plan
The frequency plan this gateway will use

no selection	⌄
Asia 920-923MHz	
Asia 923-925MHz	
Australia 915MHz	
China 470-510MHz	
Europe 868MHz	
India 865-867MHz	
Korea 920-923MHz	
Russia 864-870MHz	
United States 915MHz	

Figure 8-15. *Frequency plans for different regions*

- *Router*: Choose a router from the list to connect your gateway. To reduce latency, pick a router that is in a region that is close to the location of the gateway (Figure 8-16).

Router
The router this gateway will connect to. To reduce latency, pick a router that is in a region which is close to the location of the gateway.

ttn-router-eu	
digitalcatapult-uk-router public	ttn.thingsconnected.net
meshed-router public	thethings.meshed.com.au
switch-router public	ttn.opennetworkinfrastructure.org
ttn-router-asia-se public	asia-se.thethings.network
ttn-router-brazil public	brazil.thethings.network
ttn-router-eu public	eu.thethings.network
ttn-router-jp public	asia-se.thethings.network
ttn-router-us-west public	us-west.thethings.network

Figure 8-16. *TTN routers located in different regions*

- *Antenna Placement*: Click the "indoor" button.

6. Click the Register Gateway button to register your LG01 with the Things Network.

7. After that is successfully registered, you can see the status as "connected" (Figure 8-17). Sometimes it will take few minutes to change the status from "not connected" to "connected."

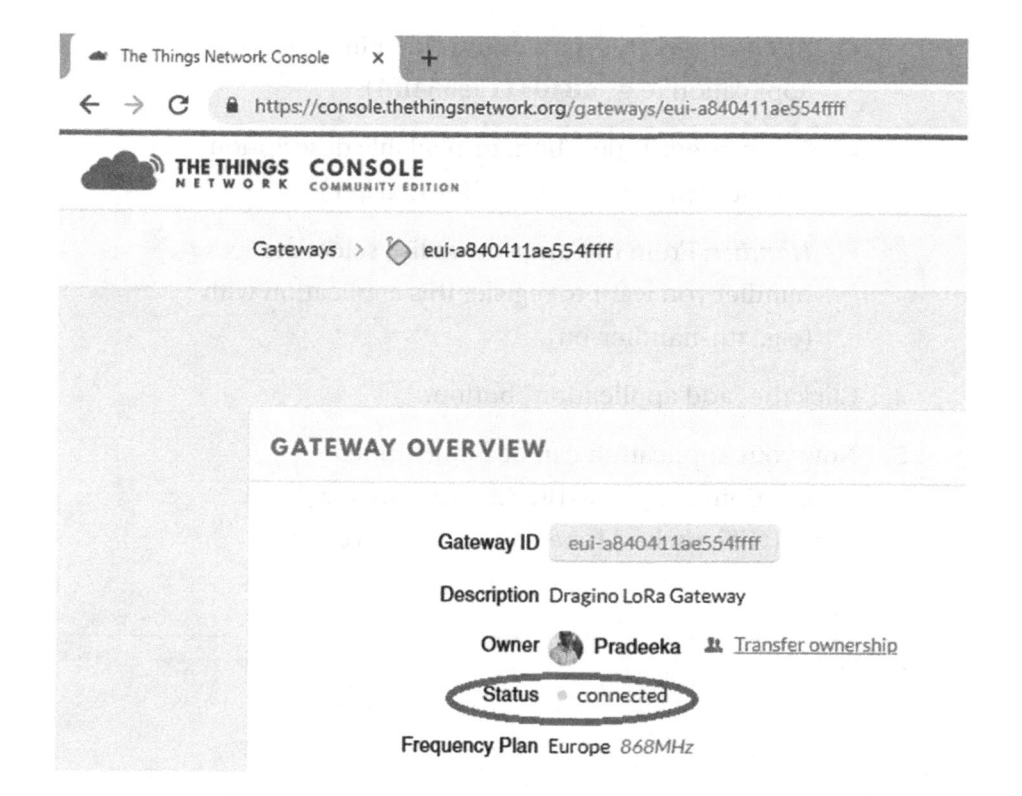

Figure 8-17. *Connection status of the gateway with the Things Network*

Creating an Application

The application allows you to decode the incoming payload to extract useful data. The following steps will guide you how to create a simple application to decode the payload and extract the ID, longitude, and latitude data. It will also trigger the IFTTT recipe for a webhook to send HTTP GET requests to the Traccar GPS server.

1. In the Things Network Console, click Application.

2. Under Applications, click the "add application" link.

3. On the Add Application page, fill out the following form fields:

    -   *Application ID*: Type a unique identifier for your application (e.g., **a840411ae554ffff**).

    -   *Description*: Type a human-readable description for your application (e.g., **GPS Tracker**).

    -   *Handler*: From the drop-down list, select the handler you want to register this application with (e.g., ttn-handler-eu).

4. Click the "add application" button.

5. Now your application can be found under Applications (Figure 8-18). Click the application name (GPS tracker) for an application overview.

Figure 8-18. *The GPS tracker application is listed under Applications*

6. Click the Payload Formats tab (Figure 8-19).

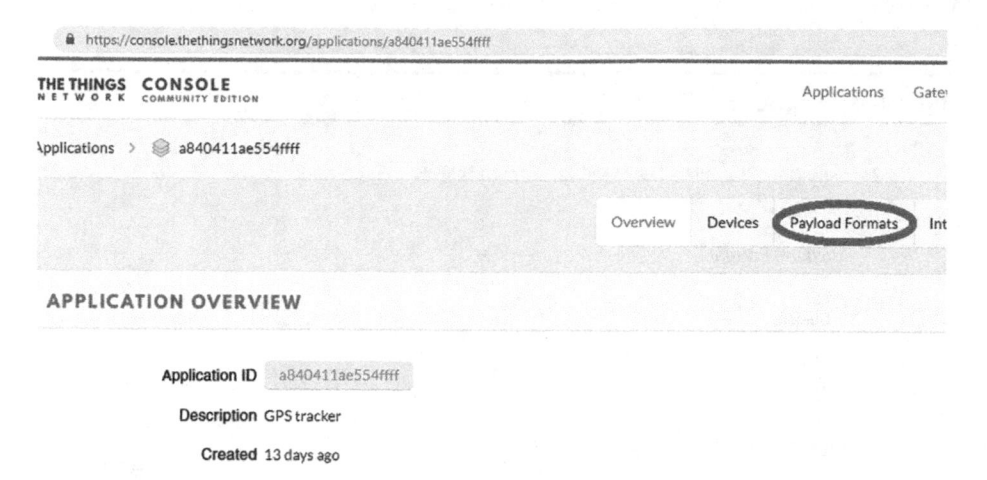

https://console.thethingsnetwork.org/applications/a840411ae554ffff

THE THINGS   CONSOLE
NETWORK   COMMUNITY EDITION

Applications   Gate

Applications > ⬡ a840411ae554ffff

Overview   Devices   Payload Formats   Int

APPLICATION OVERVIEW

Application ID   a840411ae554ffff

Description GPS tracker

Created 13 days ago

Figure 8-19. *Accessing the payload formats*

7.   On the Payload Formats page, for the payload
     format, choose Custom from the drop-down list.
     Then click the Decoder tab (Figure 8-20). Replace
     the existing JavaScript code with the following code:

```
function Decoder(b, port) {

var lng = (b[0] | b[1]<<8 | b[2]<<16 | (b[2] & 0x80 ?
0xFF<<24 : 0)) / 10000;

var lat = (b[3] | b[4]<<8 | b[5]<<16 | (b[5] & 0x80 ?
0xFF<<24 : 0)) / 10000;

return {

id: 868142, //id

lon: lng, //lng

lat: lat //lat

};

}
```

243

```
C    🔒 https://console.thethingsnetwork.org/applications/a840411ae554ffff/payload-formats

THE THINGS   CONSOLE
N E T W O R K   COMMUNITY EDITION

      Applications  >  🔷 a840411ae554ffff  >  Payload Formats


         Payload Format
         The payload format sent by your devices

           Custom



           decoder  converter  validator    encoder


        12
        13
        14
        15   function Decoder(b, port) {
        16
        17
        18   var lat = (b[0] | b[1]<<8 | b[2]<<16 | (b[2] & 0x80 ? 0xFF<<24 : 0)) / 10000;
        19
        20   var lng = (b[3] | b[4]<<8 | b[5]<<16 | (b[5] & 0x80 ? 0xFF<<24 : 0)) / 10000;
        21
        22   return {
        23
        24   id: 868142, //id
        25
```

Figure 8-20. *JavaScript function for decoding the payload and extracting the device ID, latitude, and longitude*

    8.   Click the "Save payload functions" button.

Using IFTTT

You will need an IFTTT account to create a webhook to send HTTP GET requests to the Traccar server.

    1.   Go to https://ifttt.com/ and click the "Sign up" button at the top-right corner of the page.

    2.   If you have a Google or Facebook account, you can use one of them to sign in with IFTTT. If not, click the "sign up" link at the bottom of the page (Figure 8-21).

IFTTT

Get started with **IFTTT**

G   **Continue with Google**

f   **Continue with Facebook**

Or use your password to **sign up** or **sign in**

Figure 8-21. *Sign-up options with IFTTT*

3. Type in a valid e-mail address and a password and click the "Sign up" button.

Now you have successfully created an account on IFTTT.

Integrating with IFTTT Webhooks

IFTTT webhooks allow you to make HTTP requests to a web server. The Traccar server supports HTTP GET requests. Follow these steps to integrate your application with the IFTTT webhooks:

1. In the Things Network Console, in the GPS tracker application section, click Integrations (Figure 8-22).

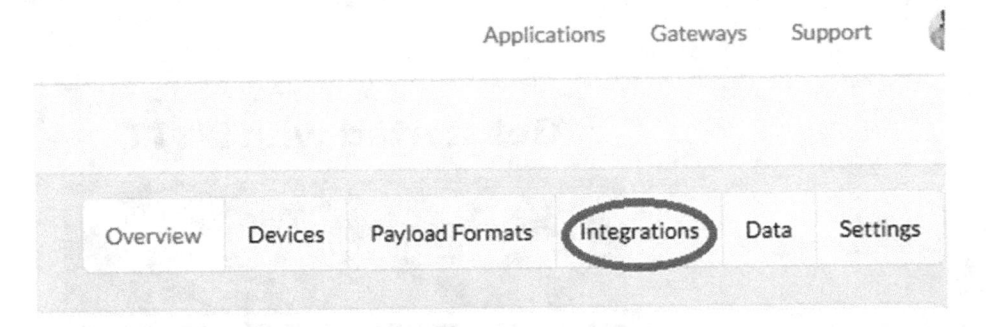

Figure 8-22. *Accessing integrations from the top navigation menu*

2. Click the "add integration" link.

3. On the Add Integration page, click IFTTT Maker (Figure 8-23).

Figure 8-23. *Choosing the integration option as IFTTT Maker channel*

4. Click the "documentation" link (Figure 8-24).

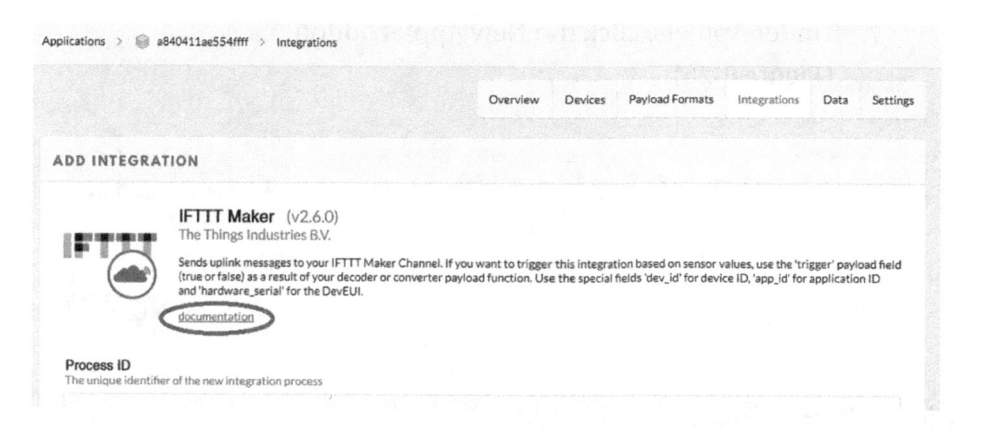

Figure 8-24. *The documentation link will open the page at* *https.//ifttt.com/maker_webhooks.*

5. This will take you to the IFTTT Webhooks page (https://ifttt.com/maker_webhooks).

6. At the top-left corner of the page, click My Applets (Figure 8-25).

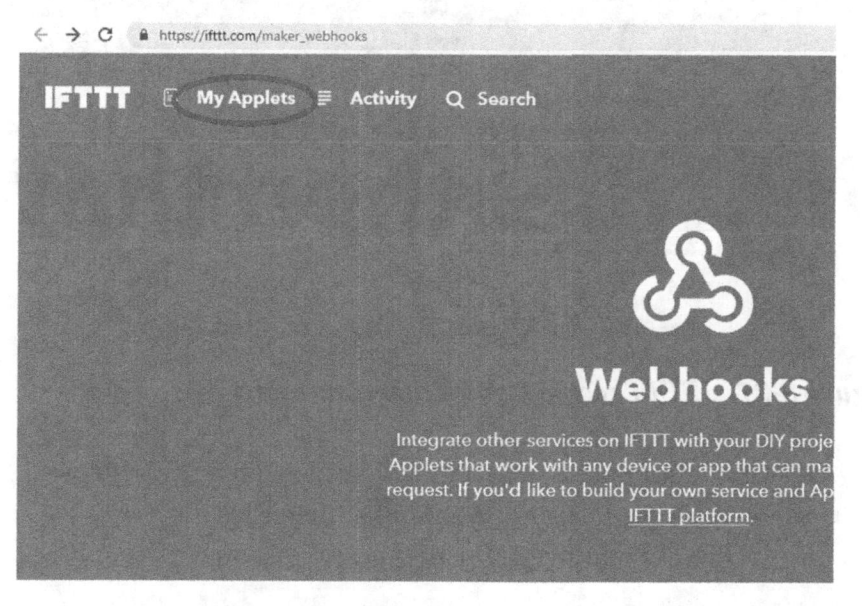

Figure 8-25. *Accessing My Applets from the top navigation menu*

7.   Under Applets, click the New Applet button
(Figure 8-26).

Figure 8-26. *Creating a new applet*

8.   On the New Applet page, you can see the IFTTT
recipe format for your webhook. Click the "+this"
link (Figure 8-27).

New Applet

if ⊞this then that

Want to build your own service? Build on the platform ⌐

Figure 8-27. *IFTTT recipe format first condition*

9.   On the "Choose a service" page, in the search
services text box, type **Webhooks**. Then click the
Webhooks button (Figure 8-28).

Choose a service

Step 1 of 6

Figure 8-28. *Choosing a service*

10. On the "Choose trigger" page, click "Receive a web request" (Figure 8-29).

‹ Back

Choose trigger

Step 2 of 6

Receive a web request

This trigger fires every time the Maker service receives a web request to notify it of an event. For information on triggering events, go to your Maker service settings and then the listed URL (web) or tap your username (mobile)

Figure 8-29. *Choosing a trigger*

11.   On the "Complete trigger fields" page, type in a name for the event (e.g., **gps_received**) and click the "Create trigger" button (Figure 8-30).

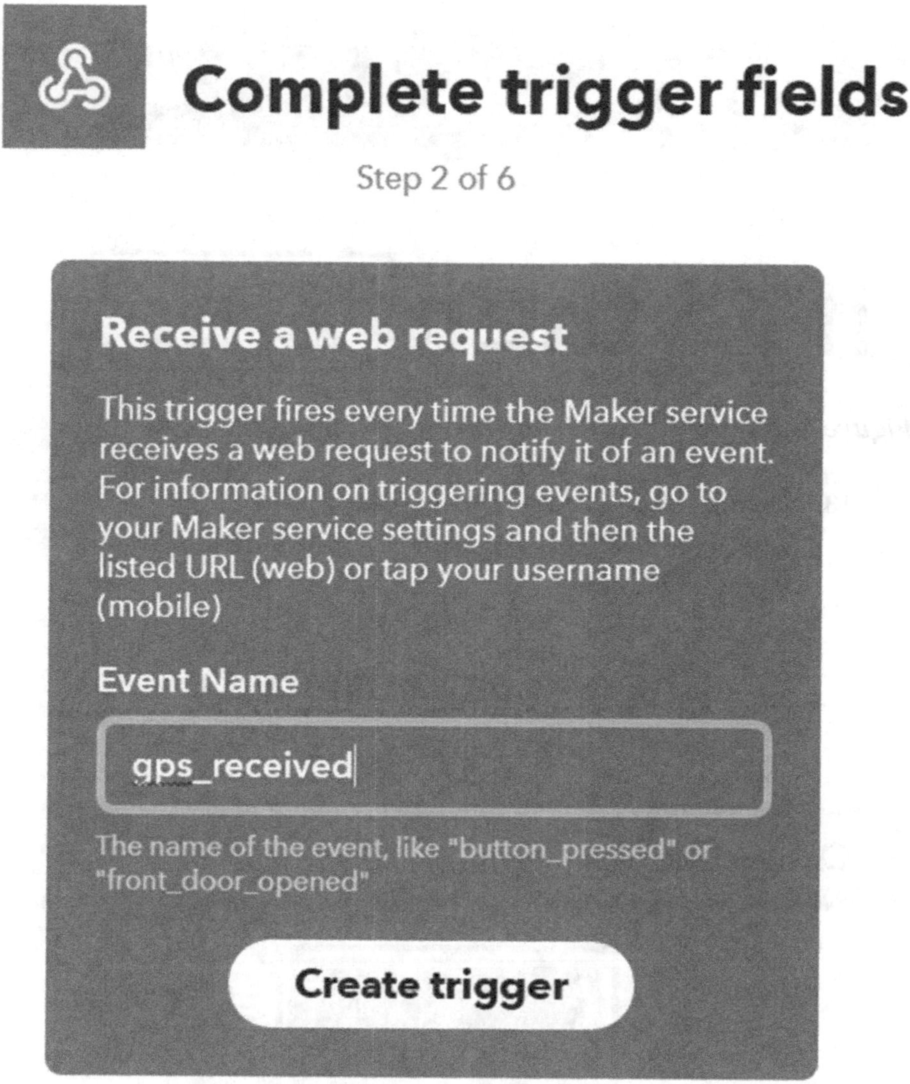

 # Complete trigger fields

Step 2 of 6

Receive a web request

This trigger fires every time the Maker service receives a web request to notify it of an event. For information on triggering events, go to your Maker service settings and then the listed URL (web) or tap your username (mobile)

Event Name

gps_received

The name of the event, like "button_pressed" or "front_door_opened"

Create trigger

Figure 8-30.   Completing the trigger fields

12.   Click the "+that" link (Figure 8-31).

ceive-a-web-request-then?sid=1

Activity   Q Search

if 🔗 then ➕that

Figure 8-31. *IFTTT recipe format second condition*

13. On the "Choose action service" page, again search for *Webhooks* (Figure 8-32). Then click the Webhooks button.

Choose action service

Step 3 of 6

Q   Webhooks

Figure 8-32. *Choosing an action service*

14. On the "Choose action" page, click the "Make a web request" box (Figure 8-33).

FTTT   ▣ **My Applets**   ☰ **Activity**   Q **Search**

‹ **Back**

⚙ **Choose action**

Step 4 of 6

Make a web request

This action will make a web request to a publicly accessible URL. NOTE: Requests may be rate limited.

Figure 8-33. *Choosing an action*

15. On the "Complete action fields" page, fill out the "Make a web request" form as explained here:

- *URL*: Type the URL for the HTTP GET request (Figure 8-1): `http://demo.traccar.org:5055/?id={{Value1}}&lat={{Value2}}&lon={{Value3}}`

- The `{{Value}}` fields can be added by clicking the "Add ingredient" button (Figure 8-34). Then choose the following:

  - *Value 1*: id

  - *Value 2*: Value 2: lat

  - *Value 3*: Value 3: lon

CAUTION   After adding the values from the drop-down list, remember to remove all the white spaces in the URL. If you don't do this, the webhook will not work as expected.

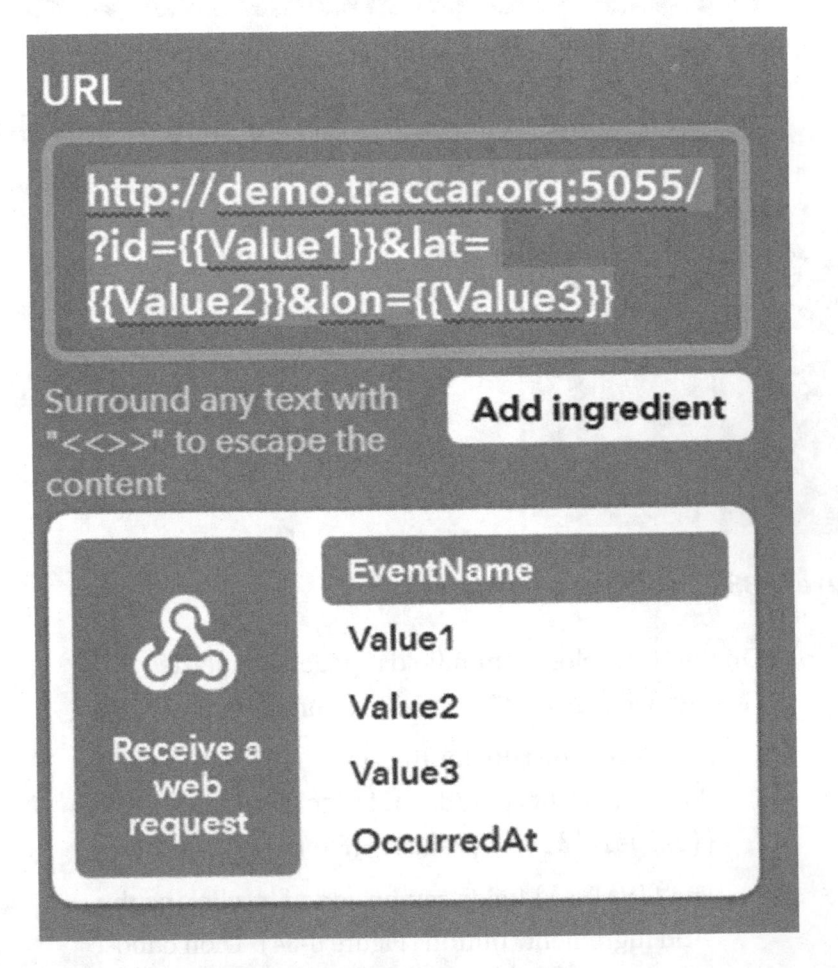

Figure 8-34. *Building an HTTP GET request*

- *Method*: GET

- *Content Type (optional)*: application/json

16.   Click the Create Action button to create the action.

17.   On the "Review and finish" page, click the Finish
button to save the recipe (Figure 8-35).

Figure 8-35.   Confirming the recipe

18.   Now you can see the summary of the webhook recipe. At any time you can turn it off by clicking the On button (Figure 8-36).

Figure 8-36. Summary of the webhook recipe

19. Now you have successfully created a recipe with
    IFTTT webhooks to make HTTP GET requests to the
    Traccar server. Still you will need to find one more
    thing: the key. On the Webhooks page (`https://`
    `ifttt.com/maker_webhooks`, click the Settings
    button (Figure 8-37).

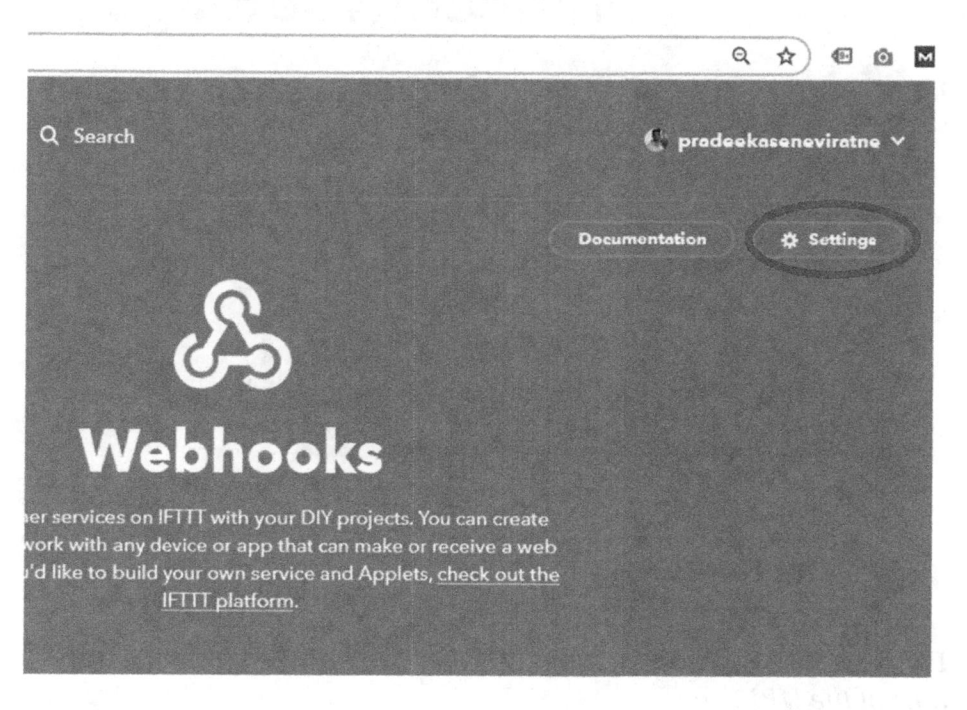

Figure 8-37. *Accessing the webhook settings*

20. On the Webhooks Settings page, under Account
    Info, copy the last part of the URL for the key
    (Figure 8-38).

257

Webhooks settings

View activity log

Account Info

Key

Connected as: pradeekaseneviratne

URL: https://maker.ifttt.com/use/mdwNeoX1Jms-
P_xDsYXN98tFC4................T7NN

Status: active

(**Edit connection**)

Figure 8-38. *Webhook settings. The key can be taken from the last
part of the URL.*

21. You will need this key to integrate the IFTTT
     webhook that is created under your IFTTT account
     with the Things Network Console.

22. Now go back to the IFTTT integration settings page
     and fill out the form as shown here (Figure 8-39):

     • *Event Name*: Enter the event name of your IFTTT
       recipe (e.g., **gps_received**).

- *Key*: Enter your key (e.g., **mdwXeoX1Jms-P_
  xDsYXN98tXXXXUb3I8pHJfiBbT7XX**).

- *Value 1*: This is the payload field name to send as
  value 1 (e.g., **id**).

- *Value 2*: This is the payload field name to send as
  value 2 (e.g., **lat**).

- *Value 3*: This is the payload field name to send as
  value 3 (e.g., **lon**).

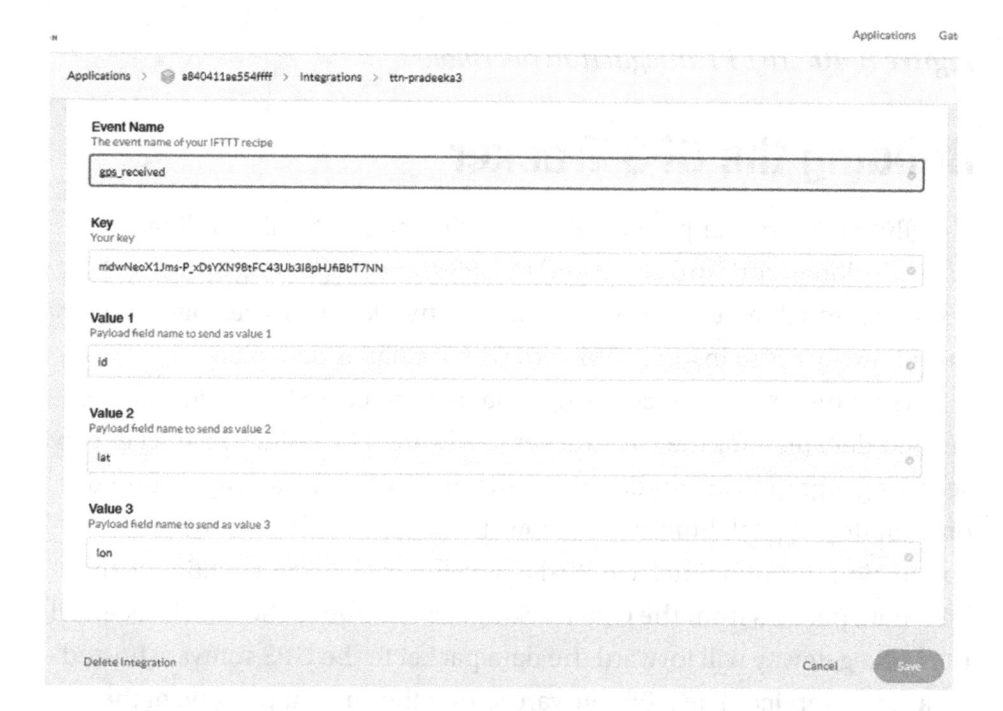

Figure 8-39. *IFTTT integration settings*

23. Click the Save button to save the integration. Now,
    under Integration Overview, you can see the status
    as Running (Figure 8-40).

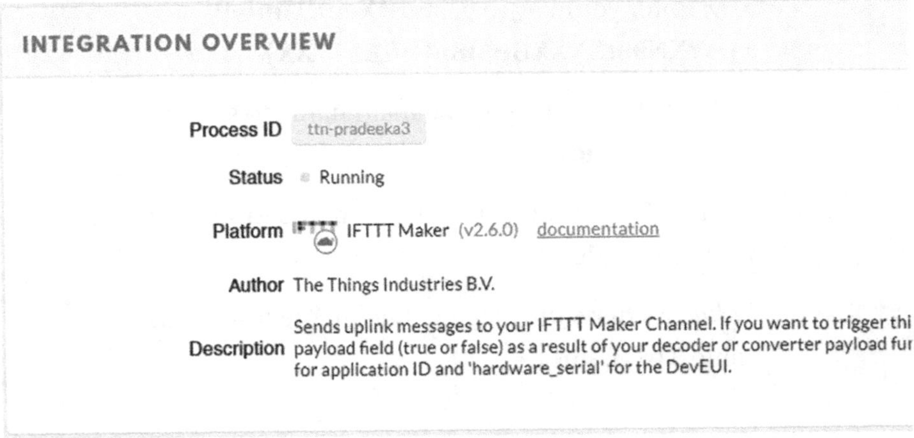

INTEGRATION OVERVIEW

Process ID   ttn-pradeeka3

Status   ● Running

Platform   IFTTT IFTTT Maker (v2.6.0)   documentation

Author   The Things Industries B.V.

Description   Sends uplink messages to your IFTTT Maker Channel. If you want to trigger thi
payload field (true or false) as a result of your decoder or converter payload fur
for application ID and 'hardware_serial' for the DevEUI.

Figure 8-40. IFTTT integartion overview

Building the GPS Tracker

Usually, a GPS tracker periodically sends its geographical coordinates
(latitude, longitude, and elevation) to GPS software (hosted on a cloud
service) through an existing GPRS/GSM network. It has a cellular module
that allows users to insert a SIM card with a cellular data plan.

With LoRa wireless technology, you don't need a SIM module and a
cellular data plan for the GPS tracker hardware. The LoRa GPS tracker can
send its geographical coordinates to the nearby LoRa gateway mounted
on a rooftop of a tall building or a tower. The gateway has an Internet
connection through Ethernet, Wi-Fi, or cellular. Gateways continuously
hear data packets from the GPS tracking devices. Once the data is received,
the LoRa gateway will forward the data packet to the GPS software hosted
on a cloud service. The GPS software shows the current position of the
device on a map using the geographical coordinates. A single gateway can
handle many GPS tracking devices simultaneously. (The Dragino LG01
gateway can handle up to 8 GPS tracking devices.)

Figure 8-41 shows the wiring diagram for the GPS tracker. The processing unit of the GPS tracker is an Arduino Uno (or Adafruit Metro) board. A GPS module and a LoRa radio transceiver module are connected to the Arduino. The GPS module receives data from GPS satellites. Then, the Arduino will process and format the GPS data. Finally, the LoRa transceiver sends data to the LoRa gateway.

Figure 8-41. Wiring diagram for the GPS tracker

Table 8-1 shows the connections between each component of the GPS tracker.

Table 8-1. *Wiring Connections Between Components*

Arduino	RFM9x	GPS module
5V	VIN	VIN
GND	GND	GND
9	RST	
2	G0	
6	G1	
7	G2	
10	CS	
3		RX
4		TX
11	MOSI	
12	MISO	
13	SCK	

If you want to place the GPS tracker inside an enclosure, you may want to use an external active antenna. Active antennas draw power from the GPS module but provide more gain and sensitivity. Figure 8-42 shows how to connect an external active antenna with a GPS module through an SMA to a full adapter cable.

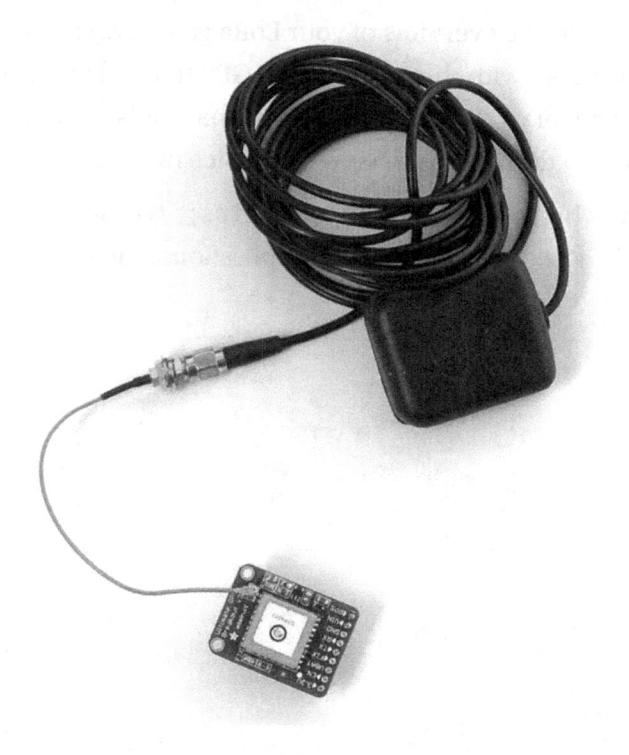

Figure 8-42. *Connecting external antenna to the U.LF connector of the GPS module (image owner: lady ada; license: Attribution-ShareAlike Creative Commons,* `https://creativecommons.org/licenses/by-sa/3.0/`*)*

Once completed, go to `https://github.com/goodcheney/Arduino-Profile-Examples/blob/patch-4/libraries/Dragino/examples/LoRa/LoRaWAN/LoRa_GPS_Shield_TTN` to get the Arduino sketch for the GPS tracking device. Copy the code and paste it in a new Arduino file. This chapter assumes you installed all the required software libraries on the Arduino IDE in Chapter 3. Before uploading the sketch to the Arduino board, edit the code to suit your hardware setup.

First, find the device overview of your LoRa gateway. The device overview is associated with the application (GPS tracker) that you created in The Things Network Console to decode the payloads coming from the GPS tracker. Follow these steps to view the device overview:

1. In the Things Network Console (`https://console.thethingsnetwork.org`), click Applications (Figure 8-43).

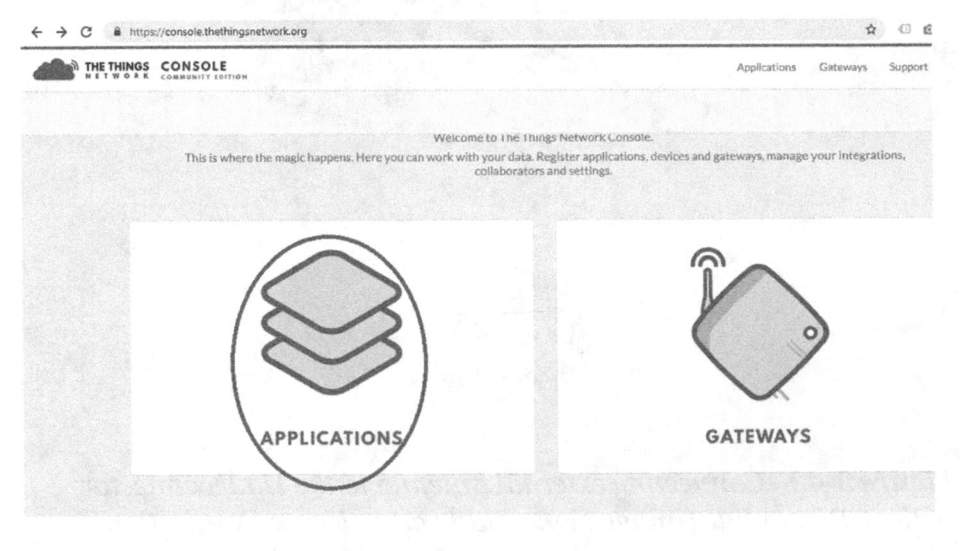

Figure 8-43. *Accessing the Applications section*

2. Under Applications, click "GPS tracker" (Figure 8-44).

Figure 8-44. *GPS tracker application showing under Applications*

3.   Click Devices (Figure 8-45).

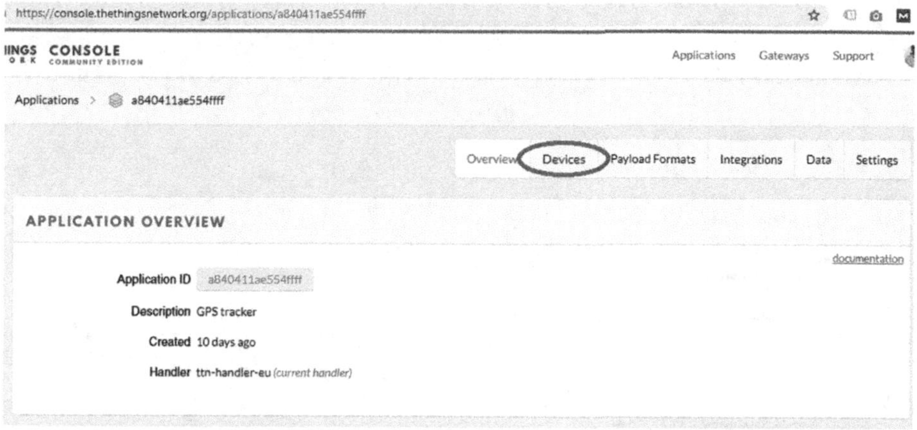

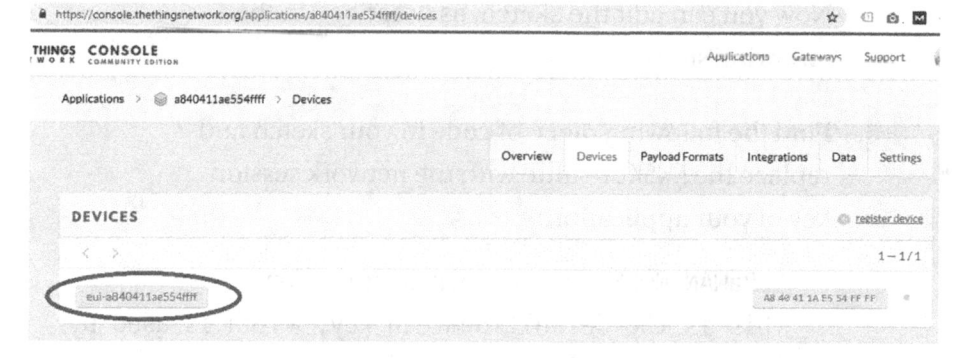

Figure 8-45. *Accessing devices*

4.   Click the Device EUI (Figure 8-46).

Figure 8-46. *Device EUI showing under Devices*

5.   Now you can see the Device Overview page (Figure 8-47).

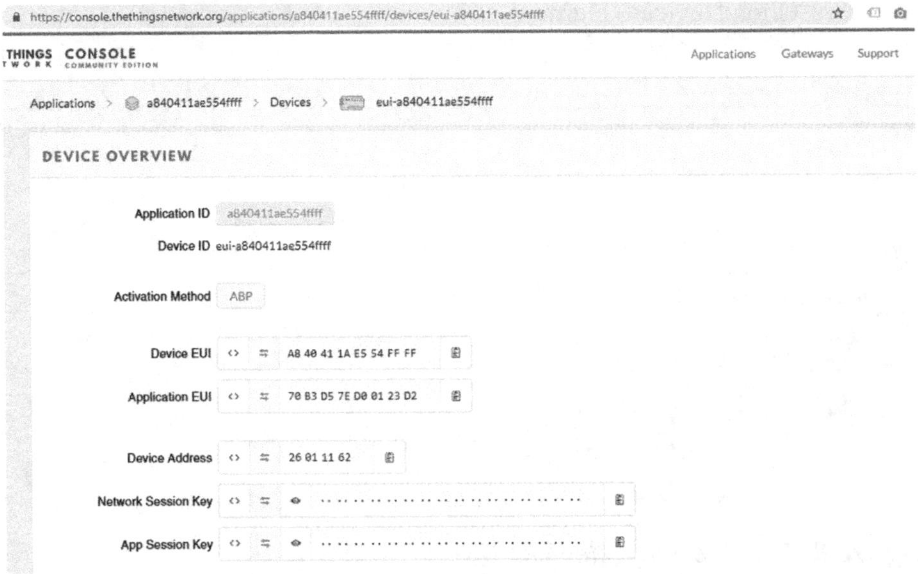

Figure 8-47. *Device Overview page*

Now you can edit the sketch, as described in the following steps.

6. Find the following piece of code in your sketch and replace the NWSKEY value with the network session key of your application:

```
/* LoRaWAN NwkSKey, network session key
   This is the default Semtech key, which is used by
   the prototype TTN
   network initially.
   ttn*/
static const PROGMEM u1_t NWKSKEY[16] = { 0xEE,0x0D,0x3
1,0x15,0x75,0x72,0x0E,0xDD,0x31,0x10,0xD3,0xFE,0x3F,0x1
0,0xFD,0xAF };
```

The network session key can be found on the Device Overview page. Click the hex/C-style button to view the network session key in C-style (Figure 8-48). Then click the Copy to Clipboard button.

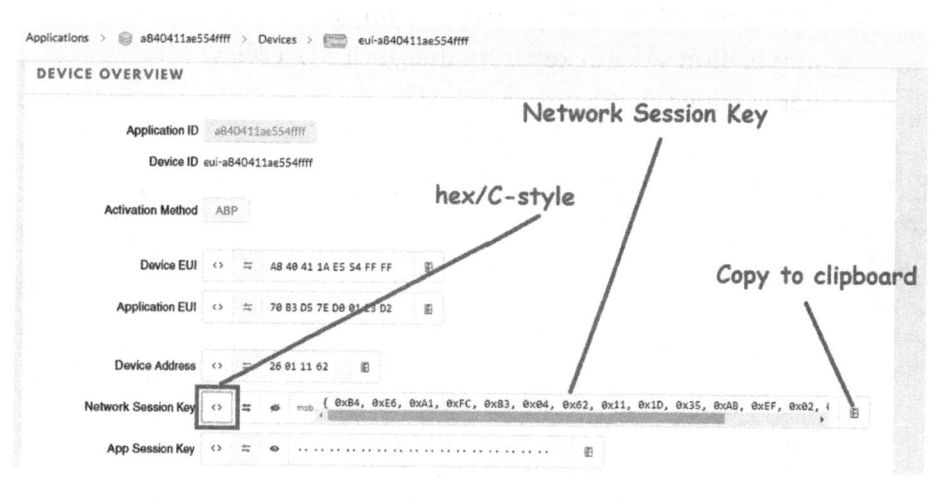

Figure 8-48. *Network session key*

7. Replace the existing NWSKEY value with the new network session key. Now your Arduino code looks similar to the following:

```
static const PROGMEM u1_t NWKSKEY[16] = { 0xB4, 0xE6,
0xA1, 0xFC, 0x83, 0x04, 0x62, 0x11, 0x1D, 0x35, 0xAB,
0xEF, 0x02, 0x5B, 0x15, 0xB1 };
```

8. Find the following code to modify the APPSKEY value:

```
/* LoRaWAN AppSKey, application session key
   This is the default Semtech key, which is used by
   the prototype TTN
   network initially.
   ttn*/
```

```
static const u1_t PROGMEM APPSKEY[16] = { 0x6A, 0x2A,
0xE6, 0xA8, 0x5C, 0xD1, 0xF0, 0xC1, 0xB9, 0xA4, 0xBD,
0xEC, 0xB4, 0x42, 0xC4,0x97 };
```

9. Replace the APPSKEY value by copying the
   application session key from the Device Overview
   page (Figure 8-49).

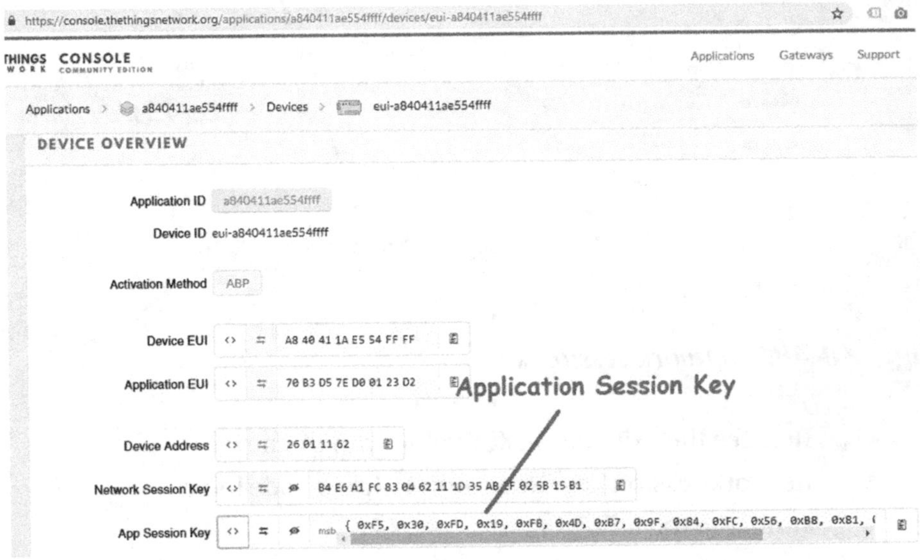

Figure 8-49. *Application session key*

10. Once modified, your Arduino code looks similar to
    the following:

```
/* LoRaWAN AppSKey, application session key
   This is the default Semtech key, which is used by
   the prototype TTN
   network initially.
   ttn*/
```

```
static const u1_t PROGMEM APPSKEY[16] = { 0xF5, 0x30,
0xFD, 0x19, 0xFB, 0x4D, 0xB7, 0x9F, 0x84, 0xFC, 0x56,
0xB8, 0x81, 0x7E, 0x08, 0x9F };
```

11. Find the code for DEVADDR and replace it with the end device address. Use C-style before copying it in to the clipboard (Figure 8-50).

```
/*
LoRaWAN end-device address (DevAddr)
See http://thethingsnetwork.org/wiki/AddressSpace
ttn*/
static const u4_t DEVADDR = 0x26011A81;
```

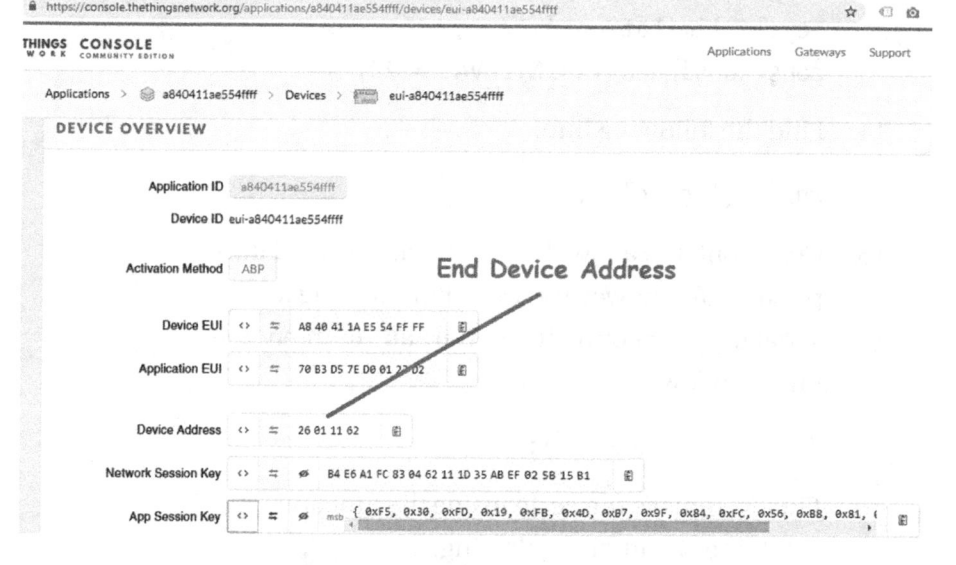

Figure 8-50. *End device address*

12. The modified code with the end device address
     looks similar to the following:

```
/*
 LoRaWAN end-device address (DevAddr)
 See http://thethingsnetwork.org/wiki/AddressSpace
 ttn*/
 static const u4_t DEVADDR = 0x26011162;
```

13. You can also change the transmission interval by
     modifying the value of the TX_INTERVAL variable.
     The default is 20 seconds.

```
/* Schedule TX every this many seconds (might become
longer due to duty
 cycle limitations).*/
const unsigned TX_INTERVAL = 20;
```

14. Find the following line:

```
while (!Console);
```

15. Comment it to allow the GPS tracker to send data
     packets after powering up without waiting for the
     serial monitor connection. You can comment the
     line as follows:

```
// while (!Console);
```

16. Finally, replace the code inside the function
     GPSWrite() with the following:

```
/*Convert GPS data to format*/
  datastring1 +=dtostrf(flat, 0, 4, gps_lat);
  datastring2 +=dtostrf(flon, 0, 4, gps_lon);
  //datastring3 +=dtostrf(falt, 0, 2, gps_alt);
```

```
if(flon!=1000.000000)
{
strcat(gps_lon,",");
strcat(gps_lon,gps_lat);
//strcat(gps_lon,",");
//strcat(gps_lon,gps_alt);
  int i = 0;
for(i = 0; i < 2; i++)
{
    //datasend.toFloat();
    atof(gps_lon);
   //Serial.println((char*)datasend);
  Serial.println("Testing converted data:");
  Serial.println(gps_lon);
  // atof(gps_alt);
  // Serial.print(gps_alt);
}

strcpy(datasend,gps_lon); //the format of datasend is
longtitude,latitude,altitude
Serial.print("##########     ");
Serial.print("NO.");
Serial.print(count);
Serial.println("   ###########");
Serial.println("The longtitude and latitude are:");
Serial.print("[");
Serial.print((char*)datasend);
Serial.print("]");
Serial.print("");
/*
for(int k = 0; k < 20;k++)
{
```

```
Serial.print("[");
Serial.print(datasend[k], HEX) ;
Serial.print("]");
}
Serial.println("");
Serial.println("");*/
count++;
}

int32_t lng = flat * 10000;
int32_t lat = flon * 10000;

datasend[0] = lat;
datasend[1] = lat >> 8;
datasend[2] = lat >> 16;

datasend[3] = lng;
datasend[4] = lng >> 8;
datasend[5] = lng >> 16;
smartdelay(1000);
```

17. After modifying the file, save it as LoRa_GPS_
     Tracker_TTN.ino.

Adding the EU433 Frequency Band

By default, the Arduino LMIC library supports only the EU868 and US915
frequency bands. However, you can modify the EU868 band to use the
EU433 band in Activation by Personalization (ABP) mode.

1. In the Arduino LMIC library folder, open the file
    lorabase.h with any text editor. The lorabase.h
    file is located in the Arduino libraries folder
    (libraries/.../scr/lmic/lorabase.h).

2. Find and comment the following code snippet in the file as shown:

```
// Default frequency plan for EU 868MHz ISM band
// Bands:
//  g1 :   1%   14dBm
//  g2 : 0.1%   14dBm
//  g3 :  10%   27dBm
//                    freq        band      datarates
/*enum { EU868_F1 = 868100000,    // g1     SF7-12
         EU868_F2 = 868300000,    // g1     SF7-12 FSK
                                            SF7/250
         EU868_F3 = 868500000,    // g1     SF7-12
         EU868_F4 = 868850000,    // g2     SF7-12
         EU868_F5 = 869050000,    // g2     SF7-12
         EU868_F6 = 869525000,    // g3     SF7-12
         EU868_J4 = 864100000,    // g2     SF7-12 used
                                            during join
         EU868_J5 = 864300000,    // g2     SF7-12
                                            ditto
         EU868_J6 = 864500000,    // g2     SF7-12
                                            ditto
};
enum { EU868_FREQ_MIN = 863000000,
       EU868_FREQ_MAX = 870000000 }; */
```

3. Add the following code snippets for EU433 support:

```
//Modify the EU868Mhz band configure for EU433Mhz temporary use.
enum { EU868_F1 = 433175000,      // g1    SF7-12
       EU868_F2 = 433375000,      // g1    SF7-12 FSK SF7/250
       EU868_F3 = 433575000,      // g1    SF7-12
       EU868_F4 = 433775000,      // g2    SF7-12
```

```
    EU868_F5 = 433975000,      // g2   SF7-12
    EU868_F6 = 434175000,      // g3   SF7-12
    EU868_J4 = 434375000,      // g2   SF7-12 used during join
    EU868_J5 = 434575000,      // g2   SF7-12   ditto
    EU868_J6 = 434775000,      // g2   SF7-12   ditto
};
enum { EU868_FREQ_MIN = 433050000,
       EU868_FREQ_MAX = 434900000 };
```

4. Save the file and close the text editor. Usually this
    is a read-only file, so first you should grant the
    permission for this file to modify.

5. Connect the Arduino Uno with your computer using
    a USB cable. Choose the correct type of USB cable
    depending on the Arduino and Adafruit Metro boards.

6. In the Arduino IDE, select Tools ➤ Board ➤
    Arduino/Genuino UNO. Select Tools ➤ Port and
    choose the correct port associated with the Arduino
    board.

7. Verify and upload the Arduino sketch to your
    Arduino board.

8. If successful, open the serial monitor in the Arduino
    IDE. You can see that the output looks similar to
    Figure 8-51. The tracker transmits data packets
    on different frequencies as configured in the
    lorabase.h file.

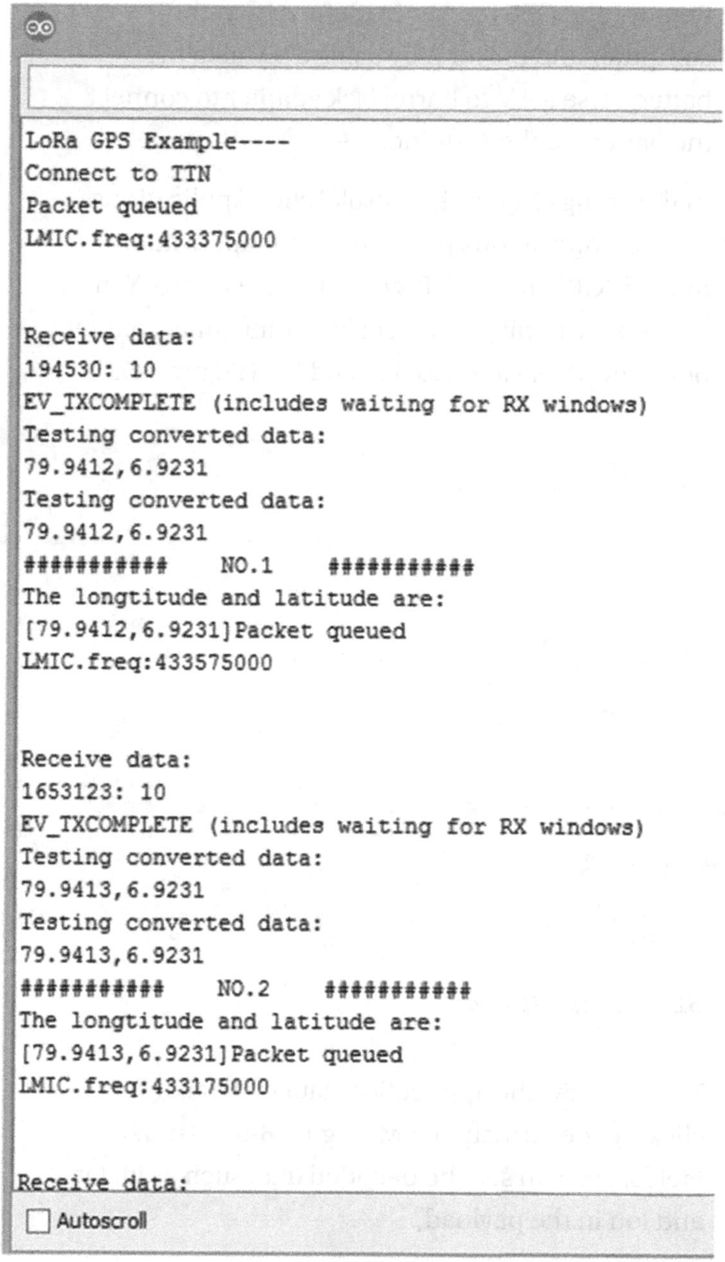

```
LoRa GPS Example----
Connect to TTN
Packet queued
LMIC.freq:433375000


Receive data:
194530: 10
EV_TXCOMPLETE (includes waiting for RX windows)
Testing converted data:
79.9412,6.9231
Testing converted data:
79.9412,6.9231
##########    NO.1    ##########
The longtitude and latitude are:
[79.9412,6.9231]Packet queued
LMIC.freq:433575000


Receive data:
1653123: 10
EV_TXCOMPLETE (includes waiting for RX windows)
Testing converted data:
79.9413,6.9231
Testing converted data:
79.9413,6.9231
##########    NO.2    ##########
The longtitude and latitude are:
[79.9413,6.9231]Packet queued
LMIC.freq:433175000


Receive data:
```
☐ Autoscroll

Figure 8-51. *Serial monitor output for the LoRa_GPS_Tracker_TTN.ino*

9. Remove the GPS tracker (Arduino) from the computer and power it by using a 9 V alkaline battery. Use a 9 V to barrel jack adapter to connect the battery to the Arduino.

10. In the Things Network Console, click Applications. On the Applications page, click your application named "GPS tracker." Then click the Data tab. You can see the application data including time, counter, port, dev id, payload, id, lat, and lon (Figure 8-52).

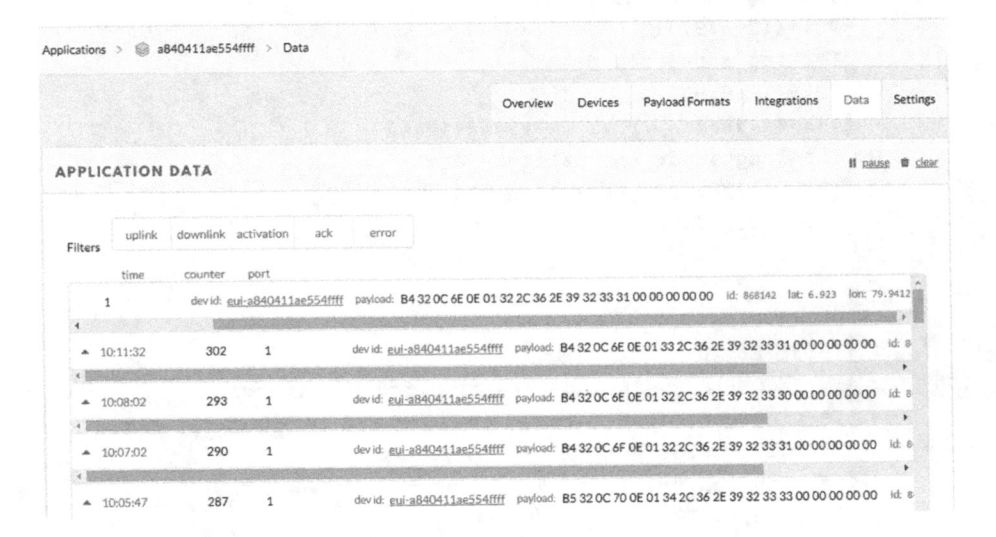

Figure 8-52. *Application data*

11. You can view the application data in detail by clicking the particular row (Figure 8-53). Under Fields, you can see the decoded data such as id, lat, and lon in the payload.

Figure 8-53. *Application data in detail*

Displaying the Real-Time Path with Traccar

Traccar (https://www.traccar.org/) is a personal, secure, open source, and modern GPS tracking platform that can be integrated with your LoRa GPS tracking system through the IFTTT webhooks.

1. Go to http://demo.traccar.org/ and click the Register button (Figure 8-54).

Figure 8-54. *Registering with Traccar server, step 1*

2. In the Register dialog box, type in a username, a
    valid e-mail address, and a password. Click the Save
    button to create the new account (Figure 8-55).

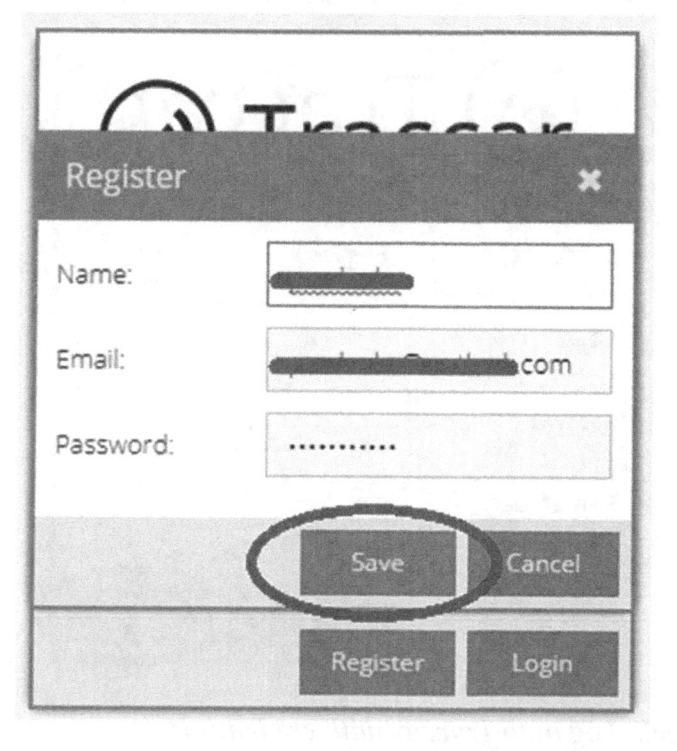

Figure 8-55. *Registering with Traccar server, step 2*

3. Once registered, type in the e-mail and password
    again. Then click the Login button (Figure 8-56).

Figure 8-56. *Log in to Traccar with credentials*

4. Once you are logged in to the demo, add a new
    device by clicking the Add button (Figure 8-57).

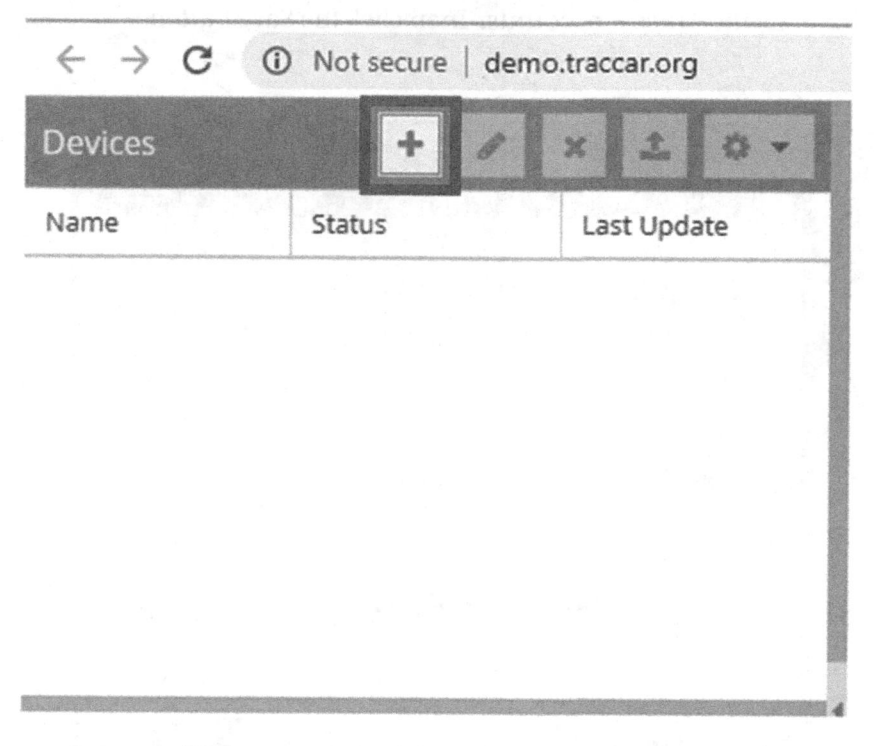

Figure 8-57. *Adding a new device, step 1*

5. In the Device dialog box, type in a name for your GPS tracker and a unique number for the identifier (Figure 8-58). The identifier is globally unique across all the Traccar accounts. Then click the Save button.

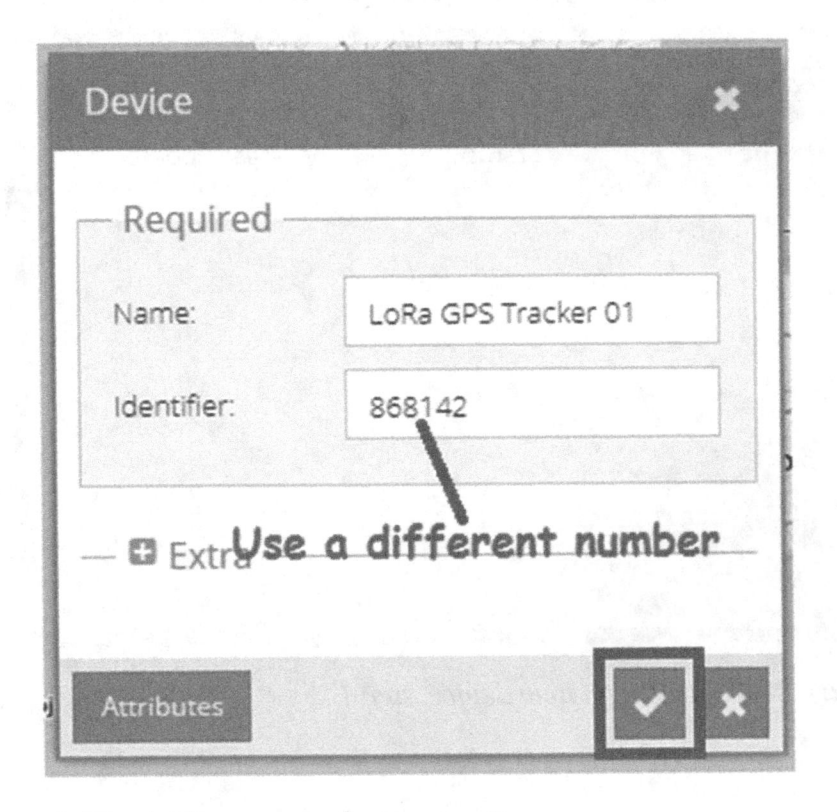

Figure 8-58. *Adding a new device, step 2*

6.   Now you can see your new GPS tracker under
     Devices. The status is Offline because it hasn't
     received any GPS data yet (Figure 8-59).

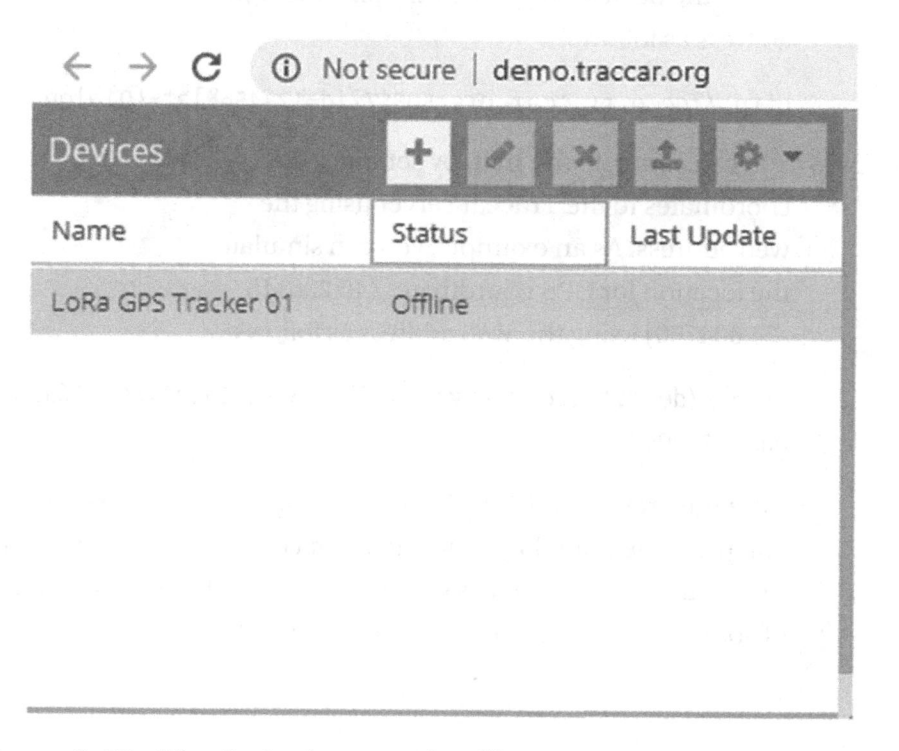

Figure 8-59. *The device is currently offline*

7.   Traccar supports the OsmAnd protocol (https://
     www.traccar.org/osmand/), and you can use this
     protocol to report your GPS data to the Traccar
     server. The OsmAnd live tracking web address
     format is as follows:

     ```
     http://demo.traccar.org:5055/?id=123456&lat={0}&lon={1}
     &timestamp={2}&hdop={3}&altitude={4}&speed={5}
     ```

8. In the web address, 123456 is the unique identifier of your device, lat is the latitude, and lon is the longitude. You will only need these three parameters to test the device, so you can simplify the web address as follows:

```
http://demo.traccar.org:5055/?id=123456&lat={0}&lon={1}
```

9. You can simulate the map by sending GPS coordinates to the Traccar server using the web address. As an example, you can simulate the location for GPS coordinates (40.726115, -74.004780) using the web address as follows:

```
http://demo.traccar.org:5055/?id=868142&lat=40.726115&l
on=-74.004780
```

Type the previous address in your web browser's address bar and press the Enter key. Then go to Traccar, and you can see that the status of your device is Online. Simply double-click the name of your device to view it on the map (Figure 8-60).

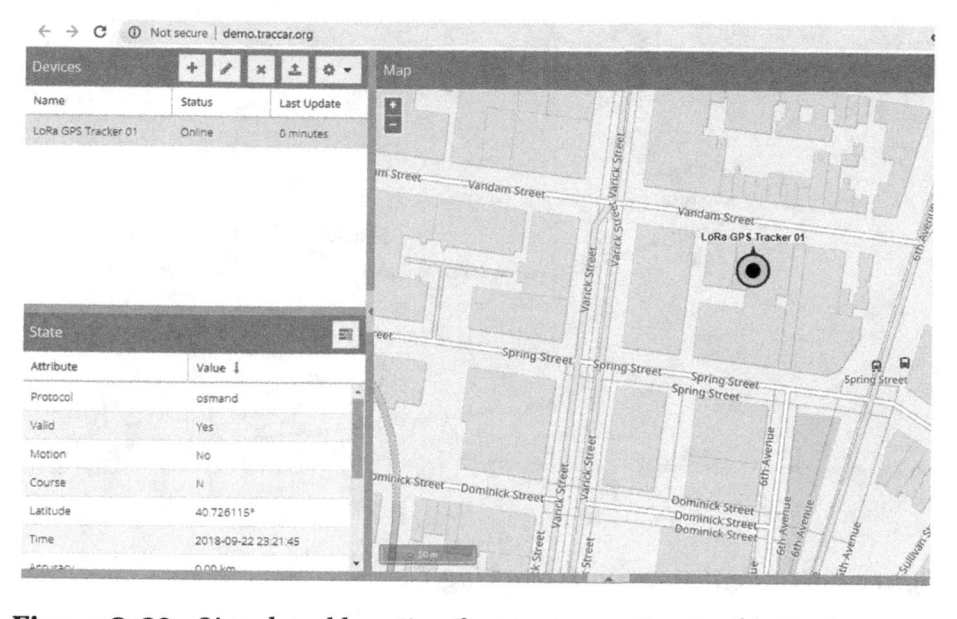

Figure 8-60. *Simulated location for GPS coordinates (latitude 40.726115, longitude -74.004780)*

Using the GPS Tracker

Figure 8-61 shows the real-time path tracking with the LoRa GPS tracker on the Traccar demo server.

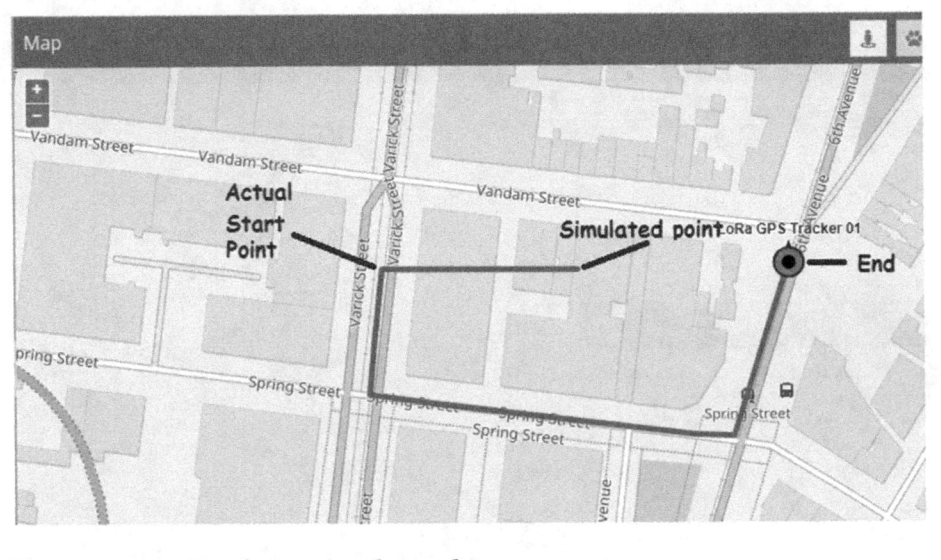

Figure 8-61. *Real-time path tracking*

You can test the GPS tracker by changing the TX_INTERVAL value in your Arduino sketch to different values. The default value is 20 seconds, which will send five pairs of GPS coordinates per minute to the LoRa gateway.

Figure 8-62 shows the completed hardware for the LoRa GPS tracker with an active antenna. Using an active antenna enables your device to receive GPS signals inside a building, but you will experience approximate location tracking.

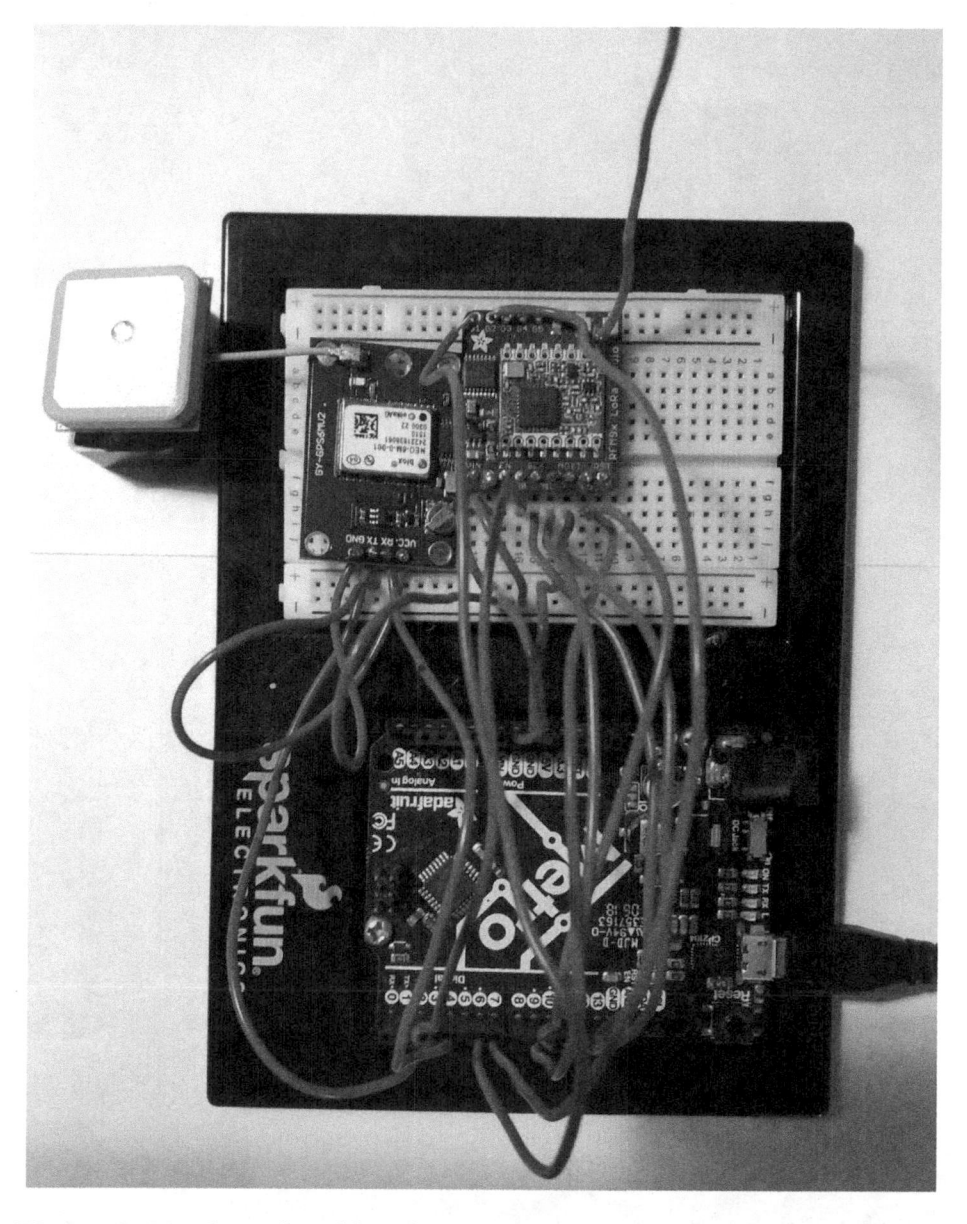

Figure 8-62. *Completed hardware setup for the LoRa GPS tracker*

APPENDIX A

LoRaWAN Channel Plans

To support the identification of LoRaWAN channel plans for a given country, Table A-1 provides a quick reference of suggested channel plans listed in priority order for each country (source: https://lora-alliance. org/resource-hub/lorawantm-regional-parameters-v11rb).

Table A-1. *Channel Plan per Country*

Country Name	Band/Channels	Channel Plan
Afghanistan		None
Albania	433.05–434.79 MHz	EU433
	863–873 MHz	EU863-870
	918–921 MHz	Other
Algeria	433.05–434.79 MHz	EU433
	870-876 MHz	Other
	880-885 MHz	Other
	915–921 MHz	Other
	925–926 MHz	Other

(continued)

© Pradeeka Seneviratne 2019
P. Seneviratne, *Beginning LoRa Radio Networks with Arduino*,
https://doi.org/10.1007/978-1-4842-4357-2

Table A-1. (*continued*)

Country Name	Band/Channels	Channel Plan
Andorra	433.05–434.79 MHz	EU433
	863–870 MHz	EU863-870
Armenia	863–870 MHz	EU863-870
	433.05–434.79 MHz	EU433
Argentina	902–928 MHz (915–928 MHz usable)	AU915-928, US902-928
Austria	433.05–434.79 MHz	EU433
	863–870 MHz	EU863-870
Australia	915–928 MHz	AU915-928, AS923
Azerbaijan	433.05–434.79 MHz	EU433
	863–868 MHz	Others
Bahrain	862–870 MHz	EU863-870
Bangladesh	433.05–434.79 MHz	EU433
	818–824 MHz	Other
	863–869 MHz	EU863-870
	925.0–927.0 MHz	Other
Belarus	433.05–434.79 MHz	EU433
	864.4–868.6 MHz	EU863-870
	869–869.2 MHz	EU863-870
Belgium	433.05–434.79 MHz	EU433
	863–870 MHz	EU863-870

(*continued*)

Table A-1. (*continued*)

Country Name	Band/Channels	Channel Plan
Burma (Myanmar)	433–435 MHz	EU433
	866–869 MHz	EU863-870
	919–923 MHz	Other
Bolivia	915–930 MHz	AU915-928, AS923
Bosnia and Herzegovina	433.05–434.79 MHz	EU433
	863–870 MHz	EU863-870
Botswana		None
Brazil	902–907.5 MHz	Other
	915–928 MHz	AU915-928
	433–435 MHz	EU433
Brunei Darussalam	866–870 MHz	EU863-870
	920–925 MHz	AS923
	433–435 MHz	EU433
Bulgaria	433.05–434.79 MHz	EU433
	863–870 MHz	EU863-870
Cambodia	866–869 MHz	EU863-870
	923–925 MHz	AS923
Cameroon		None
Canada	902–928 MHz	US902-928, AU915-928
Chile	902–928 MHz (915–928 MHz usable)	AU915-928, AS923, US902-928

(*continued*)

Table A-1. (*continued*)

Country Name	Band/Channels	Channel Plan
China	920.5–924.5 MHz	AS923
	779–787 MHz	CN779-787
	470–510 MHz	CN470-510
	433.05–434.79 MHz	EU433
	314–316 MHz	Other
	430–432 MHz	Other
	840–845 MHz	Other
Colombia	902–928 MHz	AU915-928, US902-928
Congo Rep.		None
Costa Rica	920.5–928 MHz	AS923
Croatia	433.05–434.79 MHz	EU433
	863–870 MHz	EU863-870
Cuba	433.05–434.79 MHz	EU433
	915–921 MHz	Other
Cyprus	433.05–434.79 MHz	EU433
	863–870 MHz	EU863-870
Czech Republic	433.05–434.79 MHz	EU433
	863–870 MHz	EU863-870
Denmark	433.05–434.79 MHz	EU433
	863–873 MHz	EU863-870
	918–921 MHz	Other

(continued)

Table A-1. (*continued*)

Country Name	Band/Channels	Channel Plan
Dominican Republic	915–928 MHz	AU915-928
Ecuador	902–928 MHz	AU915-928, US902-928, AS923
Egypt	433.05–434.79 MHz	EU433
	863–876 MHz	EU863-870
Estonia	433.05–434.79 MHz	EU433
	863–873 MHz	EU863-870
	918–921 MHz	Other
Finland	433.05–434.79 MHz	EU433
	863–873 MHz	EU863-870
France	433.05–434.79 MHz	EU433
	863–870 MHz	EU863-870
Georgia		None
Germany	433.05–434.79 MHz	EU433
	863–870 MHz	EU863-870
Ghana		None
Greece	433.05–434.79 MHz	EU433
	868–870 MHz	EU863-870
Guatemala	902–928 MHz (915–928 MHz usable)	AU915-928, AS923, US902-928
Haiti		None

(*continued*)

Table A-1. (*continued*)

Country Name	Band/Channels	Channel Plan
Honduras	915–928 MHz	AU915-928
Hong Kong	433.05–434.79 MHz	EU433
	865–868 MHz	Other
	920–925 MHz	AS923
Hungary	433.05–434.79 MHz	EU433
	863–873 MHz	EU863-870
	918–921 MHz	Other
Iceland	433.05–434.79 MHz	EU433
	863–873 MHz	EU863-870
India	865–867 MHz	IN765-867
Indonesia	923–925 MHz	AS923
Iraq		None
Iran	433.05–434.79 MHz	EU433
	863–873 MHz	EU863-870
	915–918 MHz	Other
Ireland	433.05–434.79 MHz	EU433
	863–873 MHz	EU863-870
	918–921 MHz	Other
Israel	433.05–434.79 MHz	EU433
	915–917 MHz	Other
Italy	433.05–434.79 MHz	EU433
	863–870 MHz	EU863-870

(*continued*)

Table A-1. (*continued*)

Country Name	Band/Channels	Channel Plan
Ivory Coast		None
Jamaica	902–928 MHz (915–928 MHz usable)	AU915-928, US902-928
Japan	920.6–928.0 MHz (steps of 200kHz)	AS923
	920.8–927.8 MHz (steps of 600kHz)	AS923
Jordan	865–868 MHz	Other
Kazakhstan	433.05–434.79 MHz	EU433
Kenya		None
Korea (DPR)		None
Kuwait	433.05–434.79 MHz	EU433
Kyrgyz Republic		None
Laos	433–435 MHz	EU433
	862–875 MHz	EU863-870
	923–925 MHz	AS923
Latvia	433.05–434.79 MHz	EU433
	863–870 MHz	EU863-870
Lebanon	433–435 MHz	EU433
	862–870 MHz	EU863-870
Liechtenstein	433.05–434.79 MHz	EU433
	863–873 MHz	EU863-870

(*continued*)

Table A-1. (*continued*)

Country Name	Band/Channels	Channel Plan
Libya		None
Lithuania	433.05–434.79 MHz	EU433
	863–870 MHz	EU863-870
Luxembourg	433.05–434.79 MHz	EU433
	863–873 MHz	EU863-870
	918–921 MHz	Other
Macao		None
Macedonia, FYR	433.05–434.79 MHz	EU433
	863–870 MHz	EU863-870
Malaysia	433–435 MHz	EU433
	919–924 MHz	AS923
Maldives		None
Malta	433.05–434.79 MHz	EU433
	863–870 MHz	EU863-870
Mauritius		None
Mexico	902–928 MHz	US902-928, AU915-928
Moldova	433.05–434.79 MHz	EU433
	863–870 MHz	EU863-870
Mongolia		None
Montenegro	433.05–434.79 MHz	EU433
	863–870 MHz	EU863-870

(*continued*)

Table A-1. (*continued*)

Country Name	Band/Channels	Channel Plan
Morocco	433.05–434.79 MHz	EU433
	867.6–869 MHz	EU863-870
Netherlands	433.05–434.79 MHz	EU433
	863–870 MHz	EU863-870
New-Zealand	915–928 MHz	AS923, AU915-928
	819–824 MHz	Other
	864–870MHz	EU863-870
	433.05–434.79 MHz	EU433
Nicaragua	902–928 MHz (915–928 MHz usable)	AU915-928, US902-928
Nigeria	863–870 MHz	EU863-870
Norway	433.05–434.79 MHz	EU433
	863–873 MHz	EU863-870
	918–921 MHz	Other
Oman	433.05–434.79 MHz	EU433
	863–870 MHz	EU863-870
Pakistan	433.05–434.79 MHz	EU433
	865–869 MHz	EU863-870
	900–925 MHz	AS923
Panama	902–928 MHz	AU915-928, US902-928, AS923
Paraguay	433.05–434.79 MHz	EU433
	915–928 MHz	AU915-928, AS923

(*continued*)

Table A-1. (*continued*)

Country Name	Band/Channels	Channel Plan
Peru	915–928 MHz	AU915-928, AS923
Papua New Guinea	915–925 MHz	AU915-928
Philippines	915–918 MHz	Other
	868–869.2 MHz	EU863-870
	869.7–870 MHz	EU863-870
	433.05–434.79 MHz	EU433
Poland	433.05–434.79 MHz	EU433
	863–873 MHz	EU863-870
	918–921 MHz	Other
Portugal	433.05–434.79 MHz	EU433
	863–870 MHz	EU863-870
Qatar	433.05–434.79 MHz	EU433
	868–868.6 MHz	EU863-870
	868.7–869.2 MHz	EU863-870
	869.4–869.65 MHz	EU863-870
	869.7–870 MHz	EU863-870
Romania	433.05–434.79 MHz	EU433
	863–870 MHz	EU863-870
Russian federation	866–868 MHz (licensed)	RU864-870
	864–865 MHz	RU864-870
	868.7–869.2 MHz	RU864-870
	433.075–434.75 MHz	EU433
	916–921 MHz (licensed)	Other

(*continued*)

Table A-1. (*continued*)

Country Name	Band/Channels	Channel Plan
Salvador	915–928	AU915-928, AS923
Saudi Arabia	863–870 MHz	EU863-870
	433.05–434.79 MHz	EU433
Senegal		None
Serbia	433.05–434.79 MHz	EU433
	863–870 MHz	EU863-870
Singapore	920–925 MHz	AS923
	433.05–434.79 MHz	EU433
	866–869 MHz	EU863-870
Slovak Republic	433.05–434.79 MHz	EU433
	863–873 MHz	EU863-870
	918–921 MHz	Other
Slovenia	433.05–434.79 MHz	EU433
	863–873 MHz	EU863-870
	918–921 MHz	Other
South Africa	433.05–434.79 MHz	EU433
	865–868.6 MHz	EU863-870
	868.7–869.2 MHz	EU863-870
	869.4–869.65 MHz	EU863-870
	869.7–870 MHz	EU863-870
	915–921 MHz	Other
South Korea	917–923.5 MHz	KR920-923

(*continued*)

Table A-1. (*continued*)

Country Name	Band/Channels	Channel Plan
Spain	433.05–434.79 MHz	EU433
	863–870 MHz	EU863-870
Sri Lanka	433.05–434.79 MHz	EU433
Sudan		None
Sweden	433.05–434.79 MHz	EU433
	868–870 MHz	EU863-870
Switzerland	433.05–434.79 MHz	EU433
	863–873 MHz	EU863-870
Syrian Arab Rep.		None
Taiwan	920–925 MHz	AS923
Tajikistan		None
Tanzania		None
Thailand	433.05–434.79 MHz	EU433
	920–925 MHz	AS923
Trinidad and Tobago		None
Tunisia	433.05–434.79 MHz	EU433
	868–868.6 MHz	EU863-870
	868.7–869.2 MHz	EU863-870
	869.4–869.65 MHz	EU863-870
	869.7–870 MHz	EU863-870
Turkey	433.05–434.79 MHz	EU433
	863–870 MHz	EU863-870
Turkmenistan		None

(*continued*)

Table A-1. (*continued*)

Country Name	Band/Channels	Channel Plan
Uganda	433.05–434.79 MHz	EU433
	865–867.6 MHz	Other
	869.25–869.7 MHz	Other
	923–925 MHz	AS923
Ukraine	433.05–434.79 MHz	EU433
	863–865 MHz	EU863-870
	868–868.6 MHz	EU863-870
United Arab Emirates	433.05–434.79 MHz	EU433
	863–870 MHz	EU863-870
	870–875.8 MHz	Other
	915–921 MHz	Other
United Kingdom	433.05–434.79 MHz	EU433
	863–873 MHz	EU863-870
	918–921 MHz	Other
United States	902–928 MHz	US902-928, AU915-928
Uruguay	902–928 MHz (915–928 MHz usable)	AU915-928, AS923, US902-928
Uzbekistan	433.05–434.79 MHz	EU433
Venezuela	922–928 MHz	AS923
Vietnam	433.05–434.79 MHz	EU433
	863–870 MHz	EU863-870
	918–923 MHz	Other
Yemen, Rep.		None
Zimbabwe		None

Table A-2 provides a quick reference of common channel plans listed for each formal plan name.

Table A-2. *Regional Parameter Common Names*

Channel Plan	Common Name
EU863-870	EU868
US902-928	US915
CN779-787	CN779
EU433	EU433
AU915-928	AU915
CN470-510	CN470
AS923	AS923
KR920-923	KR920
IN865-867	IN865
RU864-870	RU864

Index

A

Adafruit
  DHT11 library, 87–88
  metro, 76, 261
  Pi T-Cobbler Plus, 56
  RFM96W module, 30–31
  ultimate GPS breakout, 50
Amplitude modulation (AM), 2–3
Application program interface
    (API), 171
Arduino
  analog pin A0, 210
  features, 41–42
  hardware and software serial, 46
  IDE (*see* Integrated development
    environment (IDE), Arduino)
  libraries
    folder, creation, 85
    preferences dialog, 84
    sketchbook location, 83
    LMIC, 90–91
  Metro
    driver installation, 76
    silicon labs, 78
    USB/serial chip, 77
  micro-USB cable, 42–43

plastic mounting plate, 43–44
power supply unit, 47
serial monitor, 100
SPI, 44–46
Uno
  board, 261
  device manager, 70
  driver installation, 67
  driver software, searching, 73
  driver software, updation, 71
  folder, 74
  option, 72
  under ports, 76
  USB cable, connection, 68
  windows search, 69
Arduino sketch
  Arduino digital pin, 209
  Arduino/Genuino Uno, 211–212
  Adafruit Metro, 79
  board password, 219
  digital pin 13, 79
  dhtWrite() function, 210
  LG01 gateway, 209, 217–219
    charts, 193
    serial monitor output, 192–193
    ThingSpeak IoT, 189–191
    upload settings, 191

© Pradeeka Seneviratne 2019
P. Seneviratne, *Beginning LoRa Radio Networks with Arduino*,
https://doi.org/10.1007/978-1-4842-4357-2

P, Q

R

S

Printed in the United States
By Bookmasters